The Best of *Le Monde diplomatique* 2012

THE BEST OF
LE MONDE DIPLOMATIQUE
2012

Edited by
Wendy Kristianasen

PlutoPress
www.plutobooks.com

First published 2012 by Pluto Press
345 Archway Road, London N6 5AA

www.plutobooks.com

Distributed in the United States of America exclusively by
Palgrave Macmillan, a division of St. Martin's Press LLC,
175 Fifth Avenue, New York, NY 10010

British Library Cataloguing in Publication Data
A catalogue record for this book is available from the British Library

ISBN   978 0 7453 3188 1   Hardback
ISBN   978 0 7453 3187 4   Paperback

Library of Congress Cataloging in Publication Data applied for

This book is printed on paper suitable for recycling and made from fully managed
and sustained forest sources. Logging, pulping and manufacturing processes are
expected to conform to the environmental standards of the country of origin.

10   9   8   7   6   5   4   3   2   1

Designed and produced for Pluto Press by Chase Publishing Services Ltd
Typeset from disk by Stanford DTP Services, Northampton, England
Simultaneously printed digitally by CPI Antony Rowe, Chippenham, UK and
Edwards Bros in the United States of America

Contents

Introduction

Wendy Kristianasen

I travel the world every month, sitting at my computer screen, deciding which of the articles from *Le Monde diplomatique* should go into the smaller English LMD. This is a hard choice: we have just 16 smallish pages while Paris has at least 28, and they're big pages. Our 16 go out to the world monthly in print, on the internet and in digital facsimile (the favoured choice for an iPad).

Le Monde diplomatique is international, and internationalist, one of the world's great papers of the left. It thinks of itself as Paris based rather than French, covers the great global issues and has room for insights into societies and situations around the world that the mainstream media ignore. Its writers are specialists, academics, writers and journalists known for their research and reportage. Most are French, but not all: *Le Monde diplomatique*'s contributors are international too, often writing in English on their own countries, and are then translated into French.

Le Monde diplomatique started in 1954 as a journal for diplomats published by France's leading daily paper *Le Monde*. In 1996, after steady expansion and success, *Le Monde diplomatique* formed its own company, owned by its staff and readers as well as *Le Monde*. It's grown into an unlikely empire with more than 70 foreign editions in 27 languages, including Japanese, Korean, Farsi, Esperanto and two varieties of Kurdish. The empire began in Europe, spread to Latin America, Asia, the Arab world, and then went global. The English edition (LMD) began in 1997, became a joint venture with *The Guardian* and is now fully owned by *Le Monde diplomatique* Paris. The global readership is approaching three million.

International in readership, international in content, this voice of the left is fiercely independent in its views. *Le Monde diplomatique* campaigned against neoliberalism and globalisation before most of us knew what it really meant, and for the Tobin tax (through its successful lobby group Attac). The causes for which it has always fought have grown popular and now have wide appeal. Also, the paper's reputation for in-depth analysis, meticulous research and smart reporting in politics and economics, society, and many other topics, has meant that readers who may not have shared its political stance still wanted to know what it had to say.

When the English edition (LMD) began as an online monthly, I decided to discover who was reading us and why. Hundreds of people emailed within a week to tell me. They turned out to be professional people, academics and students. Their reasons for reading were interesting. They were happy to pay their internet subscription – we have always struggled to make LMD pay its way – because they needed to hear another, more critical voice, to balance the mainstream media, *The Guardian* or *The Independent*, *The New York Times* or the *Washington Post*. A reader from the United States wrote unforgettably that the 'seriousness of your reportage is startling by American standards'.

If it was always hard to choose our monthly quota it was even harder to choose the selection for this book. Many favourite articles did not fit into themed sections. For lack of space we have left aside superb pieces on the media, IT, science, popular culture and much else. The book's section on Europe is slim, for Europe has spilled into, and filled up, the opening section on the financial crisis. A year or two ago, Latin America, Asia and Africa would each have demanded sections. But in 2010–11 the Arabs unexpectedly rose up against dictatorship, old wars and conflicts in Muslim lands continued, and the question of Islam and radicalisation urgently needed better analysis; all these claimed places in this volume. The changing condition of the US empire (and of domestic America) had to have its own section, while another was ceded to intercontinental change and the growing interconnectedness of our planet. A final section addresses cities and their citizens, in expansion or decline.

A clearer understanding: that was the basis of choice for what you will read here, pieces that illuminate complex subjects, and let you see further and deeper into worlds you don't directly know. I hope you may share the excitement I sometimes feel late on some evening of editing, when I look up and think: no one has ever described this situation with such clarity before.

It takes a lot of hard work before we are ready to go to press each month. For that, thanks are due: To the authors of these fine stories for their generosity in allowing us to republish them here. To my co-editor Veronica Horwell, whose skills can bring the hardest translation to heel and make language sing. To Polly Giddings who worked on the book itself. To Ed Emery who compiled the index. To our translators, Charles Goulden, Krystyna Horko, Stephanie Irvine, George Miller and Barbara Wilson, without whose skills, patience and enthusiasm this book would not have been possible.

January 2012

Part I: The World in Crisis

❖❖❖❖❖❖❖❖❖❖❖❖❖❖❖❖❖❖❖❖❖❖❖❖❖❖❖❖❖❖❖❖❖❖

July 2011

'DON'T BE ASHAMED TO ASK FOR THE MOON: WE NEED IT'

Europe's wakeup call

The dose of austerity prescribed by the International Monetary Fund and leaders of the eurozone countries to cure the problems of sovereign debt is visibly failing ordinary people. But it suits neoliberal interests nicely. This is not just a technical and financial debate, it is a political and social battle.

Serge Halimi

The economic, and democratic, crisis in Europe raises questions. Why were policies that were bound to fail adopted and applied with exceptional ferocity in Ireland, Spain, Portugal and Greece? Are those responsible for pursuing these policies mad, doubling the dose every time their medicine predictably fails to work? How is it that in a democratic system, the people forced to accept cuts and austerity simply replace one failed government with another just as dedicated to the same shock treatment? Is there any alternative?

The answer to the first two questions is clear, once we forget the propaganda about the 'public interest', Europe's 'shared values' and being 'all in this together'. The policies are rational and on the whole are achieving their objective. But that objective is not to end the economic and financial crisis but to reap its rich rewards. The crisis means that hundreds of thousands of civil service jobs can be cut (in Greece, nine out of ten civil servants will not be replaced on retirement), salaries and paid leave reduced, tranches of the economy sold off for the benefit of private interests, labour laws questioned, indirect taxes (the most regressive) increased, the cost of public services raised, reimbursement of health care charges reduced. The crisis is heaven-sent for neoliberals, who would have had to fight long and hard for any of these measures, and now get them all. Why should they want to see the end of a tunnel that is a fast track to paradise?

The Irish Business and Employers Confederation (IBEC)'s directors went to Brussels on 15 June to ask the European Commission to pressure Dublin to dismantle some of Ireland's labour legislation, fast. After the meeting, Brendan McGinty, IBEC Director of Industrial Relations and Human Resources, warned: 'Ireland needs to show the world it is serious about economic reform and getting labour costs back into line. Foreign observers clearly see that our wage rules are a barrier to job creation, growth and recovery. Major reform is a key part of the programme agreed with the EU and the IMF. Now is not the time for government to shirk from the hard decisions.'

The decisions will not be hard for everyone, following a course that is already familiar: 'Pay rates for new workers in unregulated sectors have fallen by about 25 per cent in recent years. This shows the labour market is responding to an economic and unemployment crisis.'[1] The lever of sovereign debt enables the European Union and International Monetary Fund to impose the Irish employers' dream order on Dublin.

The same view seems to apply elsewhere. On 11 June, an *Economist* editorial observed that 'Reform-minded Greeks see the crisis as an opportunity to set their country right. They quietly praise foreigners for turning the screws on their politicians.'[2] The same issue analysed the EU and IMF austerity plan for Portugal: 'Business leaders are adamant that there should be no deviation from the IMF/EU plan. Pedro Ferraz da Costa, who heads a business think-tank, says no Portuguese party in the past 30 years would have put forward so radical a reform programme. He adds that Portugal cannot afford to miss this opportunity.'[3] Long live the crisis.

CATERING ONLY TO RENTIERS

Portuguese democracy is just 30 years old. Its young leaders were showered with carnations by crowds grateful for the end of a long dictatorship and colonial wars in Africa, the promise of agrarian reform, literacy programmes and power for factory workers. Now, with reductions in the minimum wage and unemployment benefit, neoliberal reforms in pensions, health and education and privatisation, they have had a great leap backwards. The new prime minister, Pedro Passos Coelho, has promised to go even further than the EU and the IMF require. He wants to 'surprise' investors.

US economist Paul Krugman explains: 'Consciously or not, policy makers are catering almost exclusively to the interests of rentiers – those who derive lots of income from assets, who lent large sums of money in the past, often unwisely, but are now being protected from loss at everyone else's expense.' Krugman says creditor interests naturally prevail because 'this is the class that makes big campaign contributions, it's the class that has personal access to policy makers, many of whom go to work for these people when they exit government through the revolving door'.[4] During the EU discussion on funding Greek recovery, Austrian finance minister Maria Fekter initially suggested: 'You can't leave the profits with the banks and make the taxpayers shoulder the losses.'[5] This was short-lived. Europe hesitated for 48 hours, then the interests of rentiers prevailed, as usual.

To understand the 'complex' mechanisms underlying the sovereign debt crisis, you need to know about constant innovations in financial engineering: futures, CDs (credit default swaps), etc. This level of sophistication reserves analysis for select experts who generally profit from their knowledge. They pocket the proceeds while the economically illiterate pay, as a tribute they owe to fate, or to an aspect of the modern world that is beyond them.

Let's try the simple political explanation instead. Long ago, European kings borrowed from the Doge of Venice or Florentine merchants or Genoese bankers. They were under no obligation to repay these loans and sometimes neglected to do so; a neat way of settling public debt. Many years later, the young Soviet regime announced that it would not be held accountable for money the tsars had borrowed and squandered, so generations of French savers suddenly found they had worthless Russian loans in their attics.

But there were more subtle ways of getting out of debt. In the UK, debt declined from 216 per cent of gross domestic product in 1945 to 138 per cent in 1955, and in the US it fell from 116 per cent of GDP to 66 per cent – without any austerity plan. Of course, the surge in post-war economic development automatically reduced the proportion of debt in national wealth. But that was not all. States repaid a nominal sum at the time, reduced each year by the level of inflation. If a loan subscribed at 5 per cent annual interest is repaid in currency that is depreciating at the rate of 10 per cent a year, the real interest rate becomes negative to the benefit of the debtor. Between 1945 and 1980, the real interest rate in most western countries was negative almost every year. As a result, as *The Economist* remarked: 'Savers deposited money in banks, which lent to governments at interest rates below the level of inflation.'[6] Debt was cut without much trouble. In the US, negative real interest rates were worth the equivalent of 6.3 per cent of GDP per year to the Treasury, from 1945 to 1955.[7]

Why did savers allow themselves to be cheated? They had no choice. Capital controls and the nationalisation of the banks meant that they had to lend to the state, and that is how it got its funds. Wealthy individuals did not have the option to invest on spec in Brazilian stock index linked to changes in the price of soybeans over the next three years. There was a flight of capital, suitcases of gold ingots leaving France for Switzerland the day before devaluation or an election in which the left might win. However, this was illegal.

Up to the 1980s, index-linked wage rises (sliding scales) protected most workers against the consequences of inflation, and controls on free movement of capital had forced investors to put up with negative real interest rates. After the Reagan/Thatcher years, the opposite applied.

THE SYSTEM HAS NO PITY

Sliding wage scales disappeared almost everywhere: in France, the economist Alain Cotta called this major decision, in 1982, '[Jacques] Delors' gift [to employers]'.[8] Between 1981 and 2007, inflation was destroyed and real interest rates were almost always positive. Profiting from the liberalisation of capital movements, 'savers' (this does not mean old age pensioners with a post office account in Lisbon or carpenters in Salonika) make states compete for funds and, as François Mitterrand said, 'make money in their sleep'. Moving from sliding wage scales and negative real interest rates to a reduction in the purchasing power of labour and a meteoric increase in returns on capital completely upsets the social balance.

Apparently this is not enough. The troika (European Commission, ECB and IMF) has decided to improve the mechanisms designed to favour capital at the expense of labour, by adding coercion, blackmail and ultimatum. States bled by their over-generous efforts to rescue the banks, and begging for loans to balance their monthly accounts, are told to choose between a market-led clean-up and bankruptcy. A swathe of Europe, where the dictatorships of António de Oliveira Salazar, Francisco Franco and the Greek colonels ended, has been reduced to the rank of a protectorate run by Brussels, Frankfurt and Washington, the main aim being to defend the financial sector.

These states still have their own governments, but only to ensure that orders are carried out and to endure abuse from the people who know the system will never take pity on them, however poor they are. According to *Le Figaro*, 'Most Greeks see the international supervision of the budget as a new form of dictatorship, like the old days when the colonels were in charge, between 1967 and 1974.'[9] The European ideal will not gain from being associated with a bailiff who seizes islands, beaches, national companies and public services and sells them to private investors. Since 1919 and the Treaty of Versailles, everyone knows that such public humiliation can unleash destructive nationalism – and all the more so as provocations increase. The next ECB governor, Mario Draghi, who – like his predecessor – will issue strict orders in Athens, was vice-chairman and managing director of Goldman Sachs when the bank was helping the conservative government in Greece to cook the books. The IMF, which also takes a view on the French constitution, has asked Paris to insert a 'rule to balance public finances'; Nicolas Sarkozy is already working on it.

France has let it be known that it would like the Greek political parties to follow the example of their Portuguese counterparts, 'join forces, and form an alliance'; and the prime minister, François Fillon, and European Commission president, José Barroso, have tried to persuade the Greek conservative leader, Antonis Samaras, to take this course. ECB head Jean-Claude Trichet considers that 'the European authorities could have the right to veto some national economic policy decisions'.[10]

Honduras has established an enterprise zone, in which national sovereignty does not apply. Europe is currently establishing a debate zone for all the economic and social issues no longer discussed by the political parties because these areas have gone beyond their control. Inter-party competition now concentrates on social matters: the burqa, the legalisation of cannabis, radar on motorways, the angry gestures or foul language of a reckless politician or intoxicated artist. This confirms a trend already noticeable 20 years ago: real political power is shifting to areas where democracy carries no weight, until the day when indignation finally boils over. Which is where we are.

But indignation is powerless without some understanding of the mechanisms that caused it. We know the alternatives – reject the monetarist, deflationist policies that deepen the crisis, cancel part of the debt if not all of it, take over the banks, get finance under control, reverse globalisation and recover the hundreds of billions of euros the state has lost by tax cuts that favour the wealthy (€70 billion in France in the past ten years, more than $1 trillion in the US, especially for the top 1 per cent of income earners). And knowledge of these alternatives has been shared by people who know at least as much about economics as Trichet, but do not serve the same interests.

This is not a technical and financial debate but a political and social battle. Of course, the economic liberals will claim that what progressives demand is impossible. But what have they achieved, apart from creating a situation that is unbearable? Perhaps it is time to remember how Jean-Paul Sartre summed up Paul Nizan's advice to people who bottle up their aggression: 'Do not be ashamed to ask for the moon: we need it.'[11]

Translated by Barbara Wilson

1. 'IBEC in Brussels on concerns about reform of wage rules', IBEC, 15 June 2011.
2. Charlemagne, 'It's all Greek to them', *The Economist*, London, 11 June 2011.
3. 'A grim inheritance', *The Economist*, 9 June 2011.
4. Paul Krugman, 'Rule by rentiers', *The New York Times*, 10 June 2011.
5. *International Herald Tribune*, Paris, 15 June 2011.
6. See 'The great repression', *The Economist*, London, 18 June 2011, which explains the history of this mechanism.
7. Ibid.
8. Jacques Delors was France's economic and finance minister in François Mitterrand's administration, before becoming head of the European Commission.
9. *Le Figaro*, Paris, 16 June 2011.
10. Reuters, 2 June 2011.
11. Jean-Paul Sartre, preface to *Aden Arabie*, Maspero, Paris, 1971.

❖❖❖❖❖❖❖❖❖❖❖❖❖❖❖❖❖❖❖❖❖❖❖❖❖❖❖❖❖❖

NOVEMBER 2010

NEW ECONOMIC TERRITORY

A permanent state of emergency

The explosion of anger seen on the streets of Paris, Madrid, Athens and Bucharest is a sign of people's exasperation and desire for change, with the hope that would bring. But we are in new economic territory: we do not know what we have to do, but we have to act now.

Slavoj Žižek

During this year's protests against the eurozone's austerity measures – in Greece and, on a smaller scale, Ireland, Italy and Spain – two stories have imposed themselves. The establishment story proposes a de-politicised naturalisation of the crisis: the regulatory measures are presented not as decisions grounded in political choices, but as the imperatives of a neutral financial logic – if we want our economies to stabilise, we have to swallow the bitter pill. The other story, of the protesting workers, students and pensioners, presents the austerity measures as yet another attempt by international financial capital to dismantle the last remainders of the welfare state. The International Monetary Fund appears from one perspective as a neutral agent of discipline and order: from the other, the oppressive agent of global capital.

While each story contains a grain of truth, both are fundamentally false. The European establishment's story obfuscates the fact that the huge deficits have been run up as a result of massive financial sector bailouts, as well as by falling government revenues during the recession: the big loan to Athens will be used to repay Greek debt to the great French and German banks. The true aim of the EU guarantees is to help private banks.

The protesters' story bears witness yet again to the misery of today's left: there is no positive programmatic content to its demands, just a generalised refusal to compromise the existing welfare state. The utopia here is not a radical change of the system, but the idea that one can maintain a welfare state *within* the system. But one should not miss the grain of truth in the countervailing argument: if we remain within the confines of the global capitalist system, then measures to wring further sums from workers, students and pensioners are necessary.

One thing is clear: after decades of the welfare state, when cutbacks were relatively limited and came with the promise that things would soon return to normal, we are now entering a period in which a kind of economic state of emergency is becoming permanent, turning into a constant, a way of life. It brings with it the threat of far more savage austerity measures, cuts in benefits, diminishing health and education services and more precarious employment. The left faces the difficult task of emphasising that we are dealing with *political* economy – that there is nothing 'natural' in such a crisis, that the existing global economic system relies on a series of political decisions. Simultaneously it is fully aware that, insofar as we remain within the capitalist system, the violation of its rules effectively causes economic breakdown, since the system obeys a pseudo-natural logic of its own.

It would be futile merely to hope that the ongoing crisis will be limited and that European capitalism will continue to guarantee a relatively high standard of living for a growing number of people. It would indeed be a strange radical politics, whose main hope is that circumstances will continue to render it inoperative and marginal. There is no lack of anti-capitalists today. We are even witnessing an overload of critiques of capitalism's horrors: newspaper investigations, TV reports and best-selling books abound on companies polluting our environment, corrupt bankers who continue to get fat bonuses while their firms are saved by public money, sweatshops where children work overtime.

There is, however, a catch to all this criticism, ruthless as it may appear: what is as a rule not questioned is the liberal-democratic framework within which these excesses should be fought. The goal, explicit or implied, is to regulate capitalism – through the pressure of the media, parliamentary inquiries, harsher laws, honest police investigations – but never to question the liberal-democratic institutional mechanisms of the bourgeois state of law.

THE QUESTION OF FREEDOM

It is here that Marx's key insight remains valid, perhaps today more than ever. For Marx, the question of freedom should not be located primarily in the political sphere proper, as with the criteria the global financial institutions apply when they want to pronounce a judgment on a country. Does it have free elections? Are the judges independent? Is the press free from hidden pressures? Are human rights respected? The key to actual freedom resides rather in the 'apolitical' network of social relations, from the market to the family, where the change needed for effective improvement is not political reform, but a transformation in the social relations of production. We do not vote about who owns what, or about worker-management relations in a factory; all this is left to processes outside the sphere of the political. It is illusory to expect that one can effectively change things by 'extending' democracy into this sphere, say, by organising 'democratic' banks under the people's control.

The ABC of Marxist notions of class struggle is the thesis that 'peaceful' social life is itself an expression of the (temporary) victory of one class – the ruling one. From the standpoint of the subordinated and oppressed, the very existence of the state, as an apparatus of class domination, is a fact of violence. The standard liberal motto – that it is sometimes necessary to resort to violence, but it is never legitimate – is not sufficient. From the radical-emancipatory perspective, one should turn it around: for the oppressed, violence is always legitimate – since their very status is the result of violence – but never necessary: it is always a matter of strategic consideration whether to use force against the enemy or not.

In the current economic emergency, too, we are clearly not dealing with blind market processes but with highly organised, strategic interventions by states and financial institutions, intent on resolving the crisis on their own terms – and in such conditions, are not defensive counter-measures in order?

These considerations cannot but shatter the comfortable subjective position of radical intellectuals. What if intellectuals lead basically safe and comfortable lives and, in order to justify their livelihoods, construct scenarios of radical catastrophe? For many, no doubt, if a revolution is taking place, it should occur at a safe distance – Cuba, Nicaragua, Venezuela – so that, while their hearts are warmed by thinking about faraway events, they can go on promoting their careers. But with the current collapse of properly functioning welfare states in the advanced industrial economies, radical intellectuals may be now approaching a moment of truth when they must make such clarifications: they wanted real change – now they can have it.

What has happened in the latest stage of post-68 capitalism is that the economy itself – the logic of market and competition – has progressively imposed itself as the hegemonic ideology. In education, the school system is less and less the compulsory network, elevated above the market and organised directly by the state, bearer of enlightened values – liberty, equality, fraternity. On behalf of the sacred formula of 'lower costs, higher efficiency', it is progressively penetrated by different forms of public/private partnership (PPP). In the organisation and legitimisation of power, too, the electoral system is increasingly conceived on the model of market competition: elections are like a commercial exchange where voters 'buy' the option that offers to do the job of maintaining social order, prosecuting crime, and so on, most efficiently.

On behalf of the same formula of 'lower costs, higher efficiency', functions once exclusive to the domain of state power, like running prisons, can be privatised; the military is no longer based on universal conscription, but composed of hired mercenaries. Even the state bureaucracy is no longer perceived as the Hegelian universal class, as is becoming evident in the case of Berlusconi. In today's Italy, state power is directly exerted by the base *bourgeois* who ruthlessly and openly exploits it as a means to protect his personal interests. Even the process of engaging in emotional relations is increasingly organised along the lines of a market relationship. Such a procedure relies on self-commodification: for internet dating or marriage agencies, prospective partners present themselves as commodities, listing their qualities and posting their photos.

CAN THE IMPOSSIBLE HAPPEN?

In such a constellation, the very idea of a radical social transformation may appear as an impossible dream – yet the term 'impossible' should make us stop and think. Today, possible and impossible are distributed in a strange way, both simultaneously exploding into excess. In the domains of personal freedom and scientific technology, we are told that 'nothing is impossible': we can enjoy sex in all its perverse versions, entire archives of music, films and TV series are available to download, space travel is available to everyone (at a price). There is the prospect of enhancing our physical and psychic abilities, of manipulating our basic properties through interventions into the genome; even the techgnostic dream of achieving immortality by transforming our identity into software that can be downloaded into one or another set of hardware.

On the other hand, in the domain of socio-economic relations, our era perceives itself as the age of maturity in which humanity has abandoned the old millenarian utopian dreams and accepted the constraints of reality – read: capitalist socio-economic reality – with all its impossibilities. The commandment 'you cannot' is its *mot d'ordre*: you cannot engage in large collective acts, which necessarily end in totalitarian terror; you cannot cling to the old welfare state, it makes you non-competitive and leads to economic crisis; you cannot isolate yourself from the global market, without falling prey to the spectre of North Korean *juche* ideology. In its ideological version, ecology also adds its own list of impossibilities, so-called threshold values – no more than two degrees of global warming – based on 'expert opinions'.

Today, the ruling ideology endeavours to make us accept the 'impossibility' of radical change, of abolishing capitalism, of a democracy not reduced to a corrupt parliamentary game, in order to render invisible the antagonism that cuts across capitalist societies. This is why Lacan's formula for overcoming an ideological impossibility is not 'everything is possible', but 'the impossible happens'.

The Morales government in Bolivia, the Chavez government in Venezuela and the Maoist government in Nepal came to power through 'fair' democratic elections, not through insurrection. Their situation is 'objectively' hopeless: the whole drift of history is basically against them, they cannot rely on any 'objective tendencies' pushing in their way, all they can do is to improvise, do what they can in a desperate situation. But does this not give them a unique freedom? And are we – today's left – not all in exactly the same situation?

Ours is thus the very opposite of the classical early 20th-century situation, in which the left knew what had to be done but had to wait patiently for the proper moment of execution. Today we do not know what we have to do, but we have to act now because the consequence of non-action could be disastrous. We will be forced to live 'as if we were free'.

Original text in English

Slavoj Žižek is a philosopher and author of *Living in the End Times*, Verso, London, 2010.

❖ ❖

DECEMBER 2010

BEGGAR MY NEIGHBOUR RETURNS AS A GLOBAL FINANCIAL STRATEGY

The currency wars

Once upon a time Bretton Woods ensured orderly exchange rates and the stability of the world economy. And then global currency trading mushroomed out of the control of nations' central banks. Can it still be contained and an all-out currency war averted?

Laurent L. Jacque

Brazil's finance minister, Guido Mantega, first referred to a 'currency war' in September when alerting the world to the danger of the appreciation of the Brazilian real against the US dollar and the Chinese yuan. Dominique Strauss-Kahn, managing director of the International Monetary Fund (IMF), repeated the metaphor soon after: 'I am taking very seriously the threat of a currency war, even if it is a protracted one.'

This threat takes us back to the Great Depression of the 1930s, exacerbated then by competitive, 'beggar my neighbour' devaluations among countries in recession. Today our international monetary system is radically different: there are many more protagonists and the rules of engagement have been redefined. Yet the stakes remain the same: economic growth and job creation, often driven by mercantile policies and turbo-charged by currency depreciation. Still the iron law remains true: a country with a cheap currency finds it easier to export because its goods and services are cheaper.

Fever is rising on the international monetary front. Massive intervention by the Bank of Japan on 15 September to reverse the course of the ever-rising yen went nowhere. This was followed by selective controls on capital inflows by Brazil and Thailand, and there was a threat by the US House of Representatives to impose retaliatory tariffs on imports from countries that undervalue their currency (with China the clear target). Has a currency war really broken out? We need to revisit the antecedents of the current international system.

FOUNDATIONS OF A NEW ORDER

In 1944 the Allied powers signed the Bretton Woods agreement laying the foundations for a 'new international monetary order' meant to shield the world economy from the crisis that crippled it during the inter-war period. Central banks, in close cooperation with the IMF, would be custodians of their currency values, which were publicly pegged to the US dollar in 'par value'.[1] Exchange rates were monitored by central banks that would intervene in the foreign exchange market when rates deviated by more than ±1 per cent from their par value.

From 1944 to 1971, this system enabled the rebuilding of economies devastated by the Second World War and relaunched international trade; these were the heydays of the Bretton Woods order. Over the years, tremors shook this sound edifice, principally devaluations which were necessary adjustments to the relative value of currencies to recalibrate national balances of payments. The Bretton Woods system remained stable because all foreign exchange transactions were tightly controlled by central banks.

Starting in 1958, leading member countries of the Organisation for Economic Cooperation and Development (OECD) started to decontrol foreign exchange transactions linked to their current accounts (imports and exports of goods and services), while keeping a tight control of capital flows. However, continued growth was redrawing the world economic map and the Bretton Woods system of pegged exchange rates was growing obsolete.

In 1971 the US suspended the convertibility of the dollar to gold at $35 an ounce,[2] formalising the devaluation of its currency. Major industrialised nations let their currencies float, allowing supply and demand to set the price. The foreign exchange market – not central banks – determined the value of each currency: but the float was, and is, a 'dirty' float, since central banks often intervened massively to orient exchange rates.

As exchange controls over capital movements were loosened, central banks were forced to abdicate their absolute power over exchange rates. They had little choice since their key weapon – foreign exchange reserves – were drops of water in the vast ocean of the new foreign exchange markets: today the daily turnover in those markets exceeds $4 trillion, about five times the cumulative amount of foreign exchange reserves[3] held by eurozone countries and 25 times that of the US Federal Reserve Bank. Less than 5 per cent of daily transactions can be traced to commercial operations in goods and services: 95 per cent are speculative capital movements.

That means it is almost impossible for a central bank to reverse an appreciation or depreciation of its currency: at best it can hope to slow down appreciation by accumulating massive dollar reserves. This has been true in Asia for some time: Japan once led with more than a trillion dollars in reserves but has been overtaken by China (more than two and half trillion), followed at some distance by South Korea, Taiwan, Hong Kong, Singapore and Malaysia. Other emerging market countries – BRIC, Mexico, Thailand, Indonesia, Turkey and South Africa – continue to restrain capital movements, retaining a modicum of control over the price of their currency. But that is dwindling as their foreign exchange markets are liberalised.

The declaration of war – if there ever was a currency war – goes back to China's decision in the early 1990s to peg its currency to the US dollar and resist the yuan appreciation that would have curbed its trade surplus. As the Chinese economy had a record 10–12 per cent annual growth rate, its economic boom was fuelled by exports that were largely induced by off-shoring and sub-contracting from US, Japanese and European multinationals.

This massive surplus on China's balance of trade (in large part the counterpart to the massive US trade deficit) resulted in a growing accumulation of dollar reserves mostly invested in US Treasury bonds. China maintains its exchange rate at a level that is failing to balance export revenue with import costs; this policy grants large export subsidies while imposing hefty tariffs on imports. Such a practice could incite China's trading partners to impose retaliatory tariffs, and the 'currency war' could morph into a trade war. This scenario becomes plausible in the context of an economic recovery from the sub-prime-caused financial crisis; the recovery is running out of steam as traditional economic policies, such as lowered interest rates and budget deficits, prove ineffective.

China has long been pressured by the US, and recently the European Union, to revalue the yuan by 30–40 per cent. China replies that such a revaluation could push exports-oriented firms into bankruptcy, triggering unemployment and social unrest far more difficult to contain than a commercial war. This is the classical axis of conflict; then there's the rise of currency speculators.

INVISIBLE ARMY OF CARRY TRADERS

Governors of central banks long ago abdicated their absolute power over exchange rates to an invisible army of speculators, the 'carry traders'. These footloose (and stateless) legions, from the legendary Mrs Watanabe[4] to pension or hedge fund managers, flood foreign exchange markets overwhelming the artificial dams of exchange rates defended by central banks. Carry traders simply arbitrage nominal interest rates without seeking cover against exchange rate risk.

In the early 2000s, when Japanese interest rates fell close to 0 per cent, households and institutional investors started to invest their savings in Australian or British bonds yielding 5–8 per cent. This is very profitable as long as the exchange rate remains stable during the investment period, and is even more profitable should the 'carry' currency appreciate. The carry trader can gamble further by using his capital as collateral to borrow yen at a near-zero interest rate, and then double, triple or more his bet in Australian dollars; the 'leverage' effect will multiply his gains, and possibly his losses should the yen appreciate against the Australian dollar; this is a common practice among hedge funds or trading desks of large investment banks.

Today, the carry trade comes from countries that for all practical purposes have near-zero interest rates such as the US, UK or the eurozone; it targets emerging market countries such as Brazil, Turkey or South Africa (which offer high nominal interest rates), and exacerbates the upward pressure on their currencies while pushing down the value of the financing currency, such as the US dollar. This tidal wave of capital overwhelms foreign exchange markets and marginalises central banks which – regardless of rhetoric – cannot do very much to drive the value of their currency higher or lower. The last incident was the intervention by the Bank of Japan in September, which spent $24 billion to lower the value of the yen: it did not work.

ZERO-SUM GAME

The summit meeting between heads of states of the G20 countries (90 per cent of the world economy), in Seoul in November, aimed to reduce global economic imbalances and lay foundations for 'strong, sustainable and balanced' economic growth. In fact, it was an outpouring of frustrations and recrimination, which made the fragility and vulnerability of the international monetary system even clearer.

Most countries secretly wish for a weak currency to rekindle economic growth – the 'beggar my neighbour' mercantilist spiral that could spark a currency war likely to degenerate into a trade war. Unfortunately, we are playing a zero-sum game in which one player's devaluation is others' revaluation. China, which so far has stubbornly refused to revalue its currency, is reorienting its exchange rate policy towards incremental revaluations: it is also experimenting with the internationalisation of the yuan by allowing the issuance of yuan-denominated bonds outside China.

It is an auspicious indicator of China's commitment to loosening exchange controls: over three to five years, not one to three months as the US wishes, the yuan will float more freely and appreciate against the US dollar. Emerging market countries targeted by carry traders are concerned by the progressive overvaluation of their currency and are fighting back through selective exchange controls on capital inflows to mitigate the competitive handicap inflicted on their manufacturers by too expensive a currency. The US and UK are embracing 'quantitative easing' to cure their budgetary and commercial deficits. Eurozone countries harnessed to the German locomotive and anchored to an expensive euro courtesy of the European Central Bank's tight monetary policy are waiting: the fear is that the near default of Greece and Ireland may spread to others and force a traumatic restructuring of the euro that could mean the exit of some PIIGS countries.[5] There could still be a world currency war.

Translated by the author

Laurent L. Jacque is Walter B. Wriston Professor of International Finance and Banking at the Fletcher School (Tufts University) and Professor of Economics, Finance and International Business at the HEC School of Management, France, and the author of *Global Derivative Debacles: From Theory to Malpractice*, WorldScientific, 2010.

1. And thus to gold since the US dollar was convertible into gold at $35 per ounce. A currency par value is its weight in gold and its value in US dollars.
2. Gold today trades at close to $1,500 per ounce.
3. Daily turnover is a 'flow' concept compared with foreign exchange reserves, which is a 'stock' concept.
4. The apocryphal Japanese housewife in charge of the family's finance.
5. PIIGS stands for Portugal, Ireland, Italy, Greece and Spain.

❖❖❖❖❖❖❖❖❖❖❖❖❖❖❖❖❖❖❖❖❖❖❖❖❖❖❖❖❖❖❖❖❖

JUNE 2010

'CAPITAL MUST PAY, AS WELL AS LABOUR'

The wolf pack stalks Europe

The financial sector has to be reduced in scale and importance in Europe, and the EU needs a strong central bank and an integrated fiscal system. In fact, everything that isn't being considered in the current euro panic.

James K. Galbraith

The Greek government convened an emergency meeting of expert advisers in January. A man from the IMF flatly told the prime minister George Papandreou that the only way out was to dismantle the Greek welfare state. A man from the Organisation for Economic Cooperation and Development (OECD) proposed a test: when everyone, including all your supporters, are fighting mad, he said, you'll know you've done enough. The theory behind these arguments held that markets impose discipline on states. Bond buyers judge the determination of the government's austerity programmes; then they decide whether to trust in the repayment of debt. Given sufficiently harsh and credible measures, interest rates would fall and Greece's refinancing could proceed.

But there was a problem. Promises are cheap. Even if the theory is right, for the policy to work, the cuts have actually to be carried out. But implementation takes time. Refinancing of previously existing debt is a *pre-commitment*; it depends on confidence that the government *will* carry through, long before it actually does. And how can a mere policy announcement engender such belief, in a state that has a bad reputation to begin with? Whatever was said, when Greece's current bonds matured the actual cuts would still lie ahead. And the more severe the announced cuts, the *less* credible they would be.

This argument logically destroyed the idea that *any* austerity programme could reopen private bond markets on terms acceptable to Greece. The only way to avoid default was for Europe to refinance the Greek debt, bypassing the markets. So the question became: how to persuade the EU to do that? This challenge propelled the economic crisis to the centre of a political game. The Greek government still had to announce severe cuts and other 'reforms' – not to pacify the markets, but to meet the needs of Angela Merkel. Her voters in Germany would not tolerate a 'bailout' unless they saw painful sacrifices from the Greeks. Meanwhile the Greek government declared unshakeable allegiance to its debt and to the euro – while subtly reminding France and Germany that Greek default and exit, with inevitable contagion to Portugal and Spain, could not be excluded if help did not come.

SECOND EPIPHANY

As economic policy, this game made no sense for Europe. The cuts would mean joblessness, lost tax revenues and therefore little actual deficit reduction in Greece. You cannot cut 12 per cent of GDP from total demand – as the eventual IMF programme called for – without cutting GDP itself. Falling Greek GDP would also cost jobs for German and French factory workers who make goods sold in Greece. Except relative to the unpayable interest rates on offer from private markets, Greece's ability to service its debts would not improve.

Nor – without a devaluation, made impossible by the euro – would Greece's competitiveness get better. The measures that might help over time, namely the programme of public administration and tax reforms to which the Greek government was already committed, would be much harder to implement in the atmosphere of crisis, cuts and exorbitant interest rates.

As the debt deadline neared, Europe's leaders laboured under arcane rules, an unwieldy collective process, domestic political backlash and the burden of their own limited understanding. High officials insisted fanatically that cutting public spending and deficits would *foster* economic growth. Predictably they came to the verge of disaster. After Chancellor Merkel appeared to repudiate a funding package, panic swept the eurozone. The price of credit default swaps on Portugal and Spain, and also on their banks, soared – testament to the fragility of the European financial system with its lack of EU-wide deposit guarantees. Merkel blinked and a refunding package finally went through.

But now came a second epiphany. The Greek bond bailout only made the European financial crisis worse. To see why, imagine you own a Portuguese bond. Repayment is uncertain, so you dump it, or purchase a credit default swap. The bond price then falls, making Portugal's refinancing harder. At the limit, the best way to assure payment is to *close* the private bond markets and (as with Greece) to blackmail the EU. And a rescue package is practically certain, given the general view that Portugal has not been as 'irresponsible' as Greece. And after Portugal, there is Spain, to which the same rules apply.

The speculators could thus force the Europeanisation of Mediterranean debts, and in mid-May this happened with breathtaking speed. There was panic, just as in the US in September 2008 and for the same reason: it was a panic spurred by speculators pressing reluctant political leaders to action. Like all victims of blackmail, President Sarkozy expressed anger. And Merkel announced a retaliatory ban on naked shorting on government bonds. But what can they do? A bond sale or credit default swap on Greece, Portugal or Spain can be consummated entirely outside Europe – in New York or the Cayman Islands. So the moment they came under pressure, the speculators only regrouped for another attack.

INELUCTABLE DECLINE

The trillion-dollar scale of the EU action calmed things for a moment. But then it became clear that the EU governments can only borrow from each other. They cannot create net new reserves and they cannot finance growth and bond bailouts at the same time. Only the European Central Bank (ECB) can do that. At first the actual role of the ECB seemed vague, but then it emerged that the bank really was buying up European bonds. With this, the debt problem came under control; but now the supply of euros became highly elastic, and the euro detached itself from its hard-money moorings and began an ineluctable decline. Statements by the ECB president insisting that it was only recycling term deposits, not creating new money, caused confusion and fostered a sense that Europe's leadership did not know its own mind. Flight bordering on panic continued.

And so a third pillar of financial wisdom begins to come clear. In a successful financial system, there must be a state larger than any market. That state must have monetary control – as the Federal Reserve does, without question, in the US. Otherwise the markets play divide-and-conquer against the states. Europe has devoted enormous effort to creating a single market without enlarging any state, and while pretending that the Central Bank cannot provide new money to the system. In so doing, it has created markets larger than states, and states with unbearable debts, which now consume them. Only the ECB could relieve this situation, and only by abandoning its charter in the face of the pressures of the real world.

How far the ECB will finally go, and how far it will take up the quantitative easing pioneered by the Federal Reserve in late 2008, remains unknown. But even if it finally commits to this course, ending the financial crisis for now, the *economic* crisis will deepen. Each 'rescued' country will get, in turn, just enough assistance to repay its debts. The price, each time, will be massive cuts in public budgets. The banks will be saved, but growth, jobs and the achievements of the welfare state will be destroyed. The IMF man gets his way. And the European recession grows deeper and deeper. This will be proof of the proposition that it was fiscal stabilisation – and not monetary policy – that actually brought the US economy back from the brink of a great depression.

RICH PEOPLE IN POOR COUNTRIES

This European crisis will therefore continue until Europe changes its mind. It will continue until the forces that built the welfare state in the first place rise up to defend it. It will continue until Europe faces the *constitutional* deficiencies of its system, which come from the absence of an integrated measure for macro-economic stimulation. Europe needs a single integrated tax structure, a central bank dedicated to economic prosperity and a reduction of the financial sector. But most of all it needs an automatic fiscal process to offset recession and demand shortfalls in its less-wealthy regions, and the process should work not only through governments but also directly to Europe's citizens.

From a purely technical standpoint, there are some quite easy ways to achieve this. For instance, a European Pension Union could set the goal of equalising minimum pensions across Europe, so that working people in Portugal, Greece or Spain do not retire on a material standard far below those of Germany or France. There could be a Europe-wide topping-up of minimum wages, similar to the highly effective Earned Income Tax Credit in the US. The European Investment Bank could foster the creation of transnational European universities on the US land grant model, strengthening higher education throughout the peripheral regions. Examples could be multiplied but the principle is plain: the correct response to mass unemployment and the resulting budget deficits is to *expand* public and private expenditure in the deficit regions. This is the only way to break the vicious circle of budget cutting, debt deflation and depression now under way.

Some would view this argument as a proposal to tax Germans for the benefit of Greeks, but from an economic perspective that view is entirely incorrect. The point and purpose is to mobilise unemployed resources throughout Europe and get them into employment. This imposes no cost on anyone presently employed, since it expands the flow of real goods and services, available to all. An integrated tax system, for its part, would help stem the pandemic of tax evasion in Greece and other southern countries in Europe. To the extent that there is a higher tax burden as reforms take hold, it should fall on rich people in poorer countries and not on poorer people in the rich ones.

The recent experience calls into question whether any economic recovery can occur as long as the financial markets are able to bet massively against euro assets as a whole, something that happens primarily on the credit default swap (CDS) markets. And this underlines the necessity of cutting down the financial sector until it no longer threatens the EU. Cutting down the financial sector can be achieved by regulation, by taxation and by restructuring the debts of the Mediterranean states. Regulations should prohibit CDS transactions by any European financial entity on European sovereigns, and force that kind of gambling into offshore havens. If banks fail as a result of hedged or unhedged bets, they should be taken over and run as public utilities. A common European tax on realised capital gains could (in principle, anyway) be administered by national governments; a tax on financial transactions, though no panacea, is long overdue. If capital controls must be reimposed to arrest financial contagion, so be it. In a contest between the state and the financial markets, with the survival of stable and civilised government in question, the state cannot be allowed to lose out.

FEWER INNOCENTS

To restructure public debts that cannot be paid, Europe needs a sovereign insolvency process comparable to Chapter IX covering municipal bankruptcy in US law – as long proposed by Professor Kunibert Raffer of Vienna University. That would permit national governments to maintain essential services while relieving themselves of unpayable debts. There would be consequences for the banks, avoidable only by insuring deposits and standing ready to assume control when debt restructuring for a country leads to insolvency for a bank. But losses already incurred must be recorded somewhere, and there are far fewer innocents in any bank than in any country.

These are radical steps. But can anyone seriously question that radical steps are needed? Can anyone now doubt that the architecture of neoliberal Europe is falling apart? No. The choice is between the disastrous radicalism of budget cuts and a constructive radicalism of full employment. Or between a disastrous radicalism of bank bailouts and a constructive radicalism of social development. Europe must choose.

As a very young man, I was drafted in 1975 to the Banking Committee of the US House of Representatives and I took part in a financial rescue programme for the City of New York, then in financial and economic crisis. It included, among many radical provisions, a requirement that the city's debt be restructured and that bondholders take a loss. Shortly, a call came from the former governor of New York, Averell Harriman – at one time Roosevelt's ambassador to Stalin – requesting a briefing. I was dispatched. I found Harriman – octogenarian and recovering from a hip fracture – in his pyjamas, seated on a couch in an inner room of his Georgetown mansion. On the wall to his right were Van Gogh's sunflowers. In a glass case to his left was a Degas ballerina. In this setting, I attempted to explain why the people's representatives were demanding sacrifice mainly from the rich. Presently he nodded, leaned forward on his cane, and intoned in a deep voice: 'I understand completely. Capital must pay, as well as labour.'

Original text in English

James K. Galbraith holds the Lloyd M. Bentsen, Jr, chair in government/business relations at the LBJ School of Public Affairs, University of Texas at Austin, and is the author of *The Predator State: How Conservatives Abandoned the Free Market and Why Liberals Should Too*, Simon & Schuster, 2009.

❖❖❖❖❖❖❖❖❖❖❖❖❖❖❖❖❖❖❖❖❖❖❖❖❖❖❖❖❖❖❖❖❖❖❖❖❖❖❖

AUGUST 2011

CAN'T PAY BACK, WON'T PAY BACK

Iceland's loud No

The people of Iceland have now twice voted not to repay international debts incurred by banks, and bankers, for which the whole island is being held responsible. With the present turmoil in European capitals, could this be the way forward for other economies?

Robert H. Wade and Silla Sigurgeirsdottir

The small island of Iceland has lessons for the world. It held a referendum in April to decide, more or less, whether ordinary people should pay for the folly of the bankers (and by extension, could governments control the corporate sector if they depended on it for finance). Sixty per cent of the population rejected an agreement negotiated between Iceland, the Netherlands and the UK to pay back the British and Dutch governments for the money they spent to recompense savers with the failed bank Icesave. That was less resistance than the first referendum last spring, when 93 per cent voted no.

The referendum was significant since European governments, pressured by speculators, the IMF and the European Commission, are imposing austerity policies on which their citizens have not voted. Even devotees of deregulation are worried by the degree of the western world's servitude to unconstrained financial institutions. After the Icelandic referendum, even the liberal *Financial Times* noted with approval on 13 April that it had been possible to 'put citizens before banks', an idea which does not resonate among European political leaders.

Iceland is an unusually pure example of the dynamics that blocked regulation and caused financial fragility across the developed world for 20 years. In 2007, just before the financial crisis, Iceland's average income was the fifth highest in the world, 60 per cent above US levels; Reykjavik's shops were stuffed with luxury goods, its restaurants made London seem cheap, and SUVs choked the narrow streets. Icelanders were the happiest people in the world according to an international study in 2006.[1] Much of this rested on the super-fast growth of three Icelandic banks that rose from small utility institutions in 1998 to being among the world's top 300 banks eight years later, increasing their assets from 100 per cent of GDP in 2000 to almost 800 per cent by 2007, a ratio second only to Switzerland.

The crisis came in September 2008 when money markets seized up after the Lehman meltdown. Within a week, Iceland's three big banks collapsed and were taken into public ownership. Moody's now listed them among the eleven biggest financial collapses in history.

TOWARDS MODERNISATION

After more than 600 years of foreign rule, Iceland's social structure was the most feudal of all Nordic countries at the beginning of the 20th century. Fishing dominated the economy, generating most of the foreign-currency earnings and allowing the development of an import-based commercial sector. This created urban economic activities: construction, services, light industry. After the Second World War the economy grew strongly, because of Marshall Plan aid (there was a large US-NATO military base); an abundant export commodity, cold-water fish, unusually blessed with high income elasticity of demand; and a small, literate population with a strong sense of national identity.

As Iceland became more prosperous it established a welfare state, in line with the tax-financed Scandinavian model, and by the 1980s had attained a level and a distribution of disposable income equal to the Nordic average. Yet it remained both more regulated and more patron-client-dominated than its European neighbours; a local oligopoly restricted the political and economic landscape.

There is a direct line of descent from the quasi-feudal power structures of the 19th century to the modernised Icelandic capitalism of the later 20th century, when a bloc of 14 families, popularly known as The Octopus, was the economic and political ruling elite. The Octopus controlled imports, transport, banking, insurance, fishing and supplies to the NATO base and provided most top politicians. The families lived like chieftains.

The Octopus controlled the rightwing Independence Party (IP) which dominated the media and decided on senior appointments in the civil service, police and judiciary. The local, state-owned banks were effectively run by the dominant parties, the IP and the Centre Party or CP.[2] Ordinary people had to go through party functionaries to get loans to buy a car, or for foreign exchange for travel abroad. Power networks operated as webs of bullying, sycophancy and distrust, permeated with a macho culture, something like the former Soviet Union.

This traditional order was challenged from within by a neoliberal faction, the Locomotive group, which had coalesced in the early 1970s after law and business administration students at the University of Iceland took over a journal, *The Locomotive*, and promoted free-market ideas. Their aim was not just to transform the society but also to open career opportunities for themselves, rather than wait for Octopus patronage. At the end of the cold war their position strengthened materially and ideologically, as the communists and social democrats lost public support. The future IP prime minister, Davíð Oddsson, was a prominent member.

Oddsson, born in 1948 with a middle-class background, was elected as an IP councillor to the Reykjavik municipal council in 1974; by 1982 he was mayor of Reykjavik, leading privatisation campaigns, including selling off the municipality's fishing industry, to the benefit of members of the Locomotive group. In 1991 he led the IP to victory in the general election, and reigned (not too strong a word) as prime minister for 14 years, overseeing the growth of the financial sector, before installing himself as governor of the Central Bank in 2004. He had little experience or interest in the world beyond Iceland. His Locomotive group protégé, Geir Haarde, finance minister from 1998 to 2005, took over as prime minister shortly after. These two men most directly steered Iceland's great experiment to create an international financial centre in the North Atlantic, midway between Europe and America.

ICELAND LIBERALISES

The liberalisation of the economy began in 1994, when accession to the European Economic Area, the free-trade bloc of EU countries, plus Iceland, Lichtenstein and Norway, lifted restrictions on cross-border flows of capital, goods, services and people. The Oddsson government then sold off state-owned assets and deregulated labour. Privatisation began in 1998, implemented by

Oddsson and Halldór Ásgrímsson, the leader of the CP. Of the banks, Landsbanki was allocated to IP grandees, Kaupthing to their counterparts in the CP, its coalition partner; foreign bidders were excluded. Later, Glitnir, a private bank formed from the merger of several smaller ones, joined the league.

So Iceland roared into international finance aided globally by abundant cheap credit and free capital mobility, and domestically by strong political backing for the banks. The new banks merged investment banking with commercial banking, so that both shared government guarantees. And the country had low sovereign debt, which gave the banks high marks from the international credit-rating agencies. The major shareholders of Landsbanki, Kaupthing, Glitnir and their spin-offs reversed the earlier political dominance of finance: government policy was now subordinated to the ends of finance.

Oddsson and friends relaxed the state-provided mortgage rules, allowing 90 per cent loans. The newly privatised banks rushed to offer even more generous terms. Income tax and VAT rates were lowered to turn Iceland into a low-tax international financial centre. Bubble dynamics took hold. City planners aimed to move Reykjavik from the trajectory of an ordinary city to that of a world city (despite its small population of 110,000) and approved several grandiose new public and private buildings, saying 'If Dubai, why not Reykjavik?'

Iceland's new banking elite were intent on expanding their ownership of the economy, competing and cooperating with each other. Using their shares as collateral, some took out large loans from their own banks, and bought more shares in the same banks, inflating share prices. It worked like this: Bank A lent to shareholders in Bank B, who bought more shares in B using shares as collateral, raising B's share price. Bank B returned the favour. The share prices of both banks rose, without new money coming in. The banks not only grew bigger, they grew more and more interconnected. Several dealings of this kind are now under criminal investigation by the special prosecutor, as cases of market manipulation.

Tiny Iceland soon managed to enter the big-bank league, with three banks in the world's biggest 300 by 2006. The super-abundance of credit allowed people to consume in extravagant celebration of their escape from the earlier decades of credit rationing (on top of the earlier escape from foreign rule as recently as 1944). They saw themselves as fully independent at last, which may explain their happiness ranking. The owners and managers remunerated themselves on an ever-larger scale. The richer they were, the more they attracted political support. Their private jets, roaring in and out of Reykjavik's airport, seemed to be visual and auditory proof to the part-admiring, part-envious population below. Income and wealth inequality surged, helped by government policies that shifted the tax burden to the poorer population.[3] The bankers made large financial contributions to the governing parties and giant loans to key politicians. The leading Icelandic champion of free-market economics declared in *The Wall Street Journal*: 'Oddsson's experiment with liberal policies is the greatest success story in the world.'[4]

In the euphoria, the dangers of a strategy of 'economic growth based on vast foreign borrowing' were overlooked. Icelanders lived out the dictum of Plautus, the third-century BC Roman playwright, who had one of his characters declare: 'I am a rich man, as long as I do not repay my creditors.'

THE 2006 MINI-CRISIS

In 2006 there were worries in the financial press about the stability of the big banks, which were beginning to have problems raising funds in the money markets (on which their business model depended). Iceland's current account deficit had soared from 5 per cent of GDP in 2003 to 20 per cent in 2006, one of the highest in the world. The stock market multiplied itself nine times over between 2001 and 2007.

Landsbanki, Kaupthing and Glitnir were operating far beyond the capacity of Iceland's Central Bank to support them as lender of last resort; their liabilities were real, but many of their assets were dubious. In February 2006 Fitch downgraded Iceland's outlook from stable to negative and triggered the 2006 'mini-crisis': the krona fell sharply, the value of banks' liabilities in foreign currencies rose, the stock market fell and business defaults rose, and the sustainability of foreign-currency debts became a public problem. The Danske Bank of Copenhagen described Iceland as a 'geyser economy' on the point of exploding.[5]

Icelandic bankers and politicians brushed aside the crisis. Iceland's Central Bank took out a loan to double the foreign-exchange reserves, while the Chamber of Commerce, run by representatives of Landsbanki, Kaupthing, Glitnir and their spin-offs, responded with a PR campaign. It paid the American monetary economist Frederic Mishkin $135,000 to lend his name to a report attesting to the stability of Iceland's banks. It allegedly paid the London Business School economist Richard Portes £58,000 ($95,000) to do the same for a later report. The supply-side economist Arthur Laffer assured the Icelandic business community in 2007 that fast economic growth with a large trade deficit and ballooning foreign debt were signs of success: 'Iceland should be a model to the world.'[6] The value of the banks' 'assets' was then around eight times greater than Iceland's GDP.

In the elections of May 2007, the Social Democratic Alliance (SDA) entered a coalition government with the still-dominant IP. To the consternation of many supporters, SDA leaders ditched their pre-election pledges and endorsed the continued expansion of the financial sector.

Though they had survived 2006, Landsbanki, Kaupthing and Glitnir had trouble raising money to fund their asset purchases and repay existing debts, largely denominated in foreign currencies. So Landsbanki pioneered Icesave, an internet-based service that aimed to win retail savings deposits by offering more attractive interest rates than high-street banks. Established in Britain in October 2006, and in the Netherlands 18 months later, Icesave caught the attention of best buy internet finance sites and was soon flooded with deposits. Millions of pounds arrived from Cambridge University, the London Metropolitan Police Authority, even the UK Audit Commission, responsible for overseeing local government funds, as well as 300,000 Icesave depositors in the UK alone.

Icesave entities were legally established as branches, rather than subsidiaries, so they were under the supervision of the Icelandic authorities, rather than their hosts. No one noticed that the Icelandic regulatory agency had a total staff, including receptionist, of only 45 and suffered high turnover as many went on to join the banks, which offered better pay. No one worried much that, because of Iceland's obligations as a member of the EEA deposit insurance scheme, its population of 320,000 would be responsible for compensating the depositors abroad in the event of failure. Landsbanki's shareholders reaped the short-term profits while most Icelanders didn't know anything about Icesave at all.

LOVE LETTERS

The second 'solution' to difficulties in raising new funds was a way to get more access to liquidity without pledging real assets as collateral. The Big Three sold debt securities to a smaller regional bank, which took these bonds to the Central Bank and borrowed against them, without having to supply further collateral; they then lent back to the initiating big bank. The bonds were called 'love letters' – mere promises. By participating in this game and accepting as collateral claims on other Icelandic banks the Central Bank was conniving in the banks' strategy of gambling for resurrection.

Then the banks internationalised the process: the Big Three established subsidiaries in Luxembourg and sold love letters to them. The subsidiaries sold them on to the Central Bank of Luxembourg or the European Central Bank and received cash in return, which they could pass back to the parent bank in Iceland or use themselves. The OECD calculates that just the domestic love letters, between the CBI and the Icelandic banks, incurred losses to the CBI and the Treasury of 13 per cent of GDP (OECD Economic Surveys: Iceland, June 2011).

The Icelandic banks fell two weeks after Lehman Brothers. On 29 September 2008, Glitnir approached Oddsson at the Central Bank for help with its looming liquidity problem. To restore confidence, Oddsson advised the government to buy 75 per cent of Glitnir's shares. The effect was not to boost Glitnir but to undermine confidence in Iceland. The country's rating plunged, and credit lines were withdrawn from Landsbanki and Kaupthing. A run on Icesave's overseas branches began. Oddsson moved on 7 October 2008 to peg the krona to a basket of currencies at close to the pre-crisis value. With the currency tumbling and in the absence of capital controls, the foreign-exchange reserves were exhausted: the peg lasted for only a few hours, just long enough for those in the know to change their money out of the krona at a much more favourable rate. Inside sources indicate that billions left the currency in these hours. Then the krona was floated, and sank. On 8 October the then UK prime minister, Gordon Brown, froze Landsbanki's UK assets under the anti-terrorism laws. The stock market, bank bonds, house prices and average income went into free-fall.

The IMF arrived in Reykjavik in October 2008 to prepare a crisis-management programme, the first time the Fund had been called in to rescue a developed economy since Britain in 1976. It offered a conditional loan of $2.1 billion to stabilise the krona and backed the British and Dutch governments' demands that Iceland should honour the obligations of the European deposit-guarantee scheme and recompense them for their bailouts of Icesave depositors.

Iceland's normally placid population erupted in an angry protest movement, principally targeted at Haarde, Oddsson and the IP, although the SDA's foreign minister, Ingibjörg Gísladóttir, was considered tarnished too. Thousands of people assembled in Reykjavik's main square on freezing Saturday afternoons between October 2008 and January 2009, banged saucepans, linked arms in a circle around the parliament building to demand the government's resignation, and pelted the building with food.

In January 2009, the IP-SDA coalition broke. To date, Iceland is the only country to have shifted distinctly to the left after the financial crisis. An interim SDA-LGM (Social Democrats-Left Green Movement) government was formed in January 2009 to lead until April's election. In the election the IP was reduced to 16 seats, despite the overwhelming bias of the electoral system in its favour, its worst result since its formation in 1929.

ICESAVE DEBT REJECTED

The SDA-LGM government came under immediate pressure to repay the Icesave debt; much of the IMF loan was withheld until Reykjavik agreed. The new government was also divided on whether to apply for full membership of the EU and eurozone, with most of the SDA strongly in favour. After long negotiations, the government presented the terms they had agreed on the Icesave debt to the parliament in October 2009: 5.5 billion krona ($7.8 billion), or 50 per cent of Iceland's GDP, was to be paid to the British and Dutch treasuries between 2016 and 2023.

The party's health minister resigned in protest, five dissidents refused to vote with the government. The bill was forced through on 30 December 2009, against high feelings in the country. On 5 January 2010 President Grímsson announced that he would not sign it into law, out of respect for the national sentiment. In the ensuing referendum the bill was decisively rejected. In the May 2010 Reykjavik municipal elections, the SDA slumped to 19 per cent and a comedian was elected as the city's mayor. In October, protests resumed, and the coalition conceded the election of a constitutional assembly to draw up a new constitution (the existing one having been inherited from Denmark on independence in 1944). When the election was invalidated by the Supreme Court, the assembly was reconvened as a constitutional council appointed by parliament.

The deal on the table in this April's second Icesave referendum involved substantial concessions on the part of the British and Dutch governments. After the no vote, the disagreement may have to go to international courts.

THE CRISIS POSTPONED

The cost of losses on loans and guarantees, added to the cost of restructuring financial organisations, brings the total direct fiscal costs of the crisis to about 20 per cent of GDP, higher than in any other country except Ireland (OECD Economic Surveys, Iceland, June 2011). But the postponement of major public spending cuts until this year has given the economy breathing space; and the sharp devaluation has helped to generate a trade surplus for the first time in many years. So far, Iceland has experienced smaller falls in GDP and employment than big public-spending slashers like Ireland, Estonia and Lithuania. The unemployment rate, only 2 per cent in 2006, has been between 7 per cent and 9 per cent since 2009; but the rate of outmigration, of Icelanders and other European workers (predominantly Polish), has been the highest since 1889. However, the SDA-LGM government has announced drastic cuts in public spending for 2011 and beyond. Local governments have no budget for fresh projects. Hospitals and schools are cutting salaries and sacking employees. The freeze on house repossessions expired in 2010.

The IP-SDA government's decision to provide unlimited bank deposit guarantees illustrates its debt to the financial elite. Had it limited the guarantee to five million krona ($70,000), it would have protected the entire deposits of 95 per cent of depositors; only the wealthiest 5 per cent, including many politicians, benefited from the unlimited guarantee, which now means further constraints on public spending.

Iceland's tiny scale seemed to make it easier to challenge the government's denial of the impending crisis, but the opposite was true. The Oddsson government undertook an extreme privatisation of information. Iceland's National Economic Institute had a reputation for independent thinking, and Oddsson abolished it in 2002. From then on the banks, international rating companies and the Chamber of Commerce provided almost the only information and running commentary on the state of the economy, present and future.

Paradoxically, a number of critical reports were published when the bubble was in the early stages, including one by the CBI. But by 2007–08, when the dangers were acute, reports, including those by the IMF, became noticeably softer in tone. It seems that the official financial institutions, as well as bankers and politicians, understood that the situation was so fragile that just to speak of it might trigger a run on the banks.

In October 2010 the parliament decided to charge Prime Minister Haarde for breach of ministerial responsibility. The permanent finance secretary Baldur Gudlaugsson (former member of the Locomotive group) has been given two years in prison for using inside information for his personal advantage while selling his shares in Landsbanki in September 2008. But the special prosecutor in charge of the investigation of the banks has been working with a team of 60 lawyers and others for the past two years and has so far brought no charges. Meanwhile Oddsson was appointed in September 2009 as editor-in-chief at *Morgunblaðið*, the leading Iceland daily, and orchestrated coverage of the crisis. A commentator said that was like appointing Nixon editor of *The Washington Post* after Watergate. Iceland's elite looks after its own.

Original text in English

Robert Wade is professor of political economy at the London School of Economics; Silla Sigurgeirsdottir is lecturer in public policy at the University of Iceland. This is an updated version of 'Lessons from Iceland', first published in the *New Left Review*, London, September–October 2010.

1. World Database of Happiness, 2006.
2. Among the opposition are the Social Democrat Party and the further left Common People's Party.
3. Stefán Ólafsson and Arnaldur Sölvi Kristjánsson, 'Income inequality in a bubble economy: the case of Iceland 1992–2008', paper presented at the Luxemburg Incomes Study Conference, 28–30 June 2010.
4. Hannes Gissurarson, 'Miracle on Iceland', *The Wall Street Journal*, New York, 29 January 2004.
5. Danske Bank, 'Iceland: Geyser crisis', Copenhagen, 2006.
6. Arthur Laffer, 'Overheating is not dangerous', *Morgunblaðið*, Reykjavik, 17 November 2007.

Part II: US Empire

❖❖❖❖❖❖❖❖❖❖❖❖❖❖❖❖❖❖❖❖❖❖❖❖❖❖❖❖❖❖❖❖❖❖❖❖

December 2010

Why America's democrats failed to bring change

Empire as a state of being

The US came into being within an empire, alongside other empires, and found its place in a world order rooted in European-Atlantic expansion. So, while President Obama has changed the tone and emphasis of foreign policy, his overall goal remains to ensure US power and authority.

Philip S. Golub

In the 1990s, after decades of handwringing over American 'decline', influential parts of the US power elite began dreaming of a new 'American century' and an expanded 'American peace'. This was a broad ideational trend, encompassing nationalist and internationalist segments of the foreign policy and security establishment. Despite varying prescriptions for world order and ways to assert American preferences, these segments saw the end of the cold war as a historic opportunity to reaffirm and expand US power and authority. By the end of the decade the main strands of elite opinion, casually comparing the US to the Roman or British empires at their heights, were celebrating the United States' 'unparalleled ascendancy around the globe...unrivalled by even the greatest empires of the past'.[1]

Imperial imaginings were particularly pronounced in the national security complex and the neo-conservative right, which harboured extravagant visions of 'global empire' and lasting strategic monopoly. At the turn of the century imperial outlooks pervaded a new administration that sought, in Condoleezza Rice's words, to 'capitalise on [the opportunities offered] by the shifting of the tectonic plates in international politics' and establish a new world order under exclusive US authority.[2] Striving for unbounded autonomy, the Bush administration launched a methodical assault on the UN system, abandoned international law, and initiated a new phase of military and imperial expansion in Central Asia and the

Gulf. The unintended but predictable result was a severe erosion of US legitimacy.

Today, in conditions of crisis and under more enlightened leadership, visions of empire have been replaced by greater realism and concerns of decline. Elected on a wave of rejection of the ruinous policies of the Bush administration, Barack Obama has shifted the tone and emphasis of US foreign policy in positive ways. He has made significant gestures to repair the fracture between 'Islam and the West' and acted to reduce tensions in various world regions. Yet at the same time he has slipped effortlessly into imperial presidency and framed his agenda as a way to restore US world power and authority (damaged under Bush). During the presidential campaign, in a little noticed statement, he urged American voters to 'unite in a common purpose, to make this century the next American century'. Once elected he reiterated this message, calling upon members of Congress to join him to 'make this century another American century'. In his 2010 State of the Union address, comparing the US's economic performance with that of China, India and Germany, he was more specific: 'These nations aren't playing for second place...I do not accept second place for the United States of America.'[3]

Appeals to national greatness have always been part of American political discourse in times of perceived decline or ascent. But coming from a cosmopolitan president with multicultural sensitivity, this language of national power and primacy is a troubling reflection of the weight of history on the shaping of worldviews and policy. Obama, like his predecessors, has inherited and will briefly preside over an imperial system with worldwide reach. Whatever his intimate convictions and preferences, he is caretaker of the set of interlocking institutions that have underpinned the post-1945 imperial presidency and the country's transcontinental strategic commitments.

This constraint helps to account for the continuity of US foreign policy over long periods and the difficulty of translating democratic change at home to the international level. The policy emphasis may vary from one administration to another according to prevailing social forces and international circumstances, resulting in policies that are more or less cooperative or coercive. These variations matter. As the Bush administration's behaviour shows, they matter a great deal in their impacts and outcomes.

Nonetheless, new leaders, however liberal and democratic, cannot erase the past or simply decide to liquidate the imperial system of which they become managers, and from which they derive their power and authority. They are caught in the same bind as British Liberal and Labour leaders who, in the late 19th and 20th centuries, sought to liberalise the empire and found, in Elizabeth Monroe's words, that 'a worldwide Empire...cannot change direction overnight'. Successive British governments found 'that more has gone before than [they] imagined – too much to alter quickly'.[4] Leaders of dominant countries are wedded to the accumulation of power, profit and prestige of the imperial state.

IMPERIAL COSMOLOGIES

The persistence of imperial self-conceptions should be traced back to a remoter past. Underlying the idea of the 'American century' is a set of axiomatic assumptions about historical purpose, world order and international hierarchy, an imperial cosmology that crystallised well before the mid-20th century. The notion that the present world order is a necessary one derives from historical experience of nearly continuous expansion and ascent. Erected on the debris of the 19th century European imperial order, the post-1945 American pax was the outcome of a long movement of formal and informal expansion that shaped the American historical imagination of world-empire as destiny.

The US came into being within an empire, alongside other empires, and found its place and space in the hierarchical world order that resulted from the global movement of Euro-Atlantic expansion. Fostered by transatlantic linkages, relentless US economic and territorial expansion in the 19th century was an integral, dynamic part of this global movement. Rooted in material forces and notions of cultural hierarchy common to all imperial societies, it was consistently coercive. In the course of the century, the US became an active participant in the inter-imperial system, engaging routinely in worldwide interventions in the colonial periphery, often alongside the European colonial states. Empire became a way of life, a state of being.

By the end of the century, along with the growth of the US's relative power and its new industrial ascendancy, influential segments of the American elite began dreaming of supplanting Europe and becoming 'a seat of wealth and power greater than ever was England, Rome or Constantinople'.[5] Victory in war with the decaying Spanish Empire in 1898 and the weakening of Europe with the First World War confirmed this vision, and fuelled the hope. By the late 1930s, American elite opinion entertained no doubts that the US had indeed become the 'heart of the world'. In 1939 Walter Lippmann wrote: 'In the lifetime of the generation to which we belong there has been one of the greatest events in the history of mankind. The controlling power in western civilisation has crossed the Atlantic...What Rome was to the ancient world, what Great Britain has been to the modern world, America is to the world of tomorrow.'[6] Surveying the post-war world landscape in 1946, Harry Truman said: 'From Darius I's Persia, Alexander's Greece, Hadrian's Rome, Victoria's Britain...no nation or group of nations has had our responsibilities.'[7]

This vision of historical process through imperial selection is at the root of the pervasive assumption, shared by historical actors and mainstream theorists, that pluralism is risk-laden, and that world peace requires an authoritative centre of gravity, a 'benevolent despot'. The corollary is that the perpetuation of hegemony or empire is in the universal interest. The problem for American leaders according to Stephen Walt is to get the 'rest of the world to welcome US primacy' by encouraging other 'states to see its dominant position as beneficial (or at least bearable)' and by convincing them that 'American power...will be used judiciously and for the broader benefit of mankind'.[8] Used to being at the apex, US elite opinion appears incapable of thinking outside this conceptual box.

LONG EXIT FROM EMPIRE

As Peter Cain and Anthony Hopkins point out in their study of the British Empire, the spokesmen of leading powers 'do not take readily to the idea that the end of their period of dominance is not necessarily the end of the world [and] find it hard to envisage pluralistic alternatives to the rule of a single power'.[9] If Britain's long exit from empire is anything to go by, transformation of the way the US views and deals with the world will be a difficult, drawn-out process. Late 19th-century imperialists believed that Britain had received from the 'Almighty a gift of a lease on the universe forever'. Though economically weakened by the First World War, Britain maintained its world position and empire. Indeed, Britain's 'continuing ambition and success as an imperialist power' can be seen in its expansion in the Middle East.

The decisive turn came with the Second World War, which led to Britain's financial and economic exhaustion, and the re-centring of the world capitalist economy from Europe to the US. But even then, despite the urgent need to restore the war-torn economy, in the words of Michael Blackwell, post-war 'Labour leaders sought energetically to maintain and in some cases to expand Britain's imperial role, and in so doing they used up resources that might otherwise have been allocated to domestic expenditures'.[10] So did the Conservatives, leading to Britain's ill-fated adventure in Egypt in 1956. The afterglow of empire is still not entirely gone, as shown by the revival of liberal-imperialism during Tony Blair's tenure.

The US's present position is hardly comparable to Britain's in 1945. Despite the present economic crisis, the country still accounts for over a fifth of world gross domestic product. It is the dominant world military power and remains the primary source of scientific innovation. Though it faces growing financial constraints, it is not about to become a secondary power. Unless forced to do so, it will not suddenly dismantle the internationalised security structure that gives it world leverage.

However, the coming century will not be American, and the emerging world order will not be centred. As the historical rebalancing towards non-western world regions unfolds, the US will be faced with a novel de-centred and plural configuration of world politics. How will the US accommodate itself to this new order?

Original text in English

Philip S. Golub is associate professor at the American University of Paris, lecturer at the University of Paris VIII and author of *Power, Profit and Prestige: A History of American Imperial Expansion*, Pluto Press, London 2010.

1. Henry Kissinger, *Does America Need a Foreign Policy: Toward a Diplomacy for the 21st Century*, Simon and Schuster, New York, 2001.
2. Nicholas Lemann, 'The Next World Order: the Bush Administration may have a brand-new doctrine of power', *The New Yorker*, 1 April 2002.
3. Speech in Flint, Michigan, 15 June 2008; remarks of President Barack Obama to Joint Session of Congress, White House, Washington, DC, 24 February 2009; State of the Union speech, 27 January 2010.
4. Elizabeth Monroe, *Britain's Moment in the Middle East, 1914–1956*, Chatto and Windus, London, 1963.
5. Brooks Adams, *America's Economic Supremacy*, Macmillan, New York and London, 1900.
6. Walter Lippmann, 'The American destiny', *Life Magazine*, New York, 1939.
7. Cited in Donald W. White, 'History and American internationalism: the formulation from the past after World War II', *Pacific Historical Review*, volume 58 (2), May 1989.
8. Stephen Walt, *Taming American Power: The Global Response to US Primacy*, W.W. Norton, New York, 2006.

9. Peter J. Cain and Anthony G. Hopkins, *British Imperialism, 1688–2000*, Longman Pearson, London, 2002.

10. Michael Blackwell, *Clinging to Grandeur: British Attitudes and Foreign Policy in the Aftermath of the Second World War*, Greenwood Press, London, 1993.

❖❖❖❖❖❖❖❖❖❖❖❖❖❖❖❖❖❖❖❖❖❖❖❖❖❖❖❖❖❖❖❖❖❖❖❖

DECEMBER 2010

AMERICA'S DEMOCRATS FAILED TO BRING CHANGE

Obama misses his historic moment

President Obama was elected to change US economic and social policies, and could have insisted that decisive change was not an option but a necessity. Instead, he sought to negotiate. He may now have lost his chance, as well as his supporters.

Eric Klinenberg and Jeff Manza

When Barack Obama surged to power in 2008 with a clear mandate to change the economic and social policies of the US, his election was greeted with a vast public outpouring of joy. It was a historic moment. Now, after the Democratic Party was 'shellacked' – his word – in the mid-term Congressional elections, it's hard to avoid the conclusion that President Obama has wasted that moment.

As a candidate Obama promised to govern audaciously, to restore hope by delivering progressive change. Unlike Al Gore and John Kerry, Obama managed to mobilise a broad coalition of activists into something resembling a mass movement. A substantial majority of ordinarily sceptical progressives came to embrace Obama over his Democratic primary opponent Hillary Clinton, as did millions of young people and minorities inspired by his message of hope.

Soon after the election, Obama's chief of staff pledged that the new administration would seize the political opportunity, boldly stating: 'You never want a serious crisis to go to waste.' There was to be financial reform, health care reform, media reform, a major economic stimulus package that would create jobs and repair shoddy national infrastructure, the closure of Guantanamo and the end of the unjust and unwinnable wars that the George W. Bush administration had started but could not finish. American voters were prepared for all of these changes, and Obama had promised to deliver them.

When Obama took office, most political pundits compared the situation he inherited to that of those powerful presidents Franklin Delano Roosevelt and Ronald Reagan. Both arrived with the sharp political message that the policies of their predecessors were to blame for the economic crises, and that a new policy and political agenda were required. FDR launched his 'first hundred days' with a blizzard of measures that began the process of reorienting national policy away from the protection of wealth and free markets that had led to a severe imbalance in the late 1920s. Although his early programmes did little to end the Great Depression, they laid the foundation for a 'second New Deal' that created a national welfare state, long-term economic growth and income redistribution towards the poor and the middle class.

Ronald Reagan's achievements in the 1980s, in the face of a short but severe recession that pushed unemployment over 10 per cent, accompanied by double-digit inflation, were also impressive. With control of only one of the two chambers of Congress (the Senate), Reagan charged ahead. Insisting that the New Deal era had run its course and that 'government was the problem', he successfully reframed public debate to win massive tax cuts, deregulation and significant budget cuts. Republican national political majorities, interrupted only briefly during the first two years of the Bill Clinton presidency (1993–95), pushed America steadily to the right for the next 25 years.

Like Roosevelt and Reagan before him, Obama could have insisted that decisive political change was not an option, but a necessity. He could have insisted that the Republicans, whose political agenda was all but discredited, engage in politics on his terms. Yet he did nothing like this. Instead, he sought to be a mediator, to govern in a polite, bi-partisan manner, to negotiate his way to political change.

RIPE FOR ATTACK

Consider the way that the Obama administration handled the financial sector. The crisis in the autumn of 2008 and winter of 2009 looked like a watershed for US economic policy. But when Obama took office, public outrage about the obscene levels of compensation received by the powerful men of Wall Street, and the bailout of investment banks and their affluent clients, was palpable. Far more than in any other rich democratic country, public policy in the

US had rewarded the very rich, who invest most of their money in financial instruments. The opportunity to link, productively, underlying social and political inequalities to the highly visible financial sector collapse was there, waiting to be seized. The system was ripe for attack.

Yet instead of blaming the neoliberal regime that had created the economic mess, Obama embraced it. His first key economic appointments were those close to Wall Street: Larry Summers and Timothy Geithner. Both men were associated with some of the policies that had led to the crisis, whereas prominent, Nobel Prize winning economists who had called for bolder changes – notably Paul Krugman and Joseph Stiglitz – were left off the new Democratic team. Obama and his advisers continued the unpopular Bush administration bailout policies with few significant changes.

The financial bailout in autumn 2008 generated wide public anger, in part because it suggested that the needs of the 'fat cats' were being taken care of, while ordinary Americans were suffering from the sharp economic downturn. Several of the financial institutions that the US government bailed out made record profits. In October 2010, Bloomberg reported that Goldman Sachs had reserved enough funds to pay, on average, $370,706 for each employee, while Deutsche Bank set aside enough to pay $394,499. Since these figures include support staff, who earn far less than this, the typical banker at these firms is making far more.[1]

Workers on Main Street have not fared as well. The official unemployment rate has hovered around 10 per cent since Obama took over, and is about 17 per cent for black men aged 20 and above. Since these figures only include those who haven't yet given up hope of employment, the real rates are considerably higher. In Milwaukee, a recent study found that 53 per cent of black men were unemployed in 2009. The rate for white men, at 22 per cent, was high, too.[2] In this environment, foreclosure, lost savings and insecurity have become the new norm. And the administration has offered little to help homeowners renegotiate better loans from the banks that the government bailed out.

What has the administration done to bolster the economic security of ordinary Americans? Its major achievement was a $787 billion economic stimulus package, passed in the winter of 2009. The amount of money was inadequate. In the 2010 campaign, Obama and the Democrats argued, correctly, that Americans would have been even worse off had they not passed the stimulus. But their message was easily thwarted by Republicans, who insisted that the government had squandered almost $800 billion. Not many voters could say that it had made them better off.

The failure to get a larger stimulus symbolised Obama's refusal to wage a vigorous public campaign in favour of what he claimed to believe in. His financial reform has made some modest improvements in a bankrupt system, but does nothing to solve the 'too big to fail' problem that encouraged such behaviour among financial institutions before the last crash. The new laws will make the economy even more dependent on large banks than it was before 2008.

HEALTH CARE REFORM MAY FAIL

Obama's bipartisanism led to similar problems with his greatest policy achievement, national health care reform. *Rolling Stone*'s Matt Taibbi has highlighted the administration's strategic blunders: by giving up a single-payer system before negotiations began, they lost any leverage to win an affordable public option. The policy that emerged is based on individual mandates (which force each person to buy an insurance product, regardless of its quality or affordability, from a for-profit company) that Republicans have called unconstitutional.[3] Twenty states have already filed a legal challenge against the new law, and conservative governors (whose numbers have grown since 2 November) are vowing not to enforce it. Some advocates of health care reform argue that it may provide a foundation upon which progressive leaders will someday build a more generous national policy. But for now it's not certain that it will survive Obama's first term.

Young voters who were attracted to the high principles Obama espoused in the 2008 campaign have been disappointed by his failure to live up to them while in office. (Since the midterms, 18–29 year-olds are only 11 per cent of the electorate; two years ago they were 18 per cent.) They also feel let down by his domestic policies. Economic stagnation has been devastating for college-educated 20–24-year-olds, whose unemployment level soared from 3 per cent in December 2007 to nearly 10 per cent this autumn. Yet there are no special jobs programmes for them. Media policy, which is important to the young, has gone nowhere under Obama. As a candidate, Obama called for net neutrality and promised to invest in better broadband systems, because today Americans pay more and get slower service than most Europeans. But, under the leadership of his law school pal Julius Genachowski, the Federal Communications

Commission has followed the administration's lead, engaging in endless bipartisan negotiations and accommodating the telecom industry rather than consumers.

The Obama campaign went to great lengths to mobilise progressives and disaffected American citizens. But in office, the Obama administration has acted as if it wants nothing to do with the massive movement that helped make his election possible. And now key members of this movement have made it clear that they no longer care enough to support him.

Original text in English

Eric Klinenberg and Jeff Manza are sociology professors at New York University.

1. Bloomberg, 27 October 2010.
2. 'Study shows Milwaukee unemployment for black men at record high', *The Badger Herald*, University of Wisconsin-Madison, 25 October 2010.
3. See Matt Taibbi, 'Sick and wrong', *Rolling Stone*, 5 April 2010.

❖❖❖❖❖❖❖❖❖❖❖❖❖❖❖❖❖❖❖❖❖❖❖❖❖❖❖❖❖❖❖❖

NOVEMBER 2010

CHALLENGES FOR THE ESTABLISHMENTS IN US MIDTERMS

'We the people'

A new strand of rightwing populists in the US, represented by talk show host Glenn Beck and his Tea Party followers, fear al-Qaida less than they do socialism. But in particular all Tea Partiers despise the Republican rich and the elites.

Walter Benn Michaels

Over the summer two stars of the American right had a friendly argument about who poses the greatest threat to the United States. Fox News host Bill O'Reilly went with the conventional wisdom: al-Qaida. During the Bush administration, it was the clash of cultures that organised the way American conservatives saw the world. When they worried about issues like illegal immigration, what they were afraid of was al-Qaida operatives mingling among the future valet parkers of Chicago and meatpackers of Iowa. But O'Reilly's new colleague and ratings rival, Glenn Beck,[1] had a more surprising answer: it's not the jihadists who are trying to destroy our country, it's the communists. When Beck and the Tea Party, the rightwing populists most closely tied to him, express their deepest worries, it's not terrorism they fear, it's socialism.

What's surprising is that worrying about communists was more characteristic of the Eisenhower years than of post-9/11. Even more surprising is that Beck is a generation younger than O'Reilly. He hadn't even been born in 1963 when Eisenhower's secretary of agriculture, Ezra Taft Benson, gave the speech about Krushchev's promise to keep 'feeding us socialism' mouthful by mouthful until one day (today, according to Beck, who cites this speech frequently) we wake up and realise we've 'already got communism'.

Most surprising of all is that this reinvention of the cold war is working. Tea Partiers rush to expose the communists in the Democratic Party; on Amazon's bestseller lists, the highest ranking political book is F.A. Hayek's *The Road to Serfdom*, and even the celebrated radio talk show host Rush Limbaugh has started worrying about the 'communist' spies 'who work for Vladimir Putin'.[2]

Why communism? And why now? Islamophobia at least has some pretext based in reality: jihadists really did kill thousands of Americans. But not only were there no communists on the planes that hit the World Trade Centre, today there are virtually no communists anywhere in the US, and precious few in the former USSR. Indeed, if there's one thing Vladimir Putin and Barack Obama can agree on, it's their enthusiasm for what Putin (at Davos!) called 'the spirit of free enterprise'. And yet, like anti-semitism without Jews, anti-communism without communists has come to play a significant political role on the right, especially on what we might call the anti-neoliberal right.

Beck's own biography suggests how this has happened. His parents divorced in response to stress caused (as his biographer tells it) by the recession of the late 1970s; his early success in radio was a product of the ratings wars set off by the deregulation of the radio industry begun in 1982; and his successes and failures have been in a broadcasting industry increasingly fragmented and driven by the demands of the deregulated market. Before politics became central to his performance, he was known primarily as a master of marketing, and many believe his current political views aren't deeply held: they're just another marketing device.

But, if we've learned anything from the last 30 years, it's that marketing is itself a kind of politics. Beck is a pure neoliberal baby, coming of age with the disappearance of communism and now –

confronted with the Great Recession – making his career through its reappearance. To him and his millions of viewers, it cannot be the triumph of capitalism that has produced our problems, so it must be the return of communism. And it's the 'immigrants and socialists' – not Saudis on planes but Mexicans on foot – who have spearheaded that return.

ANGRY TEA PARTIERS

You can see this structure in the stories that both Democrats (Barack Obama) and Republicans (Congressman Bob Inglis) have told about angry Tea Partiers denouncing what they take to be Obamacare's socialising of medicine while demanding that the government 'keep its hands off Medicare'. Inglis says: 'I had to politely explain that "Actually, sir, your health care is being provided by the government", but he wasn't having any of it.'[3] The reason is that he can see that Medicare and even Social Security have been put in jeopardy; what he can't see is that it's the drive to privatisation that has put them there. What he and his comrades really want is to be rescued from neoliberalism (they don't want to lose Medicare), but what they *think* they want is to be rescued from socialism (Obamacare).

In reality, there's nothing the slightest bit socialist about Obamacare, much less about immigration. In fact, unlike the Tea Party, Chicago-school economists identify open borders with free markets and argue that it's not immigration but 'immigration controls' that are 'a form of socialist central planning'. Even more to the point, there's nothing communist about *illegal* immigration which, from an economic standpoint, is preferable to legal immigration because it 'responds to market forces in ways that legal immigration does not' and thus 'benefits both the undocumented workers who desire to work…in the US and employers who want flexible, low-cost labour'.[4] So when Beck, speaking for all the Tea Partiers, pronounces his judgment – 'Immigration good; illegal immigration bad' – he may think he's opposing communism, but what he's actually opposing is neoliberalism in its purest form. The thing the Tea Party regards as the greatest threat to capitalism is capitalism itself.

Which is not to say that anyone supports illegal immigration as a principle. That would be a contradiction in terms – why not just defend the legality of open borders? But what doesn't make sense as a principle has made very good sense as a policy: it was the policy of the Bush administration and the Obama administration too, until the Tea Party began to call its bluff. For what the policy has done is allow both Democrats and Republicans to encourage a massive increase in the supply of very cheap labour, while at the same time condemning that labour for the very thing (its illegality) that makes it so cheap.

Thus the American way of dealing with illegal immigration – talk like a border guard, act like a hiring committee – has made a significant contribution to the redistribution of wealth (upwards) which closed borders used to inhibit, but which the new mobility of capital and labour brilliantly enhances. Increased mobility of labour, just like increased mobility of capital, and just like the deregulation that enables them both, are core components of that neoliberalism which, as David Harvey says, has made 'increasing social inequality structural to its whole project'.[5]

And there's every reason why this should produce anxiety in the US, at least among those American workers whose meagre share of the national income has continued to decline. As recently as the first Reagan administration (1981–85), the bottom 80 per cent of the work force was taking home a little more than 48 per cent of the nation's income; now it's now taking home a little less than 39 per cent.

But it's puzzling that Glenn Beck and the Tea Party should be so indignant. For, as the Tea Partiers are relatively wealthy and belong disproportionately to the top 20 per cent, neoliberalisation has been good for them.[6] Illegal immigration is one of the very things that has made rich Americans rich! We're used to the idea of poor people opposing their own interests: rich people taking to the streets to protest the very policies that produced their wealth is a more novel phenomenon, but not inexplicable. For if the good news for the Tea Party is that the top 20 per cent has increased its share of the national income, the bad news is that virtually all that increase has gone to the top 1 per cent. Where the top 1 per cent made 12.8 per cent of all money earned in 1982, the figure almost doubled by 2006 (21.3 per cent). Meanwhile the top 20 per cent increased only by 1 per cent (from 39.1 per cent to 40.1 per cent). So when the Tea Party sees immigration as a threat, they're not totally delusional. What they're seeing is a new set of economic norms that has taken the traditional inequalities of American life and intensified them – a capitalism in which they were winners turning into a capitalism that threatens to make them losers.

ANTI-ELITISM

What this has produced is an anti-elitism that is a little less of a sham than it usually is in US politics. Usually the millionaires who run the Republican Party manage to portray themselves as closer to the people than the millionaires who run the Democratic Party just by wearing cowboy boots, disapproving of abortion and talking a lot about Jesus. But this year, in primaries in places like New York, Delaware and of course Alaska, Jesus (though still essential) hasn't been enough. What enabled the Tea Party candidate Christine O'Donnell to defeat her conservative opponent in the Delaware Republican primary was not that she is even more Christian than he is (although she is; she used to be director of the Saviour's Alliance for Lifting the Truth Ministry, a group that advocates sexual abstinence up to and including no masturbation). It was her attacks on 'the ruling class'.

At a recent rally O'Donnell said, to sustained applause: 'The small elite don't get us. They call us wacky. They call us wingnuts' but 'we call us "We the people".' And, turning her attention from rich Republicans to rich Democrats, she contrasted herself to former presidential candidate John Kerry, recently accused of trying to avoid the taxes on his brand new $7 million yacht: 'I never had the high-paying job or the company car...I never had to worry about where to dock my yacht to reduce my taxes...And I'll bet most of you didn't either.'

Of course, the fact that Christine O'Donnell can win some votes by making fun of rich politicians doesn't mean that in office she would do any better than they have. In the unlikely event she's elected, she'll almost certainly do worse. And the Tea Party is already being bankrolled by billionaires like David Koch, whose most recent contribution to the welfare of 'We the people' was laying off 118 of them in North Carolina.

But even if we can't really trust the Tea Party's contempt for the rich or share their hostility to immigration, both these emotions are of more political interest today than any produced by the Democrats or establishment Republicans. The Census Bureau recently announced that 44 million Americans are living below the poverty line. Meanwhile the top 1 per cent – about three million people – control half the nation's wealth. An American political party that was actually serious about blaming the rich for their wealth and then took the unprecedented step of not blaming the poor for their poverty would be something new.

Original text in English

Walter Benn Michaels is a professor of English at the University of Illinois at Chicago, and author of *The Trouble with Diversity: How we Learned to Love Identity and Ignore Inequality*, Metropolitan Books, New York, 2006.

1. The long-established O'Reilly tends to get around three million viewers, the up-and-coming Beck, also a Fox News host and host of *The Glenn Beck Program*, a nationally syndicated talk-radio show, around two million.
2. MMTV, 8 July 2010.
3. *The Washington Post*, 27 July 2009.
4. Richard N. Haass, president of the Council on Foreign Relations, preface to Gordon H. Hanson, *The Economic Logic of Illegal Immigration*, Council on Foreign Relations Press, New York, 2007.
5. David Harvey, *A Brief History of Neoliberalism*, Oxford University Press, 2007.
6. Only 35 per cent of them identify themselves as making under $50,000 a year and thus being below the national median; 20 per cent identify themselves as making more than $100,000.

❖❖❖❖❖❖❖❖❖❖❖❖❖❖❖❖❖❖❖❖❖❖❖❖❖❖❖❖❖❖❖

DECEMBER 2010

AMERICA'S DEMOCRATS FAILED TO BRING CHANGE

What happened to the US left?

Since US midterm elections that were disastrous for the Democrats, attention has turned to America's left. Inside and outside the two-party system, two distinct lefts are alive if not well – the one polite and established, the other made up of grassroots activists.

Rick Fantasia

Is there any leftwing opposition in the United States? An ideologically hardened Republican Party is purging its moderate elements, prodded and encouraged by the rise of the Tea Party movement. Meanwhile an ideologically submissive Democratic Party has a centrist faction that is indistinguishable from the Republicans, and a progressive wing that is bound to a campaign finance system that demands careful attention is paid to the money people. Where is the left?

The left does exist, and operates both inside and outside of the two-party arrangement. There are in fact two lefts, and each has been in action recently, visibly so, in separate and distinct venues. One left was present at the US Social Forum in Detroit (Michigan) in June, where a gathering of over 15,000 activists from around the country and from a range of organisations met to 'continue the spirit of the World Social Forums' by holding strategic discussions, 'building relationships and collaborations across movements' and 'deepening commitments to international solidarity and common struggle'.

Some of this was accomplished over five days; there was a spirited march of more than 10,000 people through downtown Detroit full of militancy, anger, movement and colour. Factions and groups wore variously coloured T-shirts, and people of many colours marched together. Forums and workshops and panels reflected the same spirit: the Excluded Workers' Congress was one of some two dozen People's Movement Assemblies at the Forum. Several hundred people gathered from organisations like the Domestic Worker Alliance, the Taxi Alliance, the Alliance for Guest Workers, the National Day Labourers Organising Network, along with groups of restaurant and farm workers, and from local workers' centres that support workers. Up on the stage people spoke about the brutal conditions they experience at work and in their lives, and demonstrated the vitality of their resistance that had drawn them towards the organisations and unions that had brought them to Detroit.

The left represented in Detroit is one that would be recognisable anywhere in the world, but in the US context it is mostly marginal to the political debate and largely invisible to society. There was almost no media coverage of the Detroit Social Forum in the US press, before or after, though the media had been saturated throughout that summer with reports of rightwing Tea Party rallies (some of which had attracted only a few hundred people).

Although the Forum took place in the heart of the auto industry, where were the autoworkers? While their numbers have declined significantly, in Michigan there are still some 50,000 working and 128,000 retirees. But they had no visible presence in Detroit, nor did there seem to be UAW (United Auto Workers) T-shirts or banners. Indeed, there weren't many signs of the traditional labour movement at all, although many individual union activists were surely present.

Detroit was youthful and counter-cultural, with ecological concerns and global issues represented, and a hall of literature tables occupied by socialist groupings, New Age practitioners and advocacy groups. The forum drew strong representation from non-union low-waged service industries, many of them women, as well as Latin and Asian and black. They were the excluded workers, a status celebrated by the organisers and politicos and put forward to represent the 'grass roots' left.

But where were the 'included' workers? And what does it mean to be 'included' when the conditions of inclusion (stable jobs, unions able to secure higher wages and a range of social benefits, etc.) have been under sustained assault? And if the included are increasingly being excluded, what interest is served by upholding that distinction at all?

AUTOWORKERS GATHER ON THE MALL

Another US left was also recently in action, at a large demonstration in October in Washington DC called by a coalition of 'progressive' groups, including the AFL-CIO (the country's biggest trade union confederation), the NAACP (National Association for the Advancement of Colored People), the National Council of La Raza, and the National Gay and Lesbian Task Force. This was the established, institutionalised left, led by the main labour federation, the official labour movement that was able to bring well over 100,000 workers and others to Washington to show strength and draw public attention away from the Tea Party.

Here were those autoworkers absent at the Forum in Detroit. In Washington their union seemed to be everywhere, with UAW T-shirts and banners. Many thousands of workers gathered on the Washington Mall on that beautiful Saturday in October – white and black, men and women, from the UAW, SEIU, the Transport Workers Union, AFSCME, unions of government workers, teachers and service workers. The comportment of this gathering, and of this left, was different from Detroit. At this event the crowd sat almost politely, socialising and listening to speeches. Speaking from the Lincoln Memorial were media personalities, Democratic Party politicians and leaders of the established 'progressive' organisations. While one could periodically hear angry statements coming from the podium, they were mainly directed at the Republicans, and not capitalism.

There was little attempt to stir up the crowd, no march organised and no real sense of political urgency. The organisations that sponsored the event are the unions and advocacy groups whose political action mainly consists of lobbying for social legislation and contributing funds and campaign workers to liberal political candidates. Though their membership has been shrunk from plant closings, the transfer of jobs offshore, and the fierce anti-unionism of employers, they have had no inclination to mobilise their members for militant action in recent decades. They have been too close to power too often to want to jeopardise the position of their institutions.[1] If black and white workers were present in almost equal numbers in Washington, most were members of the unions and civil rights groups that brought them there. They looked as though they would easily fit into any of the mainstream cultural institutions, with a certain nationalist pride in being Americans. It frankly seemed more like a picnic on the lawn than a workers' demonstration.

IDENTITY POLITICS

If this institutional left has a bigger voice, it doesn't mean the left of the Detroit Forum has none. Though invisible in the media and with no role or influence in national politics, the groups of the grassroots left are active in hundreds of communities, working to build power at the local level along democratic lines, trying to expand their work by creating networks and coalitions between groups and across social space.

They are able to accomplish tangible things. Domestic Workers United has made significant progress toward establishing a law in New York State to give 200,000 of them the most basic labour standards (mandatory overtime pay, protection from discrimination, notice of termination). The strength of these groups is their autonomy and a pragmatic militancy that mobilises aggressively toward concrete goals, while bringing groups together to create broader networks.

Their weakness is that their aims are too often limited to an identity politics whose highest social ambition is to 'include the excluded' within arrangements that are less and less tenable for anyone. It reflects a tendency to misunderstand or misconstrue the full reality of class in the US and this, along with an avoidance of a common or even coherent worldview, is an intellectual legacy of the cold war that tends to leave only a surface-level social analysis. While Marxism may not have been enough to be able to grasp all the dynamics and complexities of society, it was at least a reasonable place to start.

Yes, the grassroots organisations were able to bring many working-class 'people of colour' to Detroit, a fact celebrated throughout the week, but there were few white working-class people there. The whites were mostly educated members of the middle class, organisers, activists, representatives of philanthropic organisations and academics. White working-class people were not well represented in Detroit, nor had they been at the previous Social Forum in Atlanta in 2007.[2]

The head of one key organisation on the grassroots left, known as a sharp analyst of movement building, offers a solution to the problem of the relative absence of white workers in a movement attempting to build social power. He says 'white folks need to organise some poor white folks', a vision filtered through the lens of identity politics. It elevates to a political principle the very racial separation that must be overcome to create the solidarity which is the foundation for any just society. Both these American lefts are weak because they must survive in a political culture dominated by the largest corporations on the planet. But they are also weakened by the self-imposed limits of their own social horizons. One has replaced exploitation with exclusion as the basis for worker mobilisation, while for the other worker mobilisation is treated as not much more than a picnic in the park.

Original text in English

Rick Fantasia is professor of sociology at Smith College, Northampton, Massachusetts.

1. See Rick Fantasia and Kim Voss, *Hard Work: Remaking the American Labor Movement*, University of California Press, Berkeley, California, 2004.
2. See Jackie Smith, Jeffrey Juris and the Social Forum Research Collective, 'The US Social Forum in context', *Mobilization*, volume 13 (4), December 2008, pp. 382–3.

❖❖❖❖❖❖❖❖❖❖❖❖❖❖❖❖❖❖❖❖❖❖❖❖❖❖❖❖❖❖❖❖❖❖

August 2011

Goodbye to Fostoria, Ohio...

A small town in the middle of everywhere

The jobs went south – to Mexicali, Mexico – after the Nafta liberalisations of the 1990s. New owners have come and gone, the last US employees are awaiting redundancy and only a very few money men have profited, handsomely.

John R. MacArthur

Pro-North American Free Trade Agreement (Nafta) forces staged on 9 November 1993 what may be remembered as the greatest salesman's trick in the annals of televised propaganda. Millions of Americans had just watched CNN's Larry King show, and its 'debate' over the ratification of the agreement, between Ross Perot, the anti-Nafta crusader and independent presidential candidate, and then Vice-President Al Gore, spokesman for mainstream political and business opinion about free trade and its alleged benefits to the US.

The professional politician Gore had bested the billionaire amateur Perot, but the show wasn't over, and neither was rhetoric about Nafta. CNN followed with a post-debate debate, in which four 'experts' argued over the plan of former President George H.W. Bush and President Bill Clinton for eliminating tariffs and integrating the Mexican, Canadian and American economies in ways they claimed would bring money and jobs to everybody – a 'win-win' scenario. One expert, a soldier for David Ricardo's economic theory of comparative advantage, was Larry Bossidy, leader of the pro-Nafta business lobby and chairman and CEO of Allied Signal, an industrial corporation with worldwide interests, including the Autolite spark plug plant in Fostoria, Ohio.

With many fearing what Perot called the 'giant sucking sound' of jobs heading to cheap labour in Mexico if Nafta passed Congress, Bossidy needed to promote the notion that the agreement would bring more work to the Midwestern rust belt, already in steep decline. So, on instructions from Gore's media adviser Carter Eskew, Bossidy held up a plug and pronounced: 'I would like to say, about the jobs, this is a spark plug, an Autolite spark plug. It's made in Fostoria, Ohio. We make 18 million of them. We're going to make 25 million of them; the question is, where are we going to make them? Right now you can't sell these in Mexico because there's a 15 per cent tariff…if this Nafta is passed, we'll make these in Fostoria, Ohio…we'll have more jobs…This is a small part of a car. We export 4,000 cars to Mexico today, we'll export 60,000 cars in the first year [of Nafta], that's 15,000 jobs.'

As of 1 November 2010 General Motors was a ward of the federal government, the country was in prolonged economic slump and there were 86 assembly jobs in the Fostoria factory. The remaining Autolite employees were there to make just the ceramic insulators around the plug. The rest of the jobs had moved to a maquilladora in Mexicali, where nearly 600 Mexicans were manufacturing mostly Motorcraft spark plugs, the house brand of Ford Motor Company, healthiest of the Big Three US auto companies.

A VERY DIFFERENT WAGE

The crucial difference between Mexicali (just south of the border from Calexico, California, on the Baja peninsula) and Fostoria was the wage scale: in Fostoria, unionised production workers made an average $22 an hour, including benefits, for a 40-hour week; in Mexicali, workers on the first two shifts made 15.5 pesos (about $1.83) an hour for a 48-hour week. Autolite's new owner was Honeywell, dominant partner of a 1999 merger with Allied Signal, and its chairman, Dave Cote, could be pleased with his investment. The maquilladora was not only less costly to operate, it was also protected against expropriation, serious environmental supervision and strikes by Nafta, the Mexican government and Mexico's corrupt national labour union, the CTM. In 2009 Cote received more than $13 million from his board of directors. Somewhat surprising was President Barack Obama's embrace of Cote as a spokesman for American employment and re-industrialisation.

When I went to Fostoria, in September 2009, long freight trains still rumbled through town regularly on the railroad lines that made the city, despite its modest size (population 13,441), such an attractive place to build a factory in the 19th and early 20th centuries. But the trains weren't stopping to pick up much and the chamber of commerce was reduced to promoting its advantages for rail photography enthusiasts. No train buffs – or anyone else – were in evidence downtown, where Readmore's Hallmark Books and Gifts was advertising a closing sale. Vast empty parking lots abutting shuttered factories and businesses – Fostoria Industries, a maker of specialty ovens; the Thyssenkrupp Atlas crankshaft plant; the GM dealership – testified to the declining fortunes of what Fostoria's boosters had dubbed 'A Small Town in the Middle of Everywhere!'

But while factory after factory had closed down, the Autolite plant seemed impregnable – not just because of Bossidy's pledge in 1993 but also because the plant was churning out vast quantities of spark plugs with stunning efficiency – as many as 1.2 million a day on 13 production lines operating over three shifts. It couldn't last with so many plants heading to Mexico and, after passage by Congress of permanent normal trade relations with China in 2000, the even cheaper labour of China. In January 2007 Autolite announced plans to build the plant in Mexicali, and in August said it would begin to lay off 350 of the plant's 650 workers.

Bob Teeple, the president of United Auto Workers Local 533, is the son of an Autolite millwright, and in 1995, at age 32, he followed his father into the plant's skilled trades, the elite of unionised blue-collar workers. There were 'close to a thousand' employees at the plant. When I visited union headquarters with Hart Perry, the documentary filmmaker, Teeple was awaiting news from the company of the shutdown of everything but the ceramics section, but he wasn't sure when most of the remaining 271 employees would have to go, since the Mexicali plant was having start-up problems.

Teeple recalled the great Nafta debate and a later visit from Larry Bossidy 'who even came to the plant and made it sound like, you know, our business is doing good. But I wasn't super-aware of what effect Nafta would have. You know, it's just one of them things that you heard on TV – pros and cons.'

Neither, it seems, were any of his co-workers super-aware of Nafta. When I sneaked inside the factory to observe one of the four production lines still in operation, I met Peggy Gillig, who was checking plugs for defects. Gillig had started work ten years earlier, when she was 46, and she wasn't very politically or union minded. Automation at Autolite had failed to kill her job, but politicians had succeeded: 'I'm disappointed in our leaders that they've more or less stabbed us in the backs – sold us out to foreign interests.'

But Gillig didn't blame poor foreigners for taking her job and preventing her from retiring at age 60, which would have been possible under the UAW contract. 'It doesn't seem like it's good for the third world countries they [the jobs] are going to. They don't pay those people…a living wage, so how is that good for them? I mean, it's better than not havin' any kind of a job…I don't understand who it is good for other than the big companies.'

Other workers, current and former, spoke with me, including Larry Capetillo, a Spanish-speaking Mexican-American whom the company lured out of retirement in 2007 to help train workers in Mexico. Morally conflicted, Capetillo kept a journal about his dilemma. The Honeywell executive who recruited him and three other retirees claimed that the Autolite plant had lost money for the past 'four to five years', according to the journal, not so much because of production costs 'but because we have 1,200 retirees'. However, if the move to Mexicali was successful, the executive had promised that 'the goal is to keep 300-and-some jobs here [in Fostoria]'. Capetillo thought of Autolite as a family affair – his wife, Fran, had taken a buyout after 29 years, and his daughter, Tracy, was still employed there with her husband.

'We all knew that people were going to dislike us very much for doing this,' Capetillo told me. But the executive had been blunt:

'Whether you go [to Mexico] or not, they're going to move this. We're going to try to make [the Mexicali plant] go if we can – if we can't, and it goes down…the rest of this is going to close.' Capetillo said: 'We decided, you know, if we can keep the plant here; if we can do something to help there, we're going to go down and try to do it then…Believe me, the four of us were not going to go, but when he said the whole operation would close if the Mexico thing did not make it, we had to make a decision.'

In his journal, Capetillo was more candid: 'Many of our fellow employees hated us for making this decision.' However, 'the longer we can keep this plant open the longer my daughter gets to keep her job.'

The company had no intention of keeping any plug production in Fostoria. After two years of commuting between Fostoria and Mexicali, Mexicali was ready to manufacture, as Bob Teeple put it, 'everything with platinum attached to it'. When negotiations began in 2009 for a contract, the company surprised Teeple with a demand: if the union wanted to keep more than 110 jobs in Fostoria, there would be a wage cut to $11 an hour plus big employee contributions to health insurance. 'We couldn't do that,' Teeple said. Better to negotiate for good severance than to take a humiliating reduction far below the UAW norm.

'I guess I felt totally betrayed by the company,' Capetillo said. 'It seems they all deal in half-truths…He did tell us that 300 jobs would stay, probably. And not even half of them stayed.'

'ALL OF US HAVE TO HELP'

Ordinarily, this story would have ended on 23 December 2009, when the last integrated production line was shut down. I felt obliged to interview Dave Cote, especially since he had appeared with Obama at the White House, just after his inauguration, to promote business-government cooperation in combating severe recession. As Cote told reporters, 'The Congress, the American people, all of us as a business community, all of us have to help. Mr President, I can say that for Honeywell you can count on us and all of our employees to be there to help support this.'

For months, Cote's PR man at corporate headquarters in Morristown, New Jersey, kept putting me off, not knowing I wanted to talk about Nafta in general and Autolite in particular. It seemed just a matter of time before the remaining 99 workers in the ceramics department in Fostoria lost their jobs.

But on 4 April 2010 a catastrophe occurred – a 7.2 earthquake struck 60 km from Mexicali, placing the region in a state of emergency and damaging the new plant. Honeywell's Consumer Products Group had no choice but to move some production back to Fostoria and rehire 70 laid-off workers to satisfy demand. Before long, Teeple said, 'they told us we were doing four times the production of the Mexican plant, 130,000 a day, and some days we got as high as 230,000 with two lines running for three shifts.' By October operations were back to normal in Mexicali and the 70 rehires were laid off again, for good: 'Not one machine is left in department 9,' Teeple said. 'All of them were shipped to the Mexicali plant.'

All Teeple had to look forward to was a 1 November 2011 contract expiration and another round of negotiations on behalf of the 86 survivors in the insulator section. 'They're telling us no, they're not setting up kilns in Mexicali,' Teeple said in December 2010, but the company had said the same things to Larry Capetillo. The ceramic insulators could easily be made by NGK, a Japanese company with a factory in Irvine, California, much closer to the Mexicali plant. It wouldn't be long before Fostoria's Autolite plant, which opened in 1936, shut forever.

Teeple was demoralised. When he called me in February, he said he wouldn't run for re-election in June as Local 533's president and would take a buyout from the company: 'I'm dead in the water. I want to change professions, go into marketing. The more you do, the more you make.' His first love, sprint-car racing, wasn't a way to support four kids and a wife. By May, Teeple had changed his mind – a sense of obligation to union members took precedence – and he was re-elected.

But Teeple had more bad news: on 28 January Honeywell announced that it had agreed to sell its Consumer Products Group (CPG), including Autolite and Fram Filters, to the Rank Group, a New Zealand-based, privately held investment company, for $950 million in cash.[1] 'While CPG is a good business,' Dave Cote said in a press release, 'it doesn't fit with our portfolio of differentiated, global technologies...we are confident that the Rank Group, with its proven track record of investing in and building established franchises, will be a good home for CPG's consumer brands, customers, and employees'.

Rank was owned by the leveraged buyout billionaire Graeme Hart, said to be worth more than $8 billion. His method for making money was to borrow heavily to buy companies with a healthy cash flow; cut costs and increase profits through layoffs or mergers; then issue more debt or resell the company for more than he paid. His purchase of Alcoa's packaging and consumer group in 2008 was exemplary: after paying $2.7 billion for the aluminium foil maker he cut more than 20 per cent of the workforce by closing facilities, including 490 unionised workers at Reynolds Wrap manufacturing plants and a distribution facility in Richmond, Virginia, and by laying off 158 employees at a printing plant, also in Richmond. Under the new corporate entity, Reynolds Group Holdings Limited, Hart has assembled other packaging companies, including SIG and Evergreen Packaging. Bob Teeple was not optimistic about management-labour relations under Rank Group ownership: he predicted that Honeywell's union-staffed Fram Filters plant in Greeneville, Ohio, would fall victim to Hart's cost-cutting after the sale of the company became official, probably this autumn.

REWARDED FOR INVESTING IN THE AMERICAN DREAM

Over the past twelve years I have heard many stories about the beneficial effects of free trade from its proponents. But the stories recounted by its victims always seemed more persuasive. Among the best storytellers were two Autolite workers who lost their jobs. When I met Jerry Faeth in 2009 he was 52 and considered himself lucky. With 32 years at the plant, he would retire with a full pension, which he had planned to do just before being laid off. Both his daughters were well on their way to graduating from college, and his house in New Riegel, southeast of Fostoria, was fully paid for. He had liked Autolite because after 28 years, 'I got into the prototype section of the plant. I loved working [there] because it's something different every day and you're not just using your hands; you're using your mind and you're working with college-graduated individuals who treat me as an equal.' Faeth had invested in the American dream and been rewarded: 'I was fortunate because of Autolite. We had good wages…and my wife was able to quit work and stay home for eight years with our two children; and I think that's key to some of the issues we're having in society today because the babysitter doesn't raise your kids like Mom or Dad.' But now he was embittered.

After the meeting at which the layoffs were announced by a Honeywell executive, Faeth said it 'felt like he hit me in the stomach…I wanted five more years [in the plant] and I'm not going to get it…I said, "You know, you talked about us [needing to be] competitive. I contribute to the 401K in Honeywell and I get this book every year and it says the top five guys in Honeywell last year made $70 million. Sir, is that competitive?"' According to Faeth, the executive replied: 'Well, I can't speak for Dave Cote's salary but, you know, that comes out of a different fund anyway.' Faeth said: '"Sir, that's not what I asked. You can't tell me that there's not a smart person down there in Mexico that wouldn't do [Cote's] job for a whole lot less. How can he tell you that we're makin' too much money here when those top five guys made $70 million. What's wrong with that picture?" He didn't have an answer for me.'

But others purported to have an answer to Faeth's question. One of them is the economist R. Glen Hubbard, dean of the Columbia University Graduate School of Business, chairman of the Council of Economic Advisors in the first two years of the George W. Bush administration and a villain in *Inside Job* (the Academy Award-winning documentary about the 2008 financial crisis). When I encountered Alison Murray at Local 533, she had read parts of his textbook, *Macroeconomics*. With a BA, Murray enrolled in night classes at the University of Findlay when layoffs loomed at Autolite. As a single mother, aged 42, with only 17 years in the plant, she couldn't retire with a pension and needed to plan for the future. But her encounter with Findlay's economics department left her troubled about post-industrial Fostoria.

SLAPPED IN THE FACE

'The ironic thing,' she said, 'was that the very first class that I took when I went back to school was a macroeconomics class. And the whole entire textbook told us how important it was that they move the manufacturing jobs from America to other countries – and that manufacturing in America was a dinosaur and that it should be outsourced to other countries because that was the only way to make money...So it was like getting slapped in the face. I was trying to go back to school...because I'm losing my job and I'm a displaced worker...and the very first class I took, the very first page of the textbook [justifies my layoff].'

Murray argued with her teacher: 'I said, "You know, that's all well and great in theory but I've lived the human side. I've seen the devastation that...is caused by these factories moving out to the other countries..." And the textbook and the teacher say, "Well, we're not talking about very many jobs." Well, to me in this town of 15,000, to have 900 jobs [roughly the number lost at Autolite since 1993] leaving, that's a lot...And it's affected every single person's life.'

But there's no arguing with Hubbard, or even Obama, who pledged to 'renegotiate' Nafta during his battle with Hillary Clinton in the 2008 Ohio primary campaign, then reversed once he entered the White House.

Hubbard's *Macroeconomics* puts together supposedly irrefutable economic truths turned into clichés in the aftermath of the 2008 financial debacle. In its orthodox advocacy of tax cuts, deregulation, free trade and free markets, it has a tone of bland authority that makes it hard to challenge unless one pays close attention to arguments, alternatives and facts he omits. His chapter on 'Comparative Advantage and the Gains from International Trade' is full of unprovable generalisations: 'Some people worry that firms in high-income countries will have to start paying much lower wages to compete with firms in developing countries. This fear is misplaced, however, because free trade actually raises living standards by increasing economic efficiency. When a country practices protectionism and produces goods and services it could obtain more inexpensively from other countries, it reduces its standard of living.'

Besides, says Hubbard, child labour isn't such a bad thing, since the 'alternatives' (such as prostitution) can be 'extremely grim'. We can be grateful that the smart rulers of developing countries resist pressure to pay higher wages or impose environmental regulation because 'jobs that seem to have very low wages based on high-income country standards are often better than the alternatives available to workers in low-income countries'. While the US has a 'comparative advantage' with many skilled workers doing 'sophisticated' manufacturing, 'other countries, such as China, have many unskilled workers and relatively little machinery...China has a comparative advantage in the production of goods...that require unskilled workers and small amounts of simple machinery.' Nowhere is mentioned Chinese wages of 50 cents an hour, the government-controlled Chinese national labour union, the absence of a formidable Chinese environmental regulator, or the sophistication of Chinese factories.

In this distorted world, we're all operating on a level playing field: 'It is true,' the book says, that 'jobs are lost' when 'more-efficient foreign firms drive less-efficient domestic firms out of business.' But the same is true when 'more-efficient domestic firms' kill off the competition – we're all playing under the same global rules of free enterprise. One shouldn't worry about the lost jobs because 'these job losses are rarely permanent'.

While Jerry Faeth, Alison Murray and Peggy Gillig awaited news of their next place of employment, and at what wage, they could contemplate Larry Bossidy's plug promise versus the Department of Labor's latest report on a programme called the Transitional Adjustment Administration. TAA is supposed to provide money to people who lost jobs directly as a result of Nafta, which became effective on 1 January 1994. TAA does not calculate actual job losses, only petitions made for assistance as a consequence of lost jobs. As of 21 June 2011 its 'estimated number of workers covered' – those eligible for government money – stood at 2,491,479. It seemed likely that before long the figure would increase by 86, the total number of UAW members left in Autolite's Fostoria plant.

Original text in English

John R. MacArthur is publisher of *Harper's Magazine* and author of *The Selling of Free Trade: NAFTA, Washington and the Subversion of American Democracy*, University of California Press, Berkeley, 2001, and *You Can't be President: The Outrageous Barriers to Democracy in America*, Melville House, 2008.

1. A spokeswoman for Honeywell's Consumer Products Group refused to verify any facts in this article, citing an ongoing anti-trust investigation by the Federal Trade Commission into the sale of the company to Rank Group.

Part III: A Smaller World

❖❖❖

MAY 2011

AN END TO ENFORCED EQUALITY

Cuba's new socialism

Fidel Castro's brother Raúl is taking a pragmatic approach to economics in his presidency, but how far will he be able to correct Cuba's situation?

Renaud Lambert

In 1994 Raúl Castro, then defence minister, voiced a rare disagreement with his brother Fidel: 'The main threat is not American guns, it's beans – beans the Cuban people can't get.'[1] Fidel opposed liberalising agriculture, which would have boosted food production. But since the collapse of the Soviet bloc, GDP had fallen by 35 per cent, the US had tightened the trade embargo and Cubans were suffering from malnutrition. Raúl was certain that if things did not change, he would have to bring the tanks out. At the end of the year, the government authorised free farmers' markets.

Raúl is president now[2] and maintains Cuba is still not out of the 'special period'.[3] In 2008 three hurricanes caused $10 billion worth of damage to infrastructure (equivalent to 20 per cent of GDP) and the international financial crisis hit the strongest sectors of the economy, especially tourism and nickel. Unable to meet its obligations, Cuba froze foreign assets and restricted imports, although this slowed the economy further. In 2009 agricultural production fell by 7.3 per cent; between 2004 and 2010 food imports soared from 50 per cent to 80 per cent.

In December 2010 Raúl told the National Assembly: 'We are treading a path that runs along the edge of a precipice; we must rectify [the situation] now, or it will be too late and we will fall.'

The president of the National Assembly, Ricardo Alarcón (once rumoured to be a prime candidate to succeed Fidel Castro), said: 'Yes, Cuba will open up to the world market – to capitalism.' Building 'socialism in one country' is not easy, especially if its domestic market is small, so would Cuba abandon the revolution? Alarcón dismissed the idea: 'We will do our utmost to preserve socialism; not the perfect socialism we all dream of, but the kind of socialism that is possible here, under the conditions we are facing. And we already have market mechanisms in Cuba.'

A FLOOD OF DOLLARS

I went shopping with Miriam. Like 70 per cent of Cuba's population, she was born after the 1959 revolution and does not know how extraordinary it is that, in Cuba, there are no children trying to sell sweets or lottery tickets to drivers at the traffic lights, and no advertising billboards. Cuba is the only country in Latin America with no child beggars, and one of the few to have banned billboards. But Miriam is aware, and proud, of Cuba's social conquests – things the state provides for free and which she believes are her right: education, health care, sport, culture, jobs and food, which she claims using her *libreta* (ration book). Her ration includes 1.2 lb (540 g) of beans for 80 centavos; half a litre of cooking oil (20 centavos); 1 kg of skimmed milk (2 pesos); 3 lb (1.36 kg) of sugar (15 centavos); 400 g of noodles (90 centavos); and 115 g of coffee (5 pesos). Each time she visits the *bodega* (shop), the shopkeeper writes the proportion of the ration handed over in the appropriate box in her *libreta*. This time she bought rice: every Cuban is entitled to 2.5 kg for 25 centavos and a further 1 kg for 90 centavos.

Miriam works in a government ministry and earns a near-average income of 450 pesos a month, which is about 20 CUC. A CUC, or 'convertible peso', is equivalent to 24 traditional pesos. This second currency was introduced in 2004 to replace the US dollar; economic realism had prompted the government to allow the use of dollars in 1993. After the collapse of the Soviet Union, the government believed it could reform the external sector of the economy without radical changes to the internal sector, 'supporting capitalism abroad but socialism at home'.[4] But opening Cuba up to investment and tourism, to secure the foreign currency needed to maintain the social fabric without changing the country, flooded the market with dollars, through tips, the payment of a part of salaries in cash, overseas remittances and the black market.

The government gave in, and opened hard currency stores (*shoppings*) to channel some of these dollars into the state coffers. A dual market developed, undermining monetary sovereignty and the egalitarian ethic of the revolution: only two-thirds of Cubans had legal access to the dollar, and later the CUC. The income gap between the best paid and worst paid widened from 4:1 in 1987 to 25:1 in 1997.[5] Today anyone is allowed to change pesos into CUC, but not everyone can. 'The government still pays me in pesos,' said Miriam. 'Have you seen the prices in the *shoppings?*' – 1 CUC (24 pesos) for a Coca-Cola, imported from Mexico; 500 CUC (12,000 pesos) for a PC.

Is the *libreta* enough to live on? 'Yes,' said Miriam, 'for 10 days, two weeks at most. But you still have to pay for all the other things.' Vegetables, transport, electricity, clothes – 130 pesos for trousers, 90 for a T-shirt, 10 for a pair of panties (not the sexiest). A car mechanic may earn 350 pesos; a lorry driver, 250; a young journalist, 380. Senior civil servants earn around 800 pesos a month, estimates Fernando Ravsberg, a BBC journalist in Havana. The average monthly income rose from 188 to 427 pesos between 1989 and 2009, but its real value fell to 48 pesos.

LOBSTER IS FOR TOURISTS ONLY

Visitors ask how the Cubans manage. They answer: '*Hay que resolver*' – you have to resolve it. A tourist orders a beer on the terrace of a hotel for 3 CUC. The waiter will not necessarily take it from the hotel's refrigerator; he may take it from his own stock, which he keeps barely hidden. Since he buys the beer at 1 CUC a bottle, this allows him to multiply his basic wages by 50 and bribe his boss to keep quiet. A hotel worker has toothache, and the dentist tells him there's a two-week waiting list, then suggests: 'If you want to come this evening, it'll be 5 CUC.' The hotel worker makes a counter-offer: 'Fit me in now and I'll let you and all your family into the buffet this evening.'

Selling apartments is prohibited. Yet some families grow and others shrink. Intermediaries put them in touch with one another, for a fee. Prices are based on a market rate that everyone knows. A studio in the relatively smart Vedado district will cost 15,000 CUC; a five-bedroom apartment a little further from the centre, 80,000 CUC.

In Cuba, lobster is reserved for tourists or for export. Fishermen sell it on the black market and typically earn $700 a month. University staff who have internet access rent out their passwords in the evenings; teachers give classes at home; nurses visit patients' homes; bus and lorry drivers siphon diesel. Many government employees use their position to supply the black market with chairs, tools or building materials.

Cubans learned to cope by using the market mechanisms that govern everyday life. The official rhetoric condemned them to put up with the situation. Fidel had said in 2003 that values determined the true quality of life, even more than food, shelter and clothing. A few years earlier, he had launched a battle of ideas to address Cuba's problems, especially corruption. This was meant to strengthen revolutionary convictions, especially those of the young, by providing employment (students were assigned to monitor petrol stations). The ideas were effective for a time, then consciences became elastic once again. Recently it was revealed that the Ministry of Construction employed 8,000 construction workers and bricklayers – and 12,000 security guards to prevent theft.

In his first speech as (interim) president Raúl Castro said: 'Wages today are clearly insufficient to satisfy all needs...This has bred forms of social indiscipline.' After an 'extensive national debate', he decided that people were expecting a different kind of reform. (Nobody knows how he reached this conclusion as no report, summary or extract of the debate was ever published.) It was no longer a matter of correcting things incompatible with Cuba's ideological rigour, but of finding a socialism stripped of 'erroneous and unsustainable concepts' and learning 'even from the positive experience of capitalists'.[6] Sly and unorthodox solutions were already turning some Cubans into entrepreneurs. The president rehabilitated private initiative by allowing people to work for themselves.

The publication of a list of 178 such activities to be permitted from September 2010 did not change anything in practical terms. Officially, bricklayers, carpenters, electricians, clockmakers and lighter repairers did not exist, yet everyone had used their services for years. Ricardo, another contact, said: 'Getting a water leak mended through the state enterprise [in charge of building repairs] was incredibly difficult. In the end, people just asked a neighbour who knew what he was doing.' Now that neighbour pays taxes: a licence fee of just under 20 CUC, 25 per cent on turnover, social security (25 per cent of profits) and a progressive rate on income over 5,000 pesos a year (rising to 50 per cent on income above 50,000 pesos a year). 'A self-employed person can even hire other Cubans and pay them according to their productivity,' said Ricardo. The constitution disapproves of this, considering it exploitation; the taxman loves it – as a 'boss', the neighbour pays a 25 per cent payroll tax.

A NEW RHETORIC

Daily life hasn't changed much; the rhetoric has. In 1968 Fidel Castro denounced the 'small segment of the population that lives off the work of others,…lazy persons in perfect physical condition who set up some kind of vending stand, any kind of small business, in order to make 50 pesos a day'.[7] In two days, nearly all private businesses – bars, grocery stores, garages, carpenters, bricklayers, plumbers – disappeared. In 2010 the Communist Party daily *Granma* described the self-employed as responsible and high-minded people whose success would 'play a large part in the successful and continued modernisation of the Cuban economic model'.[8]

In 1995 enthusiasm for making money had to be curbed by restricting private restaurants to twelve tables, but Cuba is no longer frightened of the accumulation of wealth. 'Let's be honest: if, once he has covered all his costs, a self-employed person earns more than the current average salary, is there really anything wrong with that?' asked *Granma*. After all, 'capital is something you build up little by little, by working hard, by being competent, by improving the quality of your service every day – even the smile that wins over your clients'. In January this year, a Catholic magazine rejoiced that Cuba could now face the future 'without fearing wealth'.[9]

The goal of Raúl Castro's reforms is not just to legalise what was prohibited yesterday. It is also, as Alfredo Guevara explains, the 'de-statification' of a planned economy whose rules and regulations no longer convince. Much of the 2009 tomato harvest was left to rot on the plant as government lorries were under instructions not to travel without a load and did not arrive in time. The crop could have been taken to a nearby factory to be made into purée, but the regulations did not allow for it.

'Is it really necessary for the government to set the price of a haircut?' asked Jorge Luis Valdès of the National Association of Economists and Accountants. 'Before the April 2010 reforms, all the hairdressers in Cuba belonged to a single enterprise. Transferring them to the private sector not only saved the government 630m pesos in nine months but brought in 660m pesos of extra revenue.' He produced a notebook: 'Before April 2010 the official price of a haircut was 80 centavos. That didn't stop people charging 5 to 20 pesos for men and up to 100 for women. The government provided electricity, water and the telephone, which anyone could use if they paid one peso to the salon. For every four hairdressers, there were two security guards, a cleaner, an accountant, an administrator and one or two people to prop up the wall – all employed by the state.

Now it has all changed. The hairdressers are independent and pay the government 990 pesos a month: 330 in rent for their premises, 330 in social security contributions and 330 in payroll tax. After that, they are free to do what they like and hire anyone they like: staff numbers usually fall.' In fact, 40 per cent of the working population is to be transferred to the private sector by 2020 (at present, 90 per cent of Cubans are government employees). Valdès summed up: 'Lower costs, more revenue: it's all profit for the state.'

Efficiency, productivity, savings: the language is familiar, even in countries where the word socialism is not automatically associated with Che Guevara. 'Why should Cuba be different from other countries?' asked Valdès. 'We need to do away with everything the government gives Cubans for free, from the cradle to the grave, to make sure they are equal.'

By reducing the role of income in access to welfare, the give-aways have sapped motivation and hindered economic development. Discussions of socialism in Cuba today rarely mention equality without criticising the error of egalitarianism. Raúl Castro explained in 2008 that the solution was to eliminate handouts and 'give salaries their real value. There is no alternative.'

The government no longer pays for wedding cakes and honeymoon hotels. Four government ministries no longer have free cafeterias: their employees now get 15 pesos a day for food (enough, for the present). Even the *libreta* may soon go, since the *lineamientos* (policy guidelines) document submitted to Cuba's Congress suggests replacing it with 'targeted social assistance' reserved for 'those who really need it', as elsewhere in Latin America.

Cuba's only trade union has announced that 500,000 government jobs are to be cut in the next few months. All those laid off will receive their current salary for a month. Those who have worked for 19 years or less will receive 60 per cent of their salary for a further month, those who have worked for 26–30 years for three months, those who have worked more than 30 years for five months. No doubt the intention is to motivate them to find private sector jobs quickly. But can people who have worked in ministries for years turn into farmers, barbers or bricklayers in just two months, knowing there will be no welfare system to take care of them after that? Economist Omar Everleny Pérez, whom many consider to be the father of the current reforms, said: 'Yes, there will be some losers. Yes, some people will be out of work. Yes, there will be more inequality.' But the inequalities 'are already there: what we have, at present, is a false equality. What we have to decide is who really deserves to be at the top.'

ATTACHED TO HEALTH AND EDUCATION

This February, workers at a clinic in central Havana met to discuss the *lineamientos*. Its 291 proposals include performance-based pay, legalising market prices and a review of social programmes. The document was approved unanimously, in just a few minutes. But the workers stressed their attachment to Cuba's health and education systems – some things should change, but not those. The secretary of the meeting made a note of their comments, although nobody really knew whether or how they would be taken into account.

I asked if there was a risk the government would eventually judge it necessary to modernise Cuba's social conquests. From the opening up of the Chinese economy to the reform of public services in France, there is no shortage of examples to suggest this is likely. Alarcón said: 'It is quite possible to oppose such reforms and, if necessary, vote against them.' Does this mean Cuba has an opposition? Since its establishment in 1976 the National Assembly has not registered a single vote against a government bill.

A cartoon in *Granma* earlier this year showed a youth leaning on a lamppost asking an elderly passer-by: 'Any change, Granddad?' He answers: 'Yes – time for you to change and start earning an honest living.'

Translated by Charles Goulden

Renaud Lambert is a member of *Le Monde diplomatique*'s editorial team.

1. No verbatim account of the exchange exists, but references to it by multiple sources suggest that it is authentic.
2. Since 24 February 2008, having served as interim president since 31 July 2006, owing to Fidel's ill health.
3. Raúl Castro speech, 26 July 2007.
4. Richard Gott, *Cuba: A New History*, Yale University Press, New Haven, 2004.
5. 'Fidel, the church and capitalism', *The Economist*, London, 14 August 1997.
6. Raúl Castro speech, 18 December 2010.
7. As quoted by Richard Gott, in *Cuba: A New History*, op. cit.
8. Félix López, 'Opinión por cuenta propia',*Granma*, Havana, 18 November 2010.
9. Olando Márquez, 'Sin miedo a la riqueza', *Palabra Nueva*, no. 203, Havana, January 2011.

❖ ❖

MARCH 2010

LULA DA SILVA'S RESOURCES AND AMBITION

Brazil: we've got the power

Brazil wants to broker international diplomacy, host presidential missions and ignore the US. It now has serious economic sway in South America, and it is aiming for much more and much wider influence.

Lamia Oualalou

'It is embarrassing that Brazil is receiving the head of a repressive dictatorial regime. It is one thing to have diplomatic relations with dictatorships; it is quite another to welcome their leaders to Brazil',[1] wrote José Serra, the governor of São Paulo state and one of President Luiz Inácio Lula da Silva's main political opponents. He was commenting on the visit of Iran's president Mahmoud Ahmadinejad, on 23 November 2009. Serra is rarely so vehement in his attacks on 'Lula', who enjoys an impressive level of popularity.

Apart from social programmes, foreign policy is the area in which Lula, the leader of the Workers' Party, has made the greatest changes. Lula may have abandoned part of his economic agenda under pressure from the financial sector (although he has partially revived it during his second term) but he has parted ways with the political elite, which had aligned itself with the United States in the struggle against communism.

This change of direction should not be mistaken for a clear ideological position on Lula's part, even if his two principal collaborators, Celso Amorim, the minister of foreign affairs, and Marco Aurélio García, the president's special foreign policy adviser, have unequivocally declared themselves to be leftwing. At the most, it indicates robust economical pragmatism, a preference for popular governments, a conviction that Brazil has a historic debt to Africa (because of the role of slavery in its past) and a belief that the country needs to lose its inferiority complex.

At his investiture in January 2003, Lula reserved his warmest welcome for Cuba's president, Fidel Castro. He then appeared to establish a frank and open relationship with the US president, George W. Bush, to the despair of Workers' Party militants. The Brazilian president is, first and foremost, a trade unionist who firmly believes it is important to talk to everyone and that a sound agreement requires that both parties be satisfied, even when that agreement comes at the end of a long struggle. And that, as in the 1970s, there is really no reason why he should not enjoy a whisky with the boss between bouts of industrial action.

For the outside world, it all began in September 2003 when Brazil upset the routine of the World Trade Organisation summit in Cancún by leading a revolt of 20 emerging economies (the G20). For the first time, these insisted that the rich nations (the G8) give them something in return for opening up their markets. 'When someone wants to buy something, Brazil should be on hand to sell it to them,' said Lula.

THE ELIZABETH ARDEN CIRCUIT

Since the beginning of his first term, Lula has spent 399 days on overseas visits,[2] usually accompanied by a large number of business people. His itinerary has taken in Latin America (his number one priority) and the larger emerging economies (including South Africa, India, China and Russia) but also areas of the world traditionally scorned by the economic elite, such as Central America, Africa and the Middle East. In May 2005 Brazil hosted the first ever Latin American-Arab summit from which the US was excluded (it had wanted to attend as an observer). And in 2006, Brazil attended the Africa-Latin America summit at Abuja, in Nigeria.

At first, Brazil's foreign ministry was at a loss. Politically conservative and mostly from privileged backgrounds, its diplomats preferred the glamour of what is referred to in Brazil as 'the Elizabeth Arden circuit': Rome, Paris, London, Washington. But Brazil's business leaders were delighted: the policy has brought growth for its multinationals. The state-controlled oil company Petrobras, mining giant Vale, civil engineering groups Odebrecht and Camargo Corrêa, beef giant JBS-Friboi, chicken giant BRF, aircraft manufacturer Embraer and the private bank Itaú, as well as hundreds of ethanol and soybean producers, have all seen their exports and foreign investments explode. The discovery of substantial oil deposits off the Brazilian coast has made the country even more export orientated. China has loaned $10 billion to Petrobras in a bid to guarantee its future access to Brazilian oil. This year China has for the first time supplanted the US as Brazil's largest export market.

In Latin America politics and business go hand in hand. Brazil has been the first to benefit from the explosion of demand in neighbouring Venezuela. Venezuela's poorest citizens are becoming consumers (of meat, milk, small electrical appliances) but it lacks any real agriculture or industry and has had to rely on imports from Colombia, then, as relations with Bogotá have deteriorated, from Brazil. In Argentina, the Brazilian beverage company AmBev is keeping quiet about its takeover of the Argentine brewery Quilmes. Argentina's largest meat producers have all been taken over by Brazilian companies and the situation is similar in Uruguay, where most rice production is under Brazilian control. In Bolivia, Brazilian firms control more than one-fifth of the economy, in the form of soybeans and natural gas. In Paraguay, the fertile farmlands of the departments of Alto Paraná, San Pedro, Concepción, Amambay and Canindeyú are planted with Brazilian soybeans.

Everywhere Brazilian enterprises go they are accompanied by loans from the Brazilian Development Bank (BNDES).[3] Matias Spektor, assistant professor in international relations at the Getúlio Vargas Foundation in Rio de Janeiro, says that Brazil's trade policy is not merely about making the nation wealthier, but also about making it more powerful.

This has created tensions. Brazil is used to presenting itself as a 'gentle giant' but is now being accused of imperialism – by Argentina, which complains it is being flooded with industrial products; by Ecuador, which has accused Odebrecht of shoddy workmanship; and by Bolivia, where the big Brazilian landowners in the east of the country make no secret of their alliance with political parties opposing the government of Evo Morales. Anxious to reconcile business interests with good neighbourliness, Lula has frequently had to intervene. In most cases, he has invoked regional integration, forbidding his government from taking the kind of retaliatory action the press has been demanding.

Since the demise of the Free Trade Area of the Americas, one of Washington's pet projects, Latin American integration has become a pillar of Brazilian policy. Lula repeats that Brazil has every interest in ensuring that its neighbours are robust and are not impoverished or weakened by social and political crises. He demonstrated his commitment to this position in May 2006 by calling Evo Morales' decision to nationalise Bolivia's gas fields (which were being exploited by Petrobras) 'sovereign', while some were demanding that Brazilian troops be sent in as a response to 'the stupidity of the Bolivian government'.[4]

Last July Brazil also ended a long-running dispute with Paraguay, its other fragile neighbour, by agreeing to revise the terms (very unfavourable to Paraguay) of their agreement on the exploitation of Itaipú, the gigantic bi-national hydroelectric power station on the border between the two countries. This gesture proved vital to the stability of the government of Fernando Lugo, who was able to claim a victory over his powerful neighbour.

PUBLIC EMBRACE

Lugo and Morales irritate both the Brazilian elite and Washington, but not as much as Venezuela's president Hugo Chávez, with whom Lula has established a solid alliance. The two have refused to let themselves become embroiled in the rhetoric of the 'two left wings' – the modern and responsible left, which is anxious to maintain financial stability, led by Brazil and including Chile and Uruguay; and the radical, populist, anti-American left, led by Venezuela and Cuba and including Bolivia, Ecuador and Nicaragua. When the press play on the differences between their countries, Lula and Chávez are quick to organise a meeting for the inauguration of a bridge or the laying of the foundation stone of a factory, a pretext to be seen embracing on camera. When Chávez was accused of authoritarianism, Brazil responded by backing Venezuela's application to join Mercosur (the Southern Common Market).

The alliance between the two countries is the keystone of the major Latin American institutions established in the past few years. The most important of these is Unasur (Union of South American Nations), established at Brasília in May 2008, which includes twelve South American countries and aims to replace the Organisation of American States – which has its seat in Washington DC, a sign of its dependence on the White House. Unasur has a defence council and although the organisation is as yet fragile, it managed to ease tensions between Ecuador and Colombia.[5] And in September 2008 it blocked an attempt to destabilise the Bolivian government (orchestrated by opposition parties) by reaffirming the legitimacy of the Morales administration. In both cases, it managed without intervention by the US.

Brazil also used Unasur to oppose the establishment of seven US military bases in Colombia. Brazil feels that any conflicts in the region should be settled without outside intervention. For the same reason, Lula denounced the reactivation in 2008 of the US Fourth Fleet, whose mission is to patrol South American and Caribbean waters.

But it is over Honduras that Brazil and the US are most clearly at odds. Immediately after the coup of 28 June 2009, Unasur insisted that President Manuel Zelaya should be reinstated and allowed to complete his term of office. On 21 September, with the deposed head of state ensconced in the Brazilian embassy, Lula found himself in the front line again. Foreign minister García was furious: 'Brazil has used all the sanctions and pressures it can bring to bear, but that isn't much compared with what the US could have done. If we'd had the kind of instruments they have at their disposal, we would have used them.'

The irritation increased in November, when President Obama wrote to his Brazilian counterpart to explain his decision to recognise the elections organised by the putschist government on 29 November and his positions on the WTO negotiations and the Copenhagen summit, which Brazil had openly criticised. Sent on the eve of Ahmadinejad's visit to Brazil, this letter also reminded the Brazilian president of Iran's violations of human rights and the dangers inherent in its nuclear programme.

PART OF THE CLUB

Lula was irritated by what he called the hypocrisy of the nuclear-armed nations. Last December 2010 he said that to have the moral authority to demand that others should not have the bomb, they would have to give it up themselves. He also pointed out that Brazil's constitution explicitly prohibits the development of nuclear weapons. Sources close to the president feel it is important that Iran be allowed to develop civil nuclear technology: from Brazil's viewpoint a ban would be a dangerous precedent.

Lula was obsessed with making his country a permanent member of the UN Security Council, just as he was with reforming the International Monetary Fund. (The larger emerging economies make a substantial contribution to the IMF but enjoy only a small percentage of voting rights.) In 2004 this obsession prompted Lula to agree that Brazil should lead the military side of the UN peace mission to Haiti after the expulsion of President Jean-Bertrand Aristide, so gaining admission to the club of 'grown-up' nations.

The UN has been pressing Lula to send more troops on other UN peace missions. But without a reform of the institution that would really allow them to make their voice heard, Brazil's military are refusing to get involved in missions such as those to Darfur or the Congo, over which they have no control.

Lula's next venture was participation in the Middle East peace talks. In November 2009, he received not only Ahmedinejad, but also Israel's president Shimon Peres and the head of the Palestinian Authority, Mahmoud Abbas. Thomas Trebat, executive director of the Institute of Latin American Studies at Columbia University, says: 'By not being too closely aligned with the United States, [Brazil] can still be seen as an honest broker.' Once again Lula, the seducer, hoped that his skills as a negotiator would open up new opportunities for Brazil to become a world power.

Translated by Charles Goulden

Lamia Oualalou is a journalist based in Rio de Janeiro.

1. José Serra, 'Visita indesejável', *Folha de São Paulo*, 23 November 2009.
2. 'Como o Brasil é visto lá fora', *Zero Hora*, November 2009.
3. A bank linked to the ministry of development, industry and foreign trade.
4. Two Brazilian papers, *Estado de São Paulo* and *Veja*, in May 2006 carried cartoons showing Lula with a bootprint on the seat of his trousers.
5. In March 2008 Colombia infringed Ecuador's sovereignty by attacking a guerrilla camp on Ecuadorian soil.

❖❖❖❖❖❖❖❖❖❖❖❖❖❖❖❖❖❖❖❖❖❖❖❖❖❖❖❖❖❖❖

MARCH 2011

ANOTHER WAY TO DEFY THE US

Latin America embraces Palestine

Suddenly many Central and South American countries have formally recognised Palestine. Why?

Maurice Lemoine

In December 2010 Luiz Inácio Lula da Silva, then president of Brazil, wrote to Mahmoud Abbas, head of the Palestinian Authority, saying: 'Brazil, through this letter, recognises the Palestinian state on the 1967 borders.' It was a spectacular announcement, but it didn't set a precedent. Back in November 1988, when the PLO proclaimed the creation of the Palestinian state by invoking UN Resolution 181, the state was immediately recognised by Cuba, Venezuela, Nicaragua and Costa Rica, although no other Latin American country joined them.

The Middle East was not much considered in Latin America until 2009; then in January that year, Venezuela's president Hugo Chávez broke off diplomatic relations with Israel, accusing it of 'planned use of state terrorism' against the Palestinian people in the invasion and bombardment of Gaza. Bolivia, whose president, Evo Morales, fumed about the UN's 'insecurity council', did the same. That April, Venezuela exchanged ambassadors with Palestine.

Few in Latin America forget Israel's traditional role backing up the US. When President Jimmy Carter stopped arms sales to Guatemala in 1977 because of massive human rights violations, Israel stepped in. During the 1979 Sandinista rebellion, Israel only stopped supplying the Nicaraguan national guard 15 days before its dictator Anastasio Somoza fled. Yair Klein, a former Israeli army officer and mercenary who recruited and trained Colombian rightwing paramilitaries in 1988 during the long-running guerrilla war, has recently revealed that his actions were 'approved by the Israeli and Colombian governments'.[1]

In Colombia, a land of massacres and communal graves, Juan Manuel Santos, now president, then defence minister, admitted in 2008 to close cooperation with Israel: 'Terrorism is fought above all else by intelligence and, in this matter, Israel can help us and offer much to us.'[2] The private security firm Global CST, linked to Tel Aviv's military establishment, signed lucrative contracts with the Colombian, Peruvian and Honduran governments to train internal security troops.[3]

All this led to a serious standoff between progressives in Latin America and Israel. But the speed of events since last December has been different. Argentina, Bolivia, Chile, Ecuador and Guyana (holding the presidency of the Union of South American Nations, Unasur) have followed Brazil in recognising an independent state of Palestine. Paraguay and Peru adopted the same position in January (Peru staged February's Latin America-Arab summit, ASPA), and Uruguay declared its intention of doing the same.

Not all governments are advancing at the same speed: while Brazil, Argentina, Ecuador and Bolivia mention the frontiers in place before the 1967 Six Day War in relation to the West Bank, Gaza and East Jerusalem, Chile and Peru avoid this clear condemnation of occupation. Beyond that important difference, there are factors that explain the current convergence between states considered progressive and governments seen as close to the US.

Brazil, in demanding a permanent seat on the UN Security Council, is reiterating its ambitions as an emerging power and sending an unambiguous message to the US, which in 2010 disdainfully brushed aside its joint offer with Turkey to mediate in the Iranian nuclear crisis.

Like Brazil, other Latin American countries have reasons for friendship towards Arab and Middle East countries: business has grown with them since the first ASPA summit in 2005. Chile's president Sebastián Pinera may be aligned to the US, but he is also well aware of Chile's 400,000 Palestinians, the largest foreign community.[4] Even a country as far to the right as Peru is finding it hard to neglect the regional drive for integration.

Faced with widespread recognition of Palestine, positions are being defended. The speaker of the US House of Representatives called it 'counterproductive'. Israel denounced the 'new manoeuvres' by the Palestinians. The Colombian foreign minister, Maria Ángela Holguín, said, straight-faced: 'When there is peace with Israel we will recognise Palestine.'[5]

All the same, this broad diplomatic departure reflects Latin America's independence and its growing criticism of the impasse in the direct peace talks, reinforced by the US's complicit apathy.

Translated by Robert Waterhouse

Maurice Lemoine is a journalist and author of *Cinq Cubains à Miami*, Don Quichotte, Paris, 2010.

1. See Adriaan Alsema, 'Israeli mercenary threatens to blow whistle on Colombian officials', *Colombia Reports*, 21 November 2010.
2. BBC Mundo, 5 July 2008.
3. In Honduras, those undertaking the coup of June 2009 used state-of-the-art Israeli technology to try to break the resistance of President Manuel Zelaya's supporters.
4. The Syrian/Lebanese community has high political and economic status throughout the region.
5. *El Tiempo*, Bogota, 1 January 2011.

❖❖❖❖❖❖❖❖❖❖❖❖❖❖❖❖❖❖❖❖❖❖❖❖❖❖❖❖❖❖❖❖

DECEMBER 2010

IRAN DISCOVERS LATIN AMERICA'S ECONOMIC AND GEOPOLITICAL CHARMS

A fine, and convenient, romance

Iran's blossoming relationship with the countries of Latin America may be cause for surprise, and extreme annoyance, in Washington. Yet despite divergent ideologies, they share healthy trade and industrial links, and geopolitical interests. And you don't always have to choose your friends.

Nikolas Kozloff

'A tectonic shift has occurred in the structure of international relations,' the Turkish daily *Radikal* announced excitedly following the uranium enrichment agreement signed by Brazil, Turkey and Iran on 17 May. The fuel swap deal provided Iran with a way round UN sanctions. At the time, Iran's vice-president and head of the Iranian Atomic Energy Organisation, Ali Akbar Salehi, said that for the first time western countries had to face the fact that 'emerging countries are able to defend their rights on the world stage without needing the great powers. That's hard for them to accept.'[1]

But the deal didn't turn out to be the success Iran had hoped. The US and France pushed for the rapid adoption by the UN Security Council of new sanctions (10 June 2010) and, although Brazil and Turkey voted against them, they decided to apply them (as the rules dictate). 'Brazil always abides by international law,' said the Brazilian foreign minister, Celso Amorim. This episode illustrates the difficulty of deviating from the line set by Washington, and also Brazil's desire to affirm the right of every nation to develop a civil nuclear programme. But more than that, it shows the growing importance of the links between Iran and Latin America.

Venezuela's president Hugo Chávez has made nine visits to Tehran. Presidents Correa, Lula da Silva, Morales and Ortega – leaders of Ecuador, Brazil, Bolivia and Nicaragua – have also been to Iran and hosted return visits from the Iranian leader. In addition to existing Iranian embassies in Argentina, Brazil, Cuba, Mexico and Venezuela, President Mahmoud Ahmadinejad has opened new ones in Bolivia, Chile, Colombia, Nicaragua and Uruguay. Bolivia, meanwhile, decided to relocate its only embassy in the Middle East from Cairo to Tehran.

Where politicians have led, dollars have followed. According to the *Latin Business Chronicle* research institute, between 2007 and 2008 Iran's trade with Latin America tripled to reach $2.9 billion.[2] This is a considerable sum considering that bilateral trade between them was almost non-existent when Ahmadinejad came to power in August 2005. The 'tectonic shift' referred to by *Radikal* therefore has an economic base.

In 2004, Iran's trade with Venezuela was little more than $1 million; two years later it had reached almost $51 million. Since then, Iran has increased its manufacturing base in the country: bicycles, tractors, cars and cement are all now produced there. As Venezuela suffers from a chronic shortage of expertise and technology, Iran has been helping it industrialise, especially its dairy and petrochemical sectors. Though trade between the two countries fell by 33.8 per cent in 2009 as a result of the global financial crisis, they agreed to create a joint development bank last year and signed nearly 70 new cooperation agreements (out of a total of 300). After all, the two countries have already joined forces within OPEC to revalue the price of oil, which finances their social programmes. Another symbol of the developing relationship between them is weekly flights between their two capitals since 2007.

From its Venezuelan bridgehead, Iranian involvement in Latin America gathered pace. Between 2007 and 2008 Ecuador went from seventh to third in the league table of Iran's Latin American trading partners (after Brazil and Argentina). And when Ecuadorian imports leapt from $10,000 to $168.2 million in the space of a year, in 2008, Ecuador became the biggest Latin American market for Iranian products. Iran did not merely come to sell: it has promised abundant investment especially in the hydroelectric and petrochemical industries. Rafael Correa, the Ecuadorian president, signed more than 25 bilateral agreements intended to bring the two economies closer together during his visit to Tehran in December 2008. However, after a fall of 91.7 per cent in its trade with Iran in 2009, Ecuador has now dropped to fourth place among Tehran's trading partners in Latin America, behind Venezuela but still ahead of Mexico (sixth).

In Central America meanwhile, Iran has announced a billion-dollar investment programme which will pay for the deep-water port that Nicaragua needs and provide funds for building a hydro-electric power station. In Bolivia, Iran has plans to improve natural gas extraction. It may also contribute to preliminary research into that country's vast lithium resources.

But for the moment, 94 per cent of the trade between Iran and South America – a total of $2.4 billion in 2009 – goes through Argentina and Brazil. Brazil, with a market of 200 million people and an economy that accounts for a third of South America's GDP, is one of the few countries whose trade with Iran grew in the course of 2009 (by 4 per cent, after an 80 per cent increase the previous year), to reach $1.297 billion. Even that is not enough, according to a declaration by Ahmadinejad during a visit to Brasília. He and

Lula da Silva want to see trade increase to $10 billion by 2014 through 'the efforts of entrepreneurs in both countries'.[3]

MY ENEMY'S ENEMY

It would be an understatement to say that these activities are a cause of concern in Washington. On 11 December 2009 the US Secretary of State Hillary Clinton warned that any relationship with Iran was 'a very bad idea' as Tehran 'supports, promotes and exports terrorism'. She went on: 'I think if people want to flirt with Iran, they should take a look at what the consequences might well be for them. And we hope that they will think twice.' Ahmadinejad, however, views these relationships as nothing more than the result of healthy fraternity. As he put it on 24 September 2009: 'With our friends, our relations know no limits.'[4]

The true nature of these newfound friendships is perhaps best explained by the old adage, 'My enemy's enemy is my friend'. Evidence for this is not lacking. In 2002 Chávez suffered a Washington-backed coup d'état. In 2009 Correa incurred the White House's wrath when he decided not to renew the lease on the US Manta air base on Ecuadorian soil (which expired on 18 September 2009). On 5 August 2010 the Bolivian president said the US 'is looking for pretexts such as terrorism and drug trafficking' to intervene in Latin America, and underlined that 'the central objective of this intervention is to take control of our natural resources'.[5]

The US is intensely irritated by the policies of leftwing Latin American governments which aim to reduce the economic hold of the multinationals (and aren't afraid to throw them out of their countries) and to defend their rights over their natural resources. On the Iranian side, Tehran, which is sitting on the third-largest oil reserves in the world, is well aware that, as Admiral Michael Mullen acknowledged on 1 August 2010, the US has formulated a plan of attack against their country.

The threat of US reprisals probably counts for little in the foreign policy thinking of these leaders who, if Chávez is to be believed, see themselves as 'anti-imperialist gladiators' and 'brothers in arms in the struggle'. Ahmadinejad explained the logic underpinning his own policy in June 2009: 'While the western countries are trying to isolate us, we have gone to seek support in America's backyard.'[6]

The US has reactivated the fourth fleet, which patrols Latin America's Atlantic coast. It has many military bases both in Latin America and close to Iran's borders. Conscious of this, Caracas decided to extend its military cooperation programme with Tehran, particularly in staff training and arms production. In April 2009 the Iranian defence minister, Mustafa Mohammad-Naijar, promised 'to give full support to the development of Venezuela's military capability in the context of mutual defence agreements'.[7]

Anti-imperialist solidarity is not limited to the military sphere. It also means denouncing any unwelcome manoeuvring among allies: for instance, attempts at destabilisation during elections were reputed to be 'controversial'. That is probably the logic that led Brazil, Nicaragua, Ecuador, Bolivia and Venezuela (where international observers have always praised the openness of elections) to give unconditional support to Ahmadinejad during the fraudulent June 2009 elections. Chávez was quick to claim CIA involvement behind the opposition demonstrations, without being able to produce any proof.

WINNING FRIENDS

Lula da Silva has tempered some of the anti-imperialist fervour of his supporters. He boasted that he got on as well with George W. Bush as he did with Hugo Chávez. But it didn't escape his notice that the US took away Brazil's most favoured nation status as a trading partner and granted it to China. Strong and rapidly growing, Brazil is now seeking to make its voice heard amid the chorus of emerging nations, breaking with its traditional 'Elizabeth Arden' school of diplomacy (only interested in Rome, Paris, London and Washington). In order to win the support of Southern countries for its bid to get a seat on the Security Council, Brazil needed to show that it was able to stand up to the North. That may have been one motivation for its uranium processing deal with Iran. In this field too the new president, Dilma Rousseff, has promised continuity.

Some observers, such as the Iranian presidential candidate Mir-Hossein Moussavi, express astonishment that 'instead of investing in Iran's neighbours, the government is spending time pouring money into the countries of Latin America'.[8] But this is to overlook the fact that Iranian investments in Latin America enable Tehran to support its own economy, particularly the industrial sectors it has developed autonomously, even under sanctions, such as aviation, gas and oil extraction and car manufacturing. In this last, Ahmadinejad has found a valuable salesman in Chávez. Praising the merits of the Centauro, an Iranian vehicle made and sold in Venezuela, Chávez recently explained: 'It's a vehicle that's high quality and cheap...It costs around 76,000 Bolivars [$17,700]. If you look for an equivalent model, for example the Toyota Corolla, you won't get one for less than 162,000 Bolivar [$37,700]...You see the difference? It's more than double.'[9] And the managing director of the Iran Petrochemical Commercial Company, Reza Hamzehlou, expressed his pleasure in October at having found two new potential clients: Brazil and Argentina.[10]

The relationship between Iran and the member countries of ALBA (Bolivarian Alliance for the Peoples of our America) – notably Bolivia, Ecuador, Cuba and Venezuela – led Tehran to seek observer status from the organisation. But ALBA's activities are not limited to diplomacy and economics. Since it was set up, it has pursued a political project of social emancipation. As a result, ALBA's Iranian ties have produced contradictions which the Latin American right has been quick to exploit.

But should we really be surprised when leftwing governments form relationships with countries whose views they don't necessarily share? In diplomacy, pragmatism is often the order of the day; think of the links between the Soviet Union and the Arab countries which purged their communists, or between Mao's China and Pinochet's Chile, or the alliance between the US and Saudi Arabia. 'We have no eternal allies, and we have no perpetual friends. Our interests are eternal and perpetual,' was how Lord Palmerston put it a century and a half ago.

Translated by George Miller

Nikolas Kozloff is a New York-based journalist. His books include *No Rain in the Amazon: How South America's Climate Change Affects the Entire Planet*, Palgrave-Macmillan, 2010.

1. 'Le Brésil et la Turquie demandent au Conseil de sécurité de l'ONU de ne pas sanctionner l'Iran', AFP, Thursday 20 May 2010.
2. 'Latin America: Iran trade triples', *Latin Business Chronicle*, 2 December 2009.
3. 'Iran-Brazil trade will amount to $10bn in five years', *Iran Trade News*, Tehran, 12 December 2009.
4. Fábio Moura, 'Iran's relations with Brazil have "no limits", Ahmadinejad says', *Iran Trade News*, Tehran, 12 December 2009.
5. 'Evo denuncia a Washington por los ataques a Sudamérica', AFP, 6 August 2010.
6. 'Israel and Iran compete to expand influence in Latin America', *The Sunday Times*, London, 12 November 2009.
7. Danielle Kurtzleben, 'Alliance problematic for the US, but not threatening', Inter-Press Services, 10 August 2009.
8. 'Ahmadinejad foreign policy "rattled" Iran foes', Press TV, 25 May 2009.

9. 'Chávez: "Los coches iraníes son mejores que los Toyota"', *El Mundo*, Madrid, 24 June 2010.

10. 'Iran targets South America for petchem exports', *Tehran Times*, Tehran, 18 October 2010.

❖❖❖❖❖❖❖❖❖❖❖❖❖❖❖❖❖❖❖❖❖❖❖❖❖❖❖❖❖❖❖❖❖❖

NOVEMBER 2010

A FREE SOCIETY UNDER AN AUTHORITARIAN REGIME

Russia shouldn't work but it does

Russia's post-Soviet elites of wealth and bureaucracy did a quiet deal with Putin long ago: we'll keep your governing structure stable if you keep us in the money. And that's how the country functions, even if it is storing up problems for the future.

Vladislav Inozemtsev

There have been many recent analyses drawing parallels between Russia now and during the Soviet era: a bureaucracy accountable to none, a single-party system, justice *à la carte*, democratic principles flouted and Russian imperialism reborn.

Yet Vladimir Putin's Russia is far removed from the Soviet Union of Leonid Brezhnev, even if they have much in common: the 'power vertical' of the Communist Party has given way to that of Putin's United Russia Party, 46 per cent of whose members are civil servants. The Supreme Soviet has been replaced by the Duma, whose members are elected from party lists vetted by the Kremlin (parties it does not control aren't allowed to field candidates). Expression of political opposition is repressed. Television is censored. The courts pass judgments that are favourable or useful to the regime. Economically 'neo-sovietism' is the rule: under Brezhnev, hydrocarbons and other primary products were 55 per cent of exports; today they account for 80 per cent. Numbers have risen in the civil, police and security services, although the population has fallen from 287 million in the Soviet era to 142 million today. The big business corporations are under state control. The collapse of the Soviet Union is seen by many, including Putin, as the 'major geopolitical disaster of the [20th] century'.[1]

But Russia is radically different from the Soviet Union. The current regime governs a country that is surprisingly free. Russians can leave and re-enter the country at will – if they can afford it. More than five million live abroad, while retaining their citizenship. Russia's economy is open (in 2009, foreign trade accounted for 40.7 per cent of GDP, compared with only 18.3 per cent in the US). Russia's culture and information networks are not limited by its borders. Western newspapers are available and foreign television broadcasts can be received in major cities. Unlike China, Russia does not censor the internet. Although several journalists have been assassinated, some newspapers are openly critical of the government. Business activity is unrestricted (Russia has 1.5 million small and medium enterprises). Russians can own their own house or apartment and buy plots of land without restriction as to size. Privately owned banks and industrial companies have been established.

The system is a mixture of 'quasi-Soviet' and 'pseudo-western' elements, and, according to the Russian historian Alexei Miller, allows people to enjoy a sense of personal freedom in a country that falls far short of democratic norms. Putin's model is more successful than Brezhnev's, in at least two respects.

UNFETTERED CAPITALISM

During the Soviet era, the government exercised its power in a vacuum, within tightly controlled borders, with the help of an ideology that the West saw as crude and simplistic, but which is still shared by many Russians. The Communist Party maintained its 'power vertical' and strove to suppress all alternative thought and any initiative that challenged its role as guide. This ideology has given way to a capitalism unfettered by principle. Russia's borders are open, its citizens are free to travel, criticise the government and receive and pass on any information they wish. Yet, the last decade has seen the re-emergence of many of the authoritarian principles of the Brezhnev era, without any significant resistance from the Russian people.

The Soviet system was based on poverty, and the distribution of basic commodities. The perestroika reformers and the westerners who advised Russia's first democratic government were confident that the end of poverty and the right to own property would prevent the return of authoritarian rule. But things did not turn out that way.

The growth of the last decade, in a favourable global economic climate, made many Russians rich – and loyal to the regime. The middle and upper classes realised that support for the regime would ensure they remained wealthy. There was an unprecedented (and unspoken) deal: economic prosperity in exchange for political stability. Putin, as former president and current prime minister, still basks in the glory of this achievement. To bolster this stability, the government defends Russian industry with protectionist measures and allows tens of thousands of Russian companies to exercise a virtual monopoly in the markets. The rise in costs[2] has pushed retail prices up even in the European markets, but in Russia it is offset by redistribution to the poorest of some of the country's oil profits.

Russia's leaders have established a model of government their communist predecessors did not dare dream about. They have improved the standard of living for civil servants. They have effectively put off free elections and ended the right to strike and to demonstrate. They have made the justice system subservient to the bureaucracy, and have created a closed community cut off from the people, living in a different world.

The result is a free society under the control of an authoritarian regime, which western critics say is impossible. Russians have been able to accept the erosion of their freedom, which they so passionately defended during the perestroika era, because the concept of collective action has been discredited. The secret of Putin's Russia is a sudden expansion of social space, so that citizens feel they are able to find individual solutions to systemic problems.

DAYS OF PERESTROIKA

The breadth and strength of perestroika in 1985 was due to the varied social origins of its supporters, who were able to work together because of the exceptional circumstances at the time. The Soviet system could not tolerate the emergence of large groupings within society. It censored dissent, stifled alternative cultures and repressed religious life. Soviet citizens had no access to an authentic history of their country and were not allowed to manifest their national affiliations. Atheist academics and Orthodox peasants had the same reasons to be dissatisfied with the system. Individual solutions to constraints could not be contemplated. The creaking Soviet economy prioritised the arms industry over the basic needs of citizens and was controlled by a bureaucratic system, itself controlled by the Communist Party.

When Mikhail Gorbachev introduced the idea of change, he attracted millions of supporters. Some wanted to reform and modernise the system, while others wanted to dismantle it completely; all realised that individual problems could only be solved by a general shake-up. Hence the great variety of people converted to perestroika: miners (who die today in their hundreds because the management refuses to invest in safety) fought for radical change with the same enthusiasm as the first private entrepreneurs. They were joined by regional civil servants who felt obliged to hand in their Party cards and declare the independence of their individual republics. The system was condemned because it suited nobody.

The new regime is not repeating the errors of its predecessor. In the 1990s, it allowed millions of 'overactive' citizens to leave Russia; their convictions would have created a new kind of dissidence. It has also given the vast majority of Russians access to means to accumulate wealth and attain autonomy, through commerce, social mobility (both vertical and horizontal) and through the right to leave and re-enter the country. It has also struck a judicious balance between people's interests and potential: to the talented and determined, it has offered lucrative positions in business; to others, jobs in a bureaucracy riddled with corruption. It has closed its eyes to dishonesty among low-ranking civil servants as long as they do not endanger the stability of the system.

The Soviet Union made colossal efforts to convince its citizens of its superiority. There is no point in Russia making such efforts, as it has become a society 'without citizens'. How did it become the soft, shapeless entity it is today? The answer probably lies in the characteristics of its elites, and in the 'social elevators' that have been created.

Most modernising societies have several different elites (political, entrepreneurial, intellectual, military), but in Russia the distinctions vanished during the period of transition to capitalism. The academic and military elites were declared redundant and remuneration of their work all but ended. Material success became the only social value. The political elite found it had to deal with people demanding wealth that they could not provide. The business sector began to redefine social values and, as it grew, started to penetrate the political power structure. Up to the early 2000s the state apparatus was dependent to a considerable extent on the business sector, but was still a long way from fully adopting its ideology.

DOWNHILL THIS DECADE

The situation has deteriorated over the past ten years. Putin's arrival on the political scene was accompanied by the emergence of new people, generally young, whose sole aim was to accumulate wealth and who clearly understood the opportunities that Russia's political leaders were giving them. Businessmen who had attained positions of political power earlier were declared undesirable.

The state gradually assumed the structure of a national enterprise (in the first few years, many major companies were brought back under state control) and civil servants at regional and federal level began to enter the business world.

In the 1990s, it was not unusual for a regional governor to be head of a banking group or an industrial conglomerate; by 2000 it was normal for the appointment of a new governor or minister to be followed by the appointment of family members or friends to senior management roles in regional commercial activity. The rise to power of the *siloviki* – members of the 'force structures' (intelligence agencies, armed services and law enforcement) – followed the same path, resulting in unprecedented levels of corruption. Over the past decade (since the privatisation of the arms industry, which made millionaires of some defence ministry officials), the cost of military equipment has risen by a factor of eight or nine.

Now the foundations of Russia's reality have stabilised: it has become easy to convert political power into money or property, and vice versa. The now established elite does not regard its activities as a service to the nation, but as business. The club is fairly open: new members are regularly co-opted, and members are free to leave to concentrate exclusively on business.

The West is wrong to imagine that Russian bureaucracy is inefficient: it performs very well, but it has different ideas of efficiency and of its duties. Russia functions according to its own system of laws and regulations. It is not a pale imitation of a European democracy; it is not an oriental dictatorship modified because of historic links with Europe; it is not a reincarnation of the Soviet Union with its all-powerful ideology; nor is it a model of 'power transition', since it is not shifting from capital accumulation to a post-industrial economy, but in the opposite direction.

Russia is the result of the collapse of all moral standards and social ideals in a world dominated by materialism. It has followed its own path, and it could not exist if European countries refused to buy oil from semi-criminal enterprises, if the leaders of those countries were not glad to benefit from Gazprom or if investors were not looking for speculative bubbles on the Russian stock and real estate markets. It could not exist without the offshore companies through which entrepreneurs openly (and Russian civil servants secretly) own 70 per cent of Russia's major industries.

The development of the Russian model has followed a logical path. Since there is little social dissatisfaction, it could last for a long time. Those Russians who oppose the system are free to express themselves in spheres other than politics; those who wish to make trouble are not prevented from doing so: they have no audience and fail to mobilise anyone.

Russia has adopted the cynicism that prevails, more discreetly, in western societies: the primacy of money and consumption, the levelling of cultural norms, the docility of ordinary citizens and the rapid spread of alienating technologies. The only problem with this system is its inability to produce an intellectual class, and therefore to produce vital knowledge. Intellectuals are unnecessary in a country devoted to the exploitation of natural resources, but they could become useful as global economic rivalries grow stronger. President Dmitry Medvedev knows this. Yet although he knows the current system is incompatible with technological progress, he has no intention of dismantling it. Will he initiate real reforms? And if he does, will they be able to change the system without destroying it? At the risk of offending liberals and democrats, one could argue that the chances of success are higher in Russia today than they were at the end of the Soviet era.

Translated by Charles Goulden

Vladislav Inozemtsev is director of the Centre for Post-industrial Studies in Moscow and editor of the magazine *Svobodnaya Mysl* (Free Thought).

1. Address to the Federal Assembly, 25 April 2005.
2. The price of metals and construction materials is higher in Russia than on the global markets, and the cost of extracting natural gas increased by a factor of seven between 2000 and 2009 (*Vedomosti*, Moscow, 14 August 2009, 14 April, 31 May and 1 June 2010).

❖ ❖

April 2011

No cosy ChiAmerica as planned

Can China share out the wealth?

China now has the world's second biggest economy, though its actual GDP per capita is much less than Tunisia's. But sharing the wealth and securing it for the future, while fulfilling pent-up domestic demand, represent a great challenge for China.

Martine Bulard

The Japanese rather than the Chinese government broke the news that in 2010 China had become the world's second-largest economic power, ahead of Japan. Chinese officials, not usually given to modesty, were not triumphant, as China is keen to keep its dual status of 'developing country' and 'rising superpower', allowing it to play different roles in various international organisations. With a gross domestic product of $5.9 trillion, China is still far behind the United States, which produces two-and-a-half times more. China's actual GDP per capita of $7,400[1] is almost five times less than Japan's – much less even than Tunisia's.

And yet China is powerful in finance (reserves of $2.8 trillion), industry (almost 14 per cent of the world's industrial added value, compared to 3 per cent in 1990), trade (10 per cent) and the military (it ranks third in expenditure). This is changing the world order. For a long time, the US only saw it as a 'workshop of the world', useful for constraining US salaries and increasing profits. Today it realises that China is a competitor on the political and economic level. The honeymoon that began in 1972 with US president Richard Nixon's visit to Beijing is over.

The *Financial Times* noted that some believe 'the US is in danger of re-engaging in Asia on acrimonious terms…you do not need to be a paranoid conspiracy theorist to think that the US is trying to bandwagon Asia against China'. It recalled the declaration by Secretary of State Hillary Clinton on her visit to Phnom Penh, when she advised Cambodia 'not to become too dependent on China'. As a Chinese official remarked, 'Can you imagine the Chinese government telling Mexico not to be too dependent on the US?'[2]

Last November President Barack Obama toured Asia, visiting Japan, whose relationship with China is strained; South Korea, at loggerheads with the North, Beijing's ally; Indonesia, which controls the Malacca Straits, a vital route for Chinese trade; and India, which has strong tensions with China. Clinton had previously visited Cambodia, Malaysia, Vietnam and Australia, and signed (or strengthened) military agreements. Last November and December, joint US-South Korean manoeuvres took place off the Chinese coast. The US is using the fear aroused by China's increase in power to regain control of the region. All this will feed China's paranoia and push it to react. We are far from the 'special China-US relationship' known as ChiAmerica that was supposed to characterise the start of the 21st century. It is a relationship that is neither entente cordiale nor open war, but one in which divergent interests do not prevent cooperation. It is 'conflictual cooperation'.

The General Electric group announced in January that it had signed agreements on coproduction and technology transfer to China, just as Obama was criticising the countries' trade imbalance in front of President Hu Jintao. The agreements were concerned with meeting China's domestic needs, but also production of goods for re-export. Half of Chinese sales abroad are controlled by companies that are not Chinese – companies opposed to a revaluation of the yuan, because it would make their exports more expensive. Meanwhile, General Electric's CEO, Jeff Immelt, has become chief economic adviser to the White House, chairing the Council on Jobs and Competitiveness. Chinese business circles can rest easy.

EXPORT MORE TO CHINA

Hu went so far as to invite the US to export more to China. The ministry of commerce claimed that 'restrictions on hi-tech exports to China, rather than the Chinese currency, are the "major source" of the US trade deficit'.[3] Only 7 per cent of Chinese imports of hi-tech products come from the US. Since Tiananmen Square in 1989, the US and Europe have imposed an embargo on dual-use technologies (usable in both civilian and military industries). China wants that to end and has turned it into a commercial argument, while looking to assert itself in hi-tech. Chinese leaders are deaf to US (and European) pressure to revalue the yuan and lift exchange controls. They recall that Japan gave in to such pressure in 1985, and in the following three years, the yen appreciated by 100 per cent against the dollar. Japanese export figures tumbled, relocations (especially to China) soared and the economy slumped. And it hasn't yet recovered.

China is apprehensive about this. It rebuffed France, the US and the International Monetary Fund, which had intended to impose 'good conduct' criteria at the meeting of the G20 finance ministers in Paris in February. China was supported by Germany, whose model is also focused on exports. Germany, which has a balance of payments surplus of 6.7 per cent of GDP[4] compared to China's 4.7 per cent, rejected any cap on surpluses. During his US trip in January, Hu said: 'The monetary policy of the United States has a major impact on global liquidity and capital flows and, therefore, the liquidity of the US dollar should be kept at a reasonable and stable level.'[5] He was referring to the US Federal Reserve, which has injected $600 billion into the economy while giving little support to the social sector. Low salaries and social security payments, and excess accumulated capital, were at the root of the 2008 crisis. But the US is priming the finance pump again.

This flood of liquidity has been feeding speculation on national debt in countries with high interest rates. To repay this debt, governments and the IMF are pushing for austerity measures everywhere. Capital has also been channelled into commodities (gold, oil, copper) and foodstuffs. Their prices have reached new heights, worrying the World Bank, which fears repeated food riots. Investors have rushed to buy currencies and stocks. Countries must intervene to avoid a revaluation of their currency, which would handicap their foreign sales. China's crusade against this 'dangerous disequilibrium' has been a real success in Asia (where Japan, Malaysia, South Korea and Taiwan have spent crazy amounts on buying dollars) and in Latin America (where Brazil now taxes capital entering the country). On the margins of the Paris G20, the BRIC countries (Brazil, Russia, India and China) protested against the norms that others wanted to impose on them. So far, the US and its allies have not managed to rally the South against the Chinese leadership, which, however, knows it will have to negotiate, domestically and internationally.

In Paris, China and Brazil were in agreement against the rich countries' claims. In Brasília, they confronted each other over the flood of Chinese products. If China wants to carry weight in the currency market, it needs an internationally recognised (and convertible) currency. Ending exchange controls is not the only way of achieving this. France, after all, kept its controls until 1989.

The Chinese authorities have now lifted certain prohibitions. On 11 January they extended the possibility of yuan transactions, already available in Brazil, Russia and some East Asian countries, to Central Asian countries. And they allowed multinationals such as McDonald's and Caterpillar to issue shares directly in yuan on the Hong Kong stock market. Simultaneously, they restricted the right of foreigners to buy commercial and residential property. 'If we do not control the property bubble, let a stock bubble inflate and allow the yuan to rise freely, China will face the risk of large-scale cross-border capital flows,' said Deng Xianhong, the deputy administrator of China's State Administration of Foreign Exchange.[6]

JUDGING THE PACE OF FOREIGN EXCHANGE

The governor of the central bank, Zhou Xiaochuan, said the yuan had already risen by 4 per cent against the dollar since last summer, an (unprecedented) annual rate of 8–10 per cent, and that China would continue to improve its foreign-exchange system, but at its own pace.[7] That pace must not compromise domestic growth in a country needing to create 9 million jobs each year, nor can the economy be allowed to boil over. The government has already taken measures against the rise in prices, which has affected food (and therefore purchasing power), as well as imported raw materials. Since an appreciation of the yuan might partly compensate for this, the current revaluation comes at the right moment. But it will make exports more expensive, when the trade surplus already decreased by almost 7 per cent last year, proof of a certain level of Chinese consumer dynamism.

There is also a risk of excessive borrowing. The government is trying to turn off the loans tap so as to limit wasteful investment and control the real-estate bubble. For the third time in four months, it has raised interest rates and bank reserve requirements; and it has established a resale tax on apartments not intended for personal use. But this shift toward a model more frugal with capital and centred on domestic needs has been difficult to negotiate. According to Zhou, the change 'will take a long time. It will require a radical transformation of modes of production and adequate training for workers...This kind of cycle takes a decade.'[8]

It is not clear whether the Chinese are willing to wait that long. Discontent is growing, as is the struggle for salary increases. Injustices are beginning to irritate the middle classes, previously obsessed with their own accumulation of wealth. Liu Junsheng, a researcher at an institute under the control of the Ministry of Human Resources and Social Security, wrote a piece in the official newspaper *China Daily* saying that raising workers' pay was vital for China. Pointing to inequalities, it concluded by inverting the famous government slogan: 'This is certainly incompatible with China's aim of building a harmonious society.'[9] In 2010, the number of Chinese dollar billionaires jumped from 64 (in 2009) to 115.

Hu warned the cadres of the Party School of the Central Committee of the Communist Party that the country was 'still at a stage where many conflicts are likely to arise'.[10] The twelfth five-year plan (2011–16) is testimony to such concerns: it addresses consumption, housing, the social welfare system and innovation.

At the end of National People's Congress (NPC) on 11 March, Wen said: 'I believe two figures are more important than GDP' – education and research and development in the whole production process. The five-year plan states: 'Building a fairer society has been a core goal of the government which has worked to spread the wealth more evenly among its around 1.34 billion population, but income increases have lagged behind economic growth.'

The plan was approved by the legislature, the NPC, with 2,778 out of 2,875 deputies voting for it. Adopting the plan is one thing: implementing it is another.

Translated by Tom Genrich

Martine Bulard is a member of *Le Monde diplomatique*'s editorial team responsible for Asia.

1. GDP per inhabitant at purchasing power parity. In 2010 estimates were $34,200 for Japan and $9,500 for Tunisia. Central Intelligence Agency, *The World Factbook*.
2. Geoff Dyer, 'Beijing's elevated aspirations', *Financial Times*, London, 10 November 2010.
3. 'US high-tech export curbs "cause of deficit"', *China Daily*, Beijing, 16 December 2010.
4. 'World economic outlook', IMF, Washington, October 2010.
5. Richard McGregor, 'Hu questions future role of US dollar', *Financial Times*, London, 16 January 2011.
6. Gabriel Grésillon, 'Yuan: la Chine brouille les pistes', *Les Echos*, Paris, 17 November 2010.
7. Quoted in *People's Daily*, 21 February 2011.
8. Agence France-Presse, 18 January 2011.
9. 'Raising workers' pay vital for country', *China Daily*, Beijing, 8 November 2010.
10. 'President Hu points way to harmony, stability', *China Daily*, Beijing, 21 February 2011.

❖ ❖

JUNE 2011

LOVE YOU, HATE YOU: WE GET ALONG

China and India: united against the West

India and China compete and contrast when in direct competition or conflict. But put them against the rest of the world, especially the West, and they make common cause.

Christophe Jaffrelot

Chinese president Wen Jiabao was given a cool reception in India last December, and the final communiqué from the meeting did not refer to 'One China', the usual formula for recognising Chinese sovereignty over Tibet and Taiwan. That was retaliation for China's refusal to recognise Arunachal Pradesh and Jammu and Kashmir as integral parts of India.[1] And the Indian press had publicised the fact that China has been supplying arms to rebel tribes waging a separatist war in North East India for decades.[2] Yet this April, at the third BRICS (Brazil, Russia, India, China and South Africa) summit in Sanya (China), Beijing and Delhi united to defend the interests of emerging countries, and to disapprove of western intervention in Libya.

About five years ago, Jairam Ramesh, currently India's Minister of State for Environment and Forests, coined the term 'Chindia',[3] signifying a warming in relations. The memory of the 1962 war faded after Rajiv Gandhi's historic visit to Beijing in 1988, and the rate of official visits has remained steady since. They have signed important agreements, such as the India-China strategic and cooperative partnership for peace and prosperity in 2005. India has reaffirmed the position it has held since 1954 that Tibet belongs to China, while Beijing has recognised Sikkim, annexed in 1974, as part of India. Trade shot up to $61.7 billion in 2010, compared with $3 billion in 2000, and China is now India's biggest trade partner.

But border disputes, the subject of ongoing and often laborious negotiations since 1988, have come to the fore in recent years. In 2009 Beijing tried to block a $2.9 billion loan to India by the Asian Development Bank, because $60 million would have gone to a project in Arunachal Pradesh. Unlike India, China has never recognised the McMahon Line, negotiated in 1913 by Britain and the government in Lhasa, Tibet. It calls the state South Tibet and considers it part of China. Beijing tried to dissuade the Indian prime minister, Manmohan Singh, from visiting Arunachal Pradesh; the sudden anxiety seems linked to the Tibetan Buddhist monastery at Tawang, where the sixth Dalai Lama was born; the Chinese fear the next Dalai Lama will come from there, too.

In 2009–10, in an attempt to please Pakistan, the Chinese authorities started issuing visas for people from Jammu and Kashmir on separate papers, instead of pasting them into Indian passports – a way of denying Indian sovereignty over the state.[4] When they refused a visa to the Indian general in command of Jammu and Kashmir in July last year, Delhi cancelled his official visit.

There was clearly increased tension between India and Pakistan after the Mumbai attacks of November 2008. Beijing's support for Islamabad worries Delhi, which is concerned about the Chinese-built deep sea port at Gwadar in the Pakistani province of Baluchistan,[5] and their military collaboration: China and Pakistan built the first JF-17 fighter jets together in November 2009; Sword class frigates (F-22P) and tanks will follow, and nuclear power plants, which India suspects will be for military use. There may be conflict over the Brahmaputra river: the Chinese are building a hydroelectric power station upstream, which could affect the flow of water into India.

STRING OF PEARLS

Rivalry between India and China is even stronger in the ocean than on land. Delhi fears being surrounded by China's rapidly growing 'String of Pearls' (Beijing is building ports as far away as the Straits of Hormuz), and is concerned about the deployment of missiles on the Tibetan plateau. Beijing is convinced that Delhi can block access to the China Sea, using the Andaman Islands archipelago.[6] Anxieties are all the more intense because they both get most of their oil from the Middle East, via the Indian Ocean. They are concentrating on reinforcing their naval capacities, without neglecting other areas of the military, as indicated by rising budgets.[7]

This rivalry has led to the formation of regional coalitions. China is already close to Pakistan, Burma and Sri Lanka, and is trying to woo partners that India wants, such as Iran, Nepal and Bangladesh. India is trying to exploit the anxiety over China's growing power that is felt in Vietnam, Singapore and Japan (in 2006 India signed an important economic partnership agreement with Japan). India is getting closer to the US, which offends China: considering the US-Japan axis, this further reinforces US power in Asia.

Complex bilateral relations do not prevent countries from meeting, and agreeing, at multilateral forums. The multiplicity of institutions bringing together Asian or emerging countries means these exchanges have become more frequent and intense:

India and China are members of half a dozen, at the regional and intercontinental level.

Apart from the strategic triangle of Russia, China and India, the most symbolic is the BRICS grouping. The final declaration of their first summit in Russia, in June 2009, expressed a desire for a multipolar world. The second in Brazil in April 2010 referred to specific geopolitical issues such as Iran: the BRICS agreed that the sanctions proposed by the West were not the solution. At the third summit in China this April, the club developed real political authority with the inclusion of South Africa, whose economic performance had previously disqualified it from entry. China and India united to defend the interests of emerging countries, as they had already done at the World Trade Organisation. Not only did the BRICS criticise intervention in Libya, but they demanded a greater role within the UN, including permanent seats in the Security Council for Brazil and India and senior posts in the IMF and the World Bank, traditionally held by Americans and Europeans.

OPPOSING THE WEST TOGETHER

The relative acrimony in bilateral relations between China and India is compensated by the intensity of their communication at the multilateral level, where they enjoy opposing the West. China's hostility to western policies is hardly surprising, but some of the positions India takes are ambiguous. It appears to be torn between the occidentalists who see India as a bridge power between the North and the South, and the orientalists who would replace the Washington Consensus[8] with an Asian Consensus, or even a Beijing Consensus, combining liberal economics with authoritarian politics.

The Indian elite is drawn in that direction by its fascination with China's growth. Rajiv Kumar, director general of the Federation of Indian Chambers of Commerce and Industry, came back from the China summit full of admiration: 'For me, the most remarkable feature of Chinese capitalism is the complete blurring of the distinction between the public and private sectors. The two work seamlessly under the overall regulatory gaze of the Chinese Communist Party.'[9]

For some in power in India, democracy is no longer a foreign policy ideal but a political tool: it is legitimate to intervene in the name of democracy in Afghanistan, since that weakens Pakistan, but it is not necessary to side with western protests over Russia's invasion of Georgia, or to back UN resolution 1973 authorising intervention in Libya. India seems condemned to ambivalence. Those in charge of security are obsessed with the rapid growth of China, but the elite stand together with China against the West, and India's business community believes in the Beijing Consensus.

On the fringes of the latest summit, India and China decided to renew cooperation in defence, frozen after the visa incidents of July 2010; to reduce the trade gap (India has registered a deficit of $25 billion); and to set up a mechanism to discuss border disputes. This warming in relations reflects India's desire – linked to current economic conditions – to put pressure on the US, which it has seen as too close to Pakistan. No one knows how long this will last, but India and China certainly have the capacity to separate their fluctuating bilateral relations from their partnership against the West at the multilateral level.

Translated by Stephanie Irvine

Christophe Jaffrelot is a senior research fellow at the Centre for International Studies and Research, Sciences Po/CNRS, Paris.

1. Sujit Dutta, 'Managing and engaging rising China: India's evolving posture' (PDF), *The Washington Quarterly*, vol. 34, no. 2, Spring 2011.
2. Saikat Datta, 'The Great Claw of China', *Outlook India*, Delhi, 7 February 2011.
3. Jairam Ramesh, *Making Sense of Chindia: Reflections on China and India*, India Research Press, Delhi, 2005.
4. India and Pakistan have been in dispute over Kashmir since 1947.
5. Christophe Jaffrelot, 'A Tale of Two Ports: Gwadar and Chabahar display Chinese-Indian rivalry in the Arabian Sea', Yale Global Online, 7 January 2011.
6. Mathieu Duchatel, 'The PLA Navy in the Indian Ocean', in 'China's Sea Power, Reaching Out to the Blue Waters', *China's Analysis*, March 2011.
7. China's military budget has risen by an average of 10 per cent every year for the last 30 years, and officially reached $91 billion in 2011, according to the International Institute for Security Studies, *The Military Balance*, London, 2011. India's reached $32 billion in 2009/2010, a rise of one-third compared with the previous year. The true figures may be quite different from the official ones.
8. The body of neoliberal economic measures imposed on indebted countries between 1980 and 1990.
9. Rajiv Kumar, 'Learning from Chinese capitalism', *The Hindu Business Line*, Delhi, 16 April 2011.

❖ ❖

February 2011

Africa draws its own borders

Sudan's south secedes

The tranquil referendum is over, and southern Sudan will be a nation, but it's not yet sure of its territory, its citizens or its oil income.

Gérard Prunier

Southern Sudan's referendum in January was a turning point in the history of Sudan, and of Africa. It was the first challenge to the sacrosanct principle of the inviolability of colonial borders. Since the creation of the Organisation of African Unity (OAU) in 1963, it had been accepted that the (at times absurd) boundaries imposed by colonial powers between 1885 and 1926 would not be contested. A single infringement was recognised, the independence of Eritrea in 1993. But this was an exception in appearance only, since the territory had been colonised by Italy, then entrusted to Ethiopia in 1952 by the UN.[1]

The OAU and UN rejected all attempts at secession by Katanga (the former Belgian Congo) in 1961 and Biafra (Nigeria) in 1967. Somaliland's desire in 1991 to reverse its 1960 merger with Italian Somalia has still not found a legal solution, despite its de facto independence.[2] In southern Sudan the break seems radical, for the region, which has just voted (quite legally) for its own autonomy, never had its boundaries set by colonial powers.

The idea of autonomy was already taking shape at the end of colonisation, in 1956. The enmity between north and south goes back to when southern blacks were rounded up by Arab slave traders from the north. When the British forcibly united Sudan from 1898, some southerners converted to Christianity to set themselves apart from the Muslim northerners. The result was a deeply divided colony that the British did nothing to repair, instead managing north and south as two virtually separate entities. The north received the lion's share of social and economic investment.[3]

The civil war, which began even before independence from Britain, lasted until 1972, and the south won a fairly large degree of autonomy when peace accords were signed in Addis Ababa (Ethiopia). The south's provincial government, established in Juba, managed the former rebel provinces for some ten years. And it seemed as though the rift that threatened national territorial integrity might be bridged.

But tensions resurfaced when the US company Chevron discovered oil in the south, which has 85 per cent of Sudan's oil wells. The then president, Jaafar al-Numeiry, was determined to dismantle the autonomy that had been so difficult to win. He closed the autonomous parliament in Juba, abolished the government, replacing it with a military administration, and attempted to disarm the army's black regiments. A revolt erupted in 1983, and lasted 19 years.

SUPERPOWERS INTERVENE

The Sudan People's Liberation Army (SPLA) led by Colonel John Garang, a southern officer who had deserted, proclaimed itself an 'anti-imperialist' movement. Garang was based in Ethiopia (then run by the pro-Soviet Colonel Mengistu Haile Mariam), and got his arms from Moscow and its allies. The government in Khartoum received financial and military support from the US.

The collapse of the Soviet Union in 1991 might have ensured the north's definitive victory, but the north lost US backing by turning Islamist in 1989. So between 1991 and 1994, the adversaries fought without any external support. After the end of apartheid in South Africa, Garang was discreetly backed by South Africa and its allies, including Tanzania under Julius Nyerere and Zimbabwe under Robert Mugabe.

Eventually, the US decided to get involved once more. Under pressure from the religious far right, which sided with the 'persecuted Christians of southern Sudan', President George W. Bush forced the adversaries to negotiate in 2002. The Naivasha Agreement (Comprehensive Peace Agreement, CPA) was signed in 2005, and provided for a referendum on self-determination at the end of an interim period of six-and-a-half years.

Long years of war had caused other complications – those of a vast and diverse country, which cannot be reduced to a simple north-south dichotomy. Many other regions – Darfur, South Kordofan, Blue Nile province, the Red Sea slopes – distanced themselves from the Arab Muslim 'heart' of central Sudan, which had not treated them any better than it had the south. They were home to very diverse non-native groups, all of them Muslim, and had long been considered part of an abstract 'north'. For Garang, who was not a secessionist, the deepening of these complications between centre and periphery made him rethink the domination of the Arab Muslim minority over the whole country.

A few weeks after the CPA was signed, he headed for Khartoum, where he was welcomed by an enthusiastic, mostly Arab, crowd. He then created the northern branch of his movement, and its popularity never stopped growing. His chances of winning the elections planned for 2010 seemed very high. The revolt in Darfur in February 2003 confirmed the relevance of his strategy. But Garang died in a helicopter accident in the Imatong Mountains in July 2005.

The Naivasha Agreement described in great detail how wealth, political power and military forces would be distributed – and tried hard to be as neutral and egalitarian as possible. Over six years, the former enemies were to cooperate to 'make unity attractive' before the referendum scheduled for January 2011. The six months after the vote were meant for setting up a united, democratic and egalitarian 'New Sudan' (Garang's dream), or organising secession. With Garang dead, this second option won, with his companions pinning their hopes of freedom on legal partition.[4]

From the outset, the CPA was a semi-failure, for all its diplomatic and organisational sophistication. Its security measures were efficient, despite repeated skirmishes that were finally brought under control. The allocation of half of the oil revenues to the south's semi-autonomous administration was respected. But the sharing of political and administrative power failed: the Islamists of the National Congress Party (NCP), who established an authoritarian regime in Khartoum after the coup in June 1989, had no intention of playing the CPA game. Southern ministers who took up their posts in the Government of National Unity (GoNU) in the capital quickly realised that it was impossible for them to exercise their mandate because of permanent NCP control. Part of this failure was attributable to Garang, who always led the SPLA (which became the Sudan People's Liberation Movement in 1983), in an authoritarian manner and often kept educated members of the diaspora at arm's length.

The SPLA lacked human resources for managing not just one but two states, via the autonomous southern government and the GoNU. During the interim years, the NCP succeeded only in maximising material gains from the oil wells in the south, and hampering the southern government in Juba. Nothing was done to 'make unity attractive'. Because of this, the last southern supporters of a unitary solution gradually disappeared. From 2009 it was evident that if a referendum took place, it could only lead to independence.

NEW PROBLEMS

Despite the pessimistic forecasts, the referendum passed without major incident. And yet the result – which validated the south's secession – will bring new problems:

- The border between north and south has not yet been fixed. This is serious, since the contested regions are home to a large part of the oil reserves.
- No measure has clarified how citizenship will be defined in the divided state. What will happen to millions of southerners living in the north? The same problem exists for the nomadic peoples who migrate with their livestock between north and south, following the rains and the seasons.
- It has not been decided how the debt ($38 billion) will be divided up.
- The division of oil revenues has not been settled.
- In several regions (Abey District, Blue Nile Province), the population groups that Garang categorised as 'marginalised' have won the right to 'popular consultations', to establish their relations with north and south. But there are no provisions to put the process into action.
- The CPA has no provisions concerning Darfur. The authoritarian Sudanese government, which has neither learned nor forgotten anything, obstinately refuses to resolve the conflict using viable international negotiations.

The very complexity of Sudan ensured the referendum process was adequate. In the early 2000s, the NCP-state was faced with a change in internal power relationships. Darfur rebel forces realised that their internal divisions made them vulnerable to government manipulation, and began coordinating their actions. Sudan's marginalised regions prepared to assert their rights by force, if the secession of the south left them in a difficult relationship with the NCP-state. The northern branch of the Sudan People's Liberation Movement staked everything on the referendum, knowing that it might decisively pit the forces of democracy against the Islamist regime. Northerners realised that 20 years of civil war tension and sacrifice risked ending in national humiliation – not only partition, but no more access to the only wealth from which they had some benefits, oil.

The authoritarian, corrupt Khartoum regime had claimed itself to be the promoter of national growth. But popular discontent grew to such an extent that even the old Arab political parties (despite being worn down by half a century of inept political administration) felt compelled to integrate democratic aspirations.

AIMS IN THE NORTH

In the north, all the talk was of overthrowing the regime. The NCP was divided. The vice-president Ali Osman Mohamed Taha, sidelined for a year because he was deemed too moderate, made a forceful return, catching the regime's hardliners off guard. Outside the party, the ageing Islamist leader Hassan al-Turabi publicly declared during the referendum that Sudan must follow the way now opened by Tunisia. He was immediately arrested and his supporters' homes were searched.

The government in Khartoum looked isolated. Demonstrations of Arab solidarity, much in evidence when President Omar al-Bashir had been charged by the International Criminal Court in 2009, were short-lived. Hopes of Chinese support were also dashed. Beijing, which controls 50 per cent of Sudanese oil extraction, and supplies most of the government's arms, did not wish to get involved in a crisis with the international community over an issue it considered non-crucial. The NCP dictatorship, faced with a south that, although badly organised, was determined to seize the opportunity for which it had waited 50 years, suddenly found itself on the defensive. The post-referendum period looks to be more dangerous for the north than for the south.

No doubt the perilous circumstances in the north are behind the calm of the referendum. Bashir, weakened, was honey-voiced towards the south. His visit to Juba just before the referendum process was presented, to general surprise, as a true 'declaration of peace'. Perhaps he intended to guard his rear so he could confront the war smouldering in his own realm. He made only one demand: that the leaders of the Darfur rebel forces, who have taken refuge in southern Sudan, be expelled.

Southern leaders were only too happy to pay such a modest price for a tranquil referendum, and hurried to comply. President Salva Kiir Mayardit has almost accomplished the mission he inherited upon Garang's death, and he has already announced his intention to retire once the consultation process is over.

Who will succeed him? In a politically very young southern Sudan, rivalries are dangerous. Vice-President Riak Machar looks like the favourite, but he will need the backing of politicians, including Pagan Amoun, James Wani Igga and Luka Biong Deng, who represent other tribes and other regions (Machar is a Nuer from Upper Nile). To be effective in this divided country, any future government will need to consider the ethnic-geographical balance.

The future looks uncertain. Unresolved pre-referendum problems are still on the negotiating table: drawing up the borders and concluding an oil-sharing agreement. It is obvious that Khartoum's nervousness makes the northern situation insecure and explosive. Arrangements with potentially grave consequences will need to be negotiated in a difficult atmosphere. While the south's long march has reached its destination, to make its independence concrete and lasting it still needs to surmount obstacles created by Khartoum.

Translated by Tom Genrich

Gérard Prunier is a researcher at the National Centre for Scientific Research (CNRS), Paris, and director of the French Centre for Ethiopian Studies in Addis Ababa.

1. This mandate was violated by Ethiopia when it unilaterally annexed Eritrea in 1962.
2. 'Somaliland, an African exception', *Le Monde diplomatique*, English edition, October 2010.
3. The British authorities did not encourage Christianisation. The missionaries were mostly Italian, American and French Canadian. The British government preferred to deal with the Muslims, seen as more 'advanced' and easier to administer.
4. Garang always found it difficult to 'sell' his unitarian vision to his brothers in arms, who were instinctively secessionist. Only his personal authority, and the increasing interest of Muslims opposed to the Islamist regime, had allowed him to impose his vision.

❖❖❖❖❖❖❖❖❖❖❖❖❖❖❖❖❖❖❖❖❖❖❖❖❖❖❖❖❖❖❖❖❖❖❖❖

OCTOBER 2010

ONE IS A FAILED STATE, THE OTHER WORKS

Somaliland, an African exception

The British left Somaliland functioning – unlike the Italians in Somalia. Fifty years after the end of colonialism, the breakaway region has peace and democracy, but no international recognition.

Gérard Prunier

To the south lies Somalia, the archetypal failed state. To the north, Somaliland, which in June organised one of the most democratic

SOMALILAND, AN AFRICAN EXCEPTION   101

elections Africa has seen for a long time. The explanation for this contrast lies in history. When Britain occupied the north of Somalia at the end of the 19th century, it intended only to prevent the French from gaining a strategic outlet on the Red Sea, and provide cheap food for its colony in Aden, in the Arabian Desert. The British were not concerned with making money from the territory and were content to run it at arm's length, interfering little with the indigenous system of governance and (effective) mechanisms for resolving conflict in a nomadic society.

The Italians took a radically different approach when they colonised the south. At the Berlin conference to divide Africa in 1884–85, a newly unified Italy demanded recognition, despite its political and economic backwardness as compared with the rest of western Europe. Italy's colonial ambitions were neither strategic nor economic: it sought compensatory glory (and to populate new areas to stem the emigration of its citizens, particularly to the US and Argentina). Fascism did nothing to temper Italy's pretensions; the fascist government used the imperialist project to provide its people with a compensatory psychodrama, resulting, in the 1920s, in massacres in its colonies and the destruction of indigenous mechanisms for social control.

The Somali people were divided by colonisation, but bound together by culture. They saw independence as the path to unification. Creating a Greater Somalia became a key nationalist aim, and led to the unification of the colonies under the first free Somali government in 1960. This created tension with the Organisation of African Unity, set up in 1963, which insisted on respect for colonial era borders.[1]

But the new country was built on a paradox: territories divided by history found themselves together again within the framework of an ambiguous pan-nationalist project which gave them an artificial sense of unity. The test of this came in 1977 when Somalia, under the dictator Mohamed Siad Barre,[2] invaded the Ogaden, an ethnically Somali region of neighbouring Ethiopia and the cornerstone of Greater Somalia. The war ended in a defeat with the triple effect of destroying the grand nationalist project, turning Somali clans against each other in their search for a scapegoat, and causing Siad Barre to make the clans in the north (former British Somaliland) pay for the conflict. A million refugees from the Ogaden arrived in Somalia on the heels of the retreating army. Siad Barre settled them in the north and armed them. He not only gave them wide administrative powers but a free hand to plunder.

The danger Somalis had always chosen to ignore – fragmentation of the clans – now came about, with the dictatorship's blessing. With the dream of a Greater Somalia dead, the government encouraged some clans to suppress others, redrawing the north-south border inherited from the colonial era.

REBELLION IN THE NORTH

In 1981 the north rebelled, beginning a ten-year civil war in which all those excluded from power rose up, one after another, against the dictatorship. It fell in 1991 leading to the collapse of the Somali state, since no confederation of clans proved able to replace the regime's scheming with constructive alliances.

The north took the opportunity to declare independence and withdraw from the fratricidal conflict into which the south had sunk. Although the first few years were chaotic, the 1993 Borama inter-clan conference provided the country with representative institutions which assured its democratic foundation.

While Somaliland found its feet relatively quickly, the south plunged deeper into chaos. From 1992 to 1995 the 'international community' occupied southern Somalia, at the behest of the US. Operation Restore Hope did anything but that – the 35,000 soldiers deployed by more than 30 armies, at a cost of $5 billion, achieved nothing and were evacuated after two and a half years. Weakened by outside interference, Somalia also suffered from internal stresses. Since 1992 there have been 14 attempts to reform the government. All have failed.

This is where the colonial legacy is most evident: in the north, Somaliland incorporated its ancient clan mechanisms for managing conflict into English common law to create its own form of democracy. In the south, where Italian imperialism and fascism had eroded the indigenous system but contributed no new political or legal functions, the uncontrolled clan system hindered the emergence of any form of government, even an authoritarian one.

Somalia's Transitional Federal Government (TFG), in place since 2004 and recognised internationally, only controls a few streets in the centre of the capital Mogadishu – and even that is due to the support of 6,000 soldiers from the African Union Mission in Somalia (Amisom). The TFG has been torn apart by personal quarrels and corruption, and has to deal with an Islamist insurgency which, in July, launched terrorist attacks in Kampala, Uganda, to provoke an international crisis. In fact nationalism has more influence in Somalia than Islamism, and it offers the militants of Harakat al-Shabab al-Mujahideen (movement of fighting youth) the opportunity to rebuild a national consensus around the idea of resistance, and to assuage the fears provoked by their extremism.

ABSENCE OF RECOGNITION

Up to now Somaliland has managed to keep its distance from the violence next door which has led to tens of thousands of deaths, a million refugees and two million internally displaced over the last 20 years. The irony is that the 'international community' refuses to recognise this oasis of peace and democracy, while it continues to give legitimacy to Somalia on the basis of the 1960 unification, even though it is a state in name only, incapable of meeting any democratic criteria or of re-establishing peace.

While the US, UK and France are beginning to question the wisdom of this policy, inertia and convention stand in the way of Somaliland's recognition. Western powers do not want to offend the Arab world, which sees Ethiopia – a Christian 'foreign body' in a predominantly Muslim region – as the enemy. Egypt has always wanted a strong and united Somalia to serve as an ally against Ethiopia,[3] and the existence of Somaliland interferes with this strategy.

That is why Somaliland needs to be beyond reproach. 'They will expect more from us than from others, but give us less,' predicted a former vice-president of Somaliland just before the election. But Somaliland still has a long way to go: the outgoing head of state, Hassan Dahir Riyale Kahin, who came to power in May 2002, did not have a spotless democratic career. As vice-president, he replaced President Mohamed Ibrahim Egal when Egal died of natural causes in May 2002. He then manipulated the Guurti (upper house of parliament) in order to have the elections postponed so he could stay in office. In September 2009, threatened by popular revolt and a rebellion in parliament, he asked the army chief of staff to move on the capital Hargeisa, with the probable aim of suspending parliament. But, after thinking about it for 24 hours, the head of the army refused to take part in this 'legal coup', and the president was obliged to set a date for elections.

Somaliland's constitution limits the number of political parties to three. Riyale Kahin runs Udub, a party he formed with Egal, the 'Father of the Republic'. Seventeen years in power encouraged the familiar pattern of clientelism and nepotism, but while these are common in Africa, in Somaliland they are limited by a free press, genuine freedom of speech, for which a robust civil society battled hard, and a legislative body that is not totally corrupt. Udub's old opponent, Ahmed Mohamed Silanyo, created a strong and organised opposition in the Kulmiye party. The joker in the pack is the small new party Ucid, led by Faisal Ali Warabe, which combines the positive element of openness to women, minority clans and intellectuals, with a dangerous complacency towards Islamist extremists. As a result, Ucid is often perceived as opportunist, ready to use any means to dislodge the two traditional parties.

Warabe is much younger than Kahin or Silanyo, and does not belong to the civil war generation. He does not see Somaliland as a miracle of willpower, but as a normal political entity, and this attitude has brought him support among young voters.

The election went ahead smoothly on 26 June, and on 1 July the national electoral commission declared Silanyo the winner with 49 per cent of the votes. Kahin got 33 per cent and Warabe 17 per cent. The turnout was 88 per cent of 1.09 million registered voters. The role of the 70 foreign observers was largely symbolic, to legitimise the process, which took place in a visibly calm atmosphere.

So can the goodwill and good organisation of the elections mean that Somaliland, which has lived without international aid for 20 years, will achieve the recognition it desires? Probably not, at least in the short term. Too many people are opposed – including those nostalgic for a Greater Somalia, Islamist extremists and conservative diplomats. Some of its supporters fear that, in any case, full recognition will only aggravate the antagonisms that have devastated Somalia. Perhaps an intermediate status is possible, where Somaliland would have most of the legal and commercial advantages of recognition, and not provoke too much opposition.

Translated by Stephanie Irvine

Gérard Prunier is a researcher at the National Centre for Scientific Research (CNRS), Paris, and director of the French Centre for Ethiopian Studies in Addis Ababa.

1. Article 4b of the Organisation of African Unity charter required its members to respect the borders that existed when they achieved independence. A Greater Somalia would have brought together the former British and Italian colonies as well as French Somaliland (modern day Djibouti), the Ethiopian province

of Ogaden and the Northern Frontier District of Kenya, all populated by ethnic Somalis.

2. Siad Barre was a *carabiniere* under Italian colonial rule and throughout his life maintained great respect for his 'boss', Benito Mussolini, whose style of government he shared.

3. The situation has worsened since the denunciation of the 1959 Nile Waters Treaty. The rebellion, largely anti-Egyptian, is led by Ethiopia and brings together the non-Muslim countries on the Nile (Uganda, Burundi, Tanzania and Kenya).

Part IV: European Directions

❖❖❖❖❖❖❖❖❖❖❖❖❖❖❖❖❖❖❖❖❖❖❖❖❖❖❖❖❖❖❖❖❖❖

OCTOBER 2011

GREENS NOW JUST 'LIBERALS ON BIKES'

Germany goes for sustainable capitalism

The Greens are likely to be a major part of the next German government; few seem to have noticed that they've already been a substantial part of its regional governments for 59 years.

Olivier Cyran

Hamburg's most fashionable district is also its greenest, though this is not immediately apparent from the foot of the Marco Polo Tower – 16 storeys of luxury apartments that look like a sliced loaf. (They cost an average €3.7 million.) A love of nature isn't obvious either at the nearby offices of Unilever, but the agri-food and cosmetics giant has fitted low-energy light bulbs in its new 25,000 square metre headquarters, the biggest area ever so equipped. 'The whole building has been designed to the strictest environmental standards,' said the receptionist. The ground floor atrium has even been fitted with a heat recapture system, he told me, pointing at the glass ceiling.

The Marco Polo Tower and the Unilever headquarters are the pride of HafenCity, Hamburg's 155-hectare business district, with offices and apartments slotted in alongside the brick warehouses of the old Speicherstadt on the banks of the Elbe. By the time the building work is complete in 2025, this Dubai of the north should be a workplace to 40,000 people and home to 12,000 members of the 'creative classes', according to the project's promoters. Culture will be catered for by the Elbphilharmonie, a concert hall that the city is financing to the tune of €351 million. The cranes are still at work in some places, but the lots already completed are buzzing with senior managers nibbling Thai tapas on café terraces or drinking mediocre wine in expensive bars.

But appearances can be deceptive: just because the 'biggest urban development project in Europe' is part of the reclamation of the waste land by bankers and city whiz kids, as was London's Docklands, doesn't mean it runs counter to the principles of sustainable development. Quite the reverse. 'With its geothermal heating, low-pollution building materials, green spaces, pedestrian streets and cycle routes, it's really a pioneer development in terms of sustainability,' said Harald Müller, 53, an engineer who lives and works in HafenCity. Sitting in Carl's with a plate of pickled herring (which he favours over the other house speciality, truffle risotto), Müller made no secret of the fact that he has voted Green since 1997. The Greens didn't conceive the project but they backed it all the way, he said, and 'without them, the district certainly wouldn't have this ecological dimension'.

GREEN CREDENTIALS

Hamburg, European Green Capital 2011, certainly has environmental credentials. The Greens have twice participated in coalitions that ran the city, with the Social Democrat SPD (1997–2001) and the Conservative CDU (2008–10). Their impact is nowhere more evident than in HafenCity. Even the street names bear their mark; the Greens insisted that names given to public places should respect gender equality.

'Yes, it's a district for high earners, but the buildings are very creative and I think it's great for the image of the city,' said Katharina Fegebank, general secretary of Hamburg's Greens. Her colleague, Anja Hajduk, a member of the Bundestag from 2002 to 2008, said: 'On the whole it's a success, even if the prices are high. What was important to us when we were in government was ensuring that the district was open to all the people of Hamburg so that they could walk there. We got a guarantee that the ground floor of the Unilever building would be open to the public.'

Is this low-energy community of millionaires an early gain in the green revolution sweeping Germany? Leader writers have begun assessing the possibility of a Green Chancellor in 2013. The rise of the Greens in the past few months is spectacular: 'a mixture of Blitzkrieg and the Long March' according to their critics' jokes.

First, the self-reinforcing effect of constant opinion polls helped their stock throughout 2010, from 19 per cent support in Berlin in December 2009 to 30 per cent by October 2010. The press enthused over the 'green miracle' (*Der Spiegel*): 'The Greens are more popular than ever' (*Die Zeit*), 'The party of wellbeing' (*Stern*), 'Greens already dreaming of the Chancellery' (*Die Welt*). The Greens also benefited from sustained attention in the media after the former prodigy of German political life, the FDP (Liberal Party), went into freefall following the fall from grace of its golden boy, Guido Westerwelle, minister for foreign affairs in the Merkel government.

On 27 March 2011 the Greens won 24.2 per cent of the vote in Baden-Württemberg, the richest and third most populous of Germany's 16 states, which was traditionally CDU. By doubling their share of the vote (from 11.7 per cent in 2006), the Greens established themselves as the second political power after the CDU, overtaking their allies in the SPD and becoming senior partners in a coalition which is no longer 'red and green' but now 'green and red'. For the first time in German history, a Green assumed the presidency of a regional government. Winfried Kretschmann, 62, who sings in a church choir on Sundays, became a national star. On television he was described as a 'bearer of hope' and the 'political sensation of the year'.

Kretschmann's success was important enough to register on the stock market: the day after the Green victory, shares in E.on and RWE – Germany's two main nuclear energy companies – fell slightly, as did those of Daimler, BMW and Volkswagen. The ÖkoDAX, which monitors the top ten green investments, jumped eight points. It wasn't a revolution, since the less ecological markets soon surpassed their previous level. 'We are going to follow the path we promised within a bourgeois society,' Kretschmann was careful to reassure them on the night of his victory.

CHANGED DAYS

Back in the 1980s, it was different: the Greens then embodied the radical left in a West Germany opposed to communism. In the early 1980s the CDU came close to calling for the disbanding of the Green Party, accusing it of supporting armed struggle and anti-constitutional ideas. Middle-class Germany frowned at *grüne Chaoten* (green vandals) who claimed they were tackling social justice and environmental issues. Now Baden-Württemberg's new head says he is 'neither of the left nor the right' and has cordial relations with Erwin Teufel, the local CDU's leading light, whose 'moderate, centrist' orientation he says he shares.[1] Hamburg – the first German administration to try a 'black and green' coalition (in Germany, black symbolises the right) – shows that such a relationship is no longer outlandish. Even Chancellor Merkel has acknowledged she would not rule out a Green-Christian Democrat alliance after the legislative elections in 2013.

That scenario could become a reality next October, when it will be tested in Berlin's municipal elections. On a wave of dazzling opinion poll ratings, Renate Künast, who leads the Greens in the Bundestag, envisions herself running the capital and is not ruling out any possible partner, centre-left or right. Eberhard Diepgen, Berlin's former CDU mayor, has already begun his courtship: 'We have enough in common to make plans for a government with the Greens.'[2] *Süddeutsche Zeitung* said mockingly (5 November 2010): 'Green fever is spreading to conservative circles. Entrepreneurs and the rich are making eyes at the Greens.'

The Fukushima effect undoubtedly helped the rise of the Greens, at last able to capitalise on their opposition to a nuclear industry that most Germans don't want. The planned closure of nuclear power stations is their achievement. But radioactive leaks in Japan don't explain the transformation of a protest group into a 'neoliberal party on bikes', to quote Jutta Ditfurth, a co-founder of the Greens, who left the party in 1991. She is astonished in her new book[3] at the attractiveness of her former colleagues: 'Some commentators sound as though they have been living on Mars for the past 25 years. They say: let's see what the Greens do. Let them get on with governing. It's an astonishing position given that the Greens have already been in government on many occasions.'

The list is long: seven years as part of Gerhard Schröder's federal government (1998–2005), eleven years in coalition in North Rhine-Westphalia (1995–2005 and again from 2010), ten years in Hesse (1985–87, 1991–99), nine years in Schleswig-Holstein (1996–2005), six in Hamburg (1997–2001, 2008–10), four in Lower Saxony (1990–94), four in Saxony-Anhalt (1994–98), four in Bremen (from 2007), two in Saarland (from 2009) and two in Berlin (1989–90 and 2001–02). 'That's a total of 59 years of governmental experience,' Ditfurth calculates. 'It's doubtless in their own interests that the media pretend to regard the Greens as new and inexperienced and hold their breath to see how they will behave now they are in power, as if the suspense were unbearable…Those 59 years of experience are never subjected to detailed critical analysis.'

In Hamburg last February the electorate punished the incumbent majority (21.9 per cent voted for the CDU, 11.2 per cent for the Greens) and voted the SPD (48.3 per cent) into power, though that party was in poor shape everywhere else. Apart from walks in the HafenCity, the Greens did not have an attractive record. The coalition agreement with the right in 2008 contained plans for a tram system, the scrapping of a coal-fired power station project and an ambitious education reform to set up a single type of primary school for all. None of those promises has been kept. The tram project collapsed under budget cuts after the financial crisis of 2008 and the power station construction went ahead following a legal ruling. The school reform was rejected by the electorate in a referendum in July 2010. Following internal tensions caused by this failure, the black and green coalition collapsed, two years before its term was up.

The Greens left local bigwigs of the right with fond memories. Gregor Jaecke, the leader of Hamburg's CDU, recalled: 'Being Green means having a taste for life, and that is a value that we share. We have the same concerns about tomorrow: we have it in the Christian sense of respect for life and they have it in the more modern sense of sustainable development. That's why the need for a balanced economic policy is acknowledged more by the Greens than the SPD.'

The 2008 coalition agreement attests to that 'taste for life', reformulated in the language of budgetary orthodoxy. When the financial crisis broke, Greens and Christian Democrats immediately agreed to rein in public spending, by raising nursery charges for example. They pumped €1.5 billion into HSH Nordbank, rushed to aid the Hapag-Lloyd shipping group and took measures to cajole investors. 'The Greens fully understood that a climate of confidence had to be restored,' Jaecke said.

Weren't there any issues on which they disagreed? Perhaps a young, sexy party such as the Greens would not have the same regard for security and law and order as the CDU. 'Domestic security questions were in the hands of our conservative allies,' Fegebank said, 'but there weren't any problems.' The CDU's Jaecke confirmed that: 'We had a fairly strict stance on public order questions, but after examining them, the Greens completely accepted them.' He admitted that 'a sector of the middle-class electorate which forms the base of the CDU are today tempted to vote for the Greens'.

'NO CYCLE TRACKS HERE'

Working class districts are less tempted. In February the Greens won 9.2 per cent of the vote in the affluent Blankenese district, but only 6 per cent in the poor suburbs of Rothenburgsort, where more than half the electorate abstained. Here there are no cycle tracks and lofts with geothermal heating, but dirty concrete blocks heated with oil, and rundown shops. 'Vote Green? Me? Do you take me for an idiot?' said Joachim Riepke, 32, unemployed, whom I met as he was mending his scooter on the pavement. He is one of the 6.7 million Germans within the Hartz IV system, created by amalgamating the unemployment benefit and social security systems. 'Three hundred and fifty-nine euros a month. And you have to work for almost nothing. At the moment, the Jobcentre is leaving me in peace, but two months ago they called me in to wash dishes in an old people's home for two weeks. You can't say no otherwise it's goodbye to your benefit. Would you want me to vote for that?'

By 'that', Piepke means the SPD-Green majority, which in 2005 set up the harshest unemployment benefit system in Europe. Hartz IV forces those eligible to take 'one-euro jobs', move house if their accommodation is judged too costly and obey a long list of bureaucratic stipulations on pain of losing their allowance. 'The most drastic cut in social security since 1949' was what the conservative *Frankfurter Allgemeine Zeitung* called it when it was presented (on 30 June 2004).

Devised by Peter Hartz, then HR director of the Volkswagen group and friend of Chancellor Schröder, the reform[4] now serves as a model to reformers in France and elsewhere who want to replace a system of handouts with a system in which wage earners do without wages. But Hartz IV set a record that will be hard to beat: its architects fixed the single allowance at such a low level that the constitutional court in Karlsruhe partially outlawed it last October, judging that the families who received it could not meet their children's basic needs.

The responses of Hamburg's Greens to Hartz IV are sometimes surprising. 'The level is certainly too low,' said Fegebank, 'but we still think that it was a good idea to bring together social and unemployment benefits to encourage people back to work.' When the debate became heated, she came out with a decisive argument: 'Such a reform could only have been launched by a red and green alliance. If the CDU and the FDP had taken the initiative, it would have caused a revolution.'

BEREFT OF PASSION

Driven by the conviction that 'the economy and ecology are made for mutual understanding', Hamburg's Greens are a perfect illustration of change during the past 15 years among the party's members and supporters. Long anchored on the left, the Green Alternative List (or GAL, as the local Hamburg party used to be known) saw some of its long-term members walk out in 1999 in protest at the federal authorities' decision to approve German participation in NATO's Kosovo campaign.

The abandonment of pacifism and loss of members left the way clear for a new generation of wealthy and educated activists favourably disposed towards institutions and business circles. Their spokesman Anja Hajduk, a psychologist, typifies this change: she had never been an activist 'other than voting Green' before she got her party membership card in 1995. Elected to the Bundestag in 2002, she voted with all her party colleagues to lower taxation for the most affluent households, who saw their tax burden fall from 53 per cent to 42 per cent during the Schröder years. 'I've never been convinced by the right-left divide. It's a good thing that the Greens are taking an interest in economics.'

'Anja Hajduk is a typical representative of these new Greens who have the wind in their sails, they're pragmatic administrators, bereft of passion and totally indifferent to social issues,' said Norbert Hackbusch, who left the Greens in 1999 after 16 years. He sits today on the city council as a member of Die Linke, Germany's most leftwing party. 'Hamburg is one of the richest cities in the country, but it also has one of the highest poverty rates. Here, one child in five lives below the poverty line, but poor families don't vote, or at least not for the Greens.'

One of his major complaints against his former colleagues is their lack of action in fiscal matters. According to the latest league table in *Manager* magazine, 26 of Germany's 300 richest people live in Hamburg. Their combined wealth amounts to €44 billion, equal to half the city's GDP. 'Hamburg may be European Green Capital, but above all it's the tax evasion capital of Germany,' he said. The number of tax inspectors is inadequate: in 2010, out of 627 taxpayers who declared an annual income of over €1 million, the tax authorities were able to check up on only 31 of them. The lost tax revenues amount to hundreds of millions of euros. 'We asked for 150 additional tax inspectors to be taken on,[5] but the Greens wouldn't hear of it.'

The fat cats who live in Marco Polo Tower may not vote Green in the elections. The tower was built on a natural promontory in the port that gives residents a bird's eye view of the landing stage for liners. But the designers forgot that these floating palaces belch out toxic smoke that the wind blows back on to the balconies and windows of the tower. According to an investigation by *Der*

Spiegel, a 'breath of fresh air' for Marco Polo's residents contains the equivalent of the emissions from '50,000 lorries travelling at 130 kph, with significant quantities of sulphur dioxide, nitrogen dioxide and other carcinogenic particles'.[6] Multi-millionaires poisoned by luxury cruises: sustainable development has some surprising twists.

Translated by George Miller

Olivier Cyran is a journalist.

1. *Tagblatt Online*, 14 April 2011.
2. *Der Tagesspiegel*, Berlin, 7 November 2010.
3. Jutta Ditfurth, *Krieg, Atom, Armut. Was sie reden, was sie tun: die Grünen*, Rotbuch, Berlin, 2011.
4. In January 2007, Peter Hartz received a two-year suspended sentence and a fine of €576,000 from the court in Braunschweig for having given bribes to and treated members of the Volkswagen works council to travel and prostitutes.
5. In Germany, budget control falls within the responsibility of the *Länder*.
6. 'Luxusprobleme in Hamburg' (Luxury problem in Hamburg), *Der Spiegel*, Hamburg, 5 March 2010.

❖❖❖❖❖❖❖❖❖❖❖❖❖❖❖❖❖❖❖❖❖❖❖❖❖❖❖❖❖❖❖❖❖

May 2011

France's thinkers in the business of living

Academia's rebel alliance

One of the surprises of last autumn's public activism against French pension reform was the silence of intellectuals. Yet we have witnessed a surge of critical thought in recent years. Could the alliance be reformed between ordinary working people and academics who now have as much to lose as everyone else?

Pierre Rimbert

The unified fight against pension reform in France last autumn – with streets full of people, slogans, chants and raised fists, and union rank and file outpacing their leaders – mobilised more people than the events of the winter of 1995, when two million people demonstrated against the 'reform' of social security and pensions planned by the prime minister, Alain Juppé. Those strikes had a strange climate, familiar and unknown. Workers were suddenly back in fashion, although philosophers, journalists and politicians thought they had dissolved with the industrial restructuring of the 1980s. Government critics from inside academia were back too, determined to fight a war of ideas on economic and social issues. One of the 1995 speakers was the sociologist Pierre Bourdieu, addressing railway workers in Paris at the crowded Gare de Lyon. Famous French intellectuals didn't do that much after the 1970s. 'I am here to express support for all those who have been fighting for the past three weeks against the destruction of a civilisation linked to the existence of public services,' he said. There was a great split in French intellectual circles over the plans, and this was shown in completely opposed petitions. The first welcomed the Juppé plan, 'which [would] lead to social justice'; its signatories were recruited from the journal *Esprit*, the Saint-Simon Foundation, the French Democratic Trade Union (CFDT) and sections of the left won over by the market. The 'intellectuals' appeal in favour of the strikers' grouped previously unconnected researchers, academics and activists from trade unions and associations into a loose rebel alliance.

Last autumn's fight was so much less divided and divisive. Fifteen years after Bourdieu's speech, it's worth asking how the relationship has evolved in France between those who produce anti-Establishment ideas, the institutions to which they belong and industrial action. Two contradictory movements seem to coexist, seen in bookshop displays, among the ranks at meetings and in social-science seminars. There is more critical thought and it has increased; it has also become more specialised and aligned itself with academic norms.

The 1995 mobilisations helped renew independent publishing, and some 30 publishing houses now popularise critical works. All their catalogues feature translations; without the persistence of often unpaid teams of translators, works that were disdained by mainstream publishing would not have been published in French, including the historian Howard Zinn and Noam Chomsky. Now these are widely available. The translations include the cultural, historical and sociological analyses by the British 'New Left' in the 1960s and 1970s (Stuart Hall, Raymond Williams, Perry Anderson); the neo-Marxist books of the economist Giovanni Arrighi and geographer David Harvey; studies on gender, sexuality and dominated identities; and the now well-known names of Judith Butler, Michael Hardt, Toni Negri, Slavoj Žižek. Several critical journals introduced and discussed these texts, ensuring their transposition into the French context. One important detail: almost all the authors and commentators were involved in higher education or research.

A REJUVENATED MARXISM FOR INTELLECTUALS

The British historian Perry Anderson noted that 'the "crisis of Marxism" was a quintessentially Latin phenomenon…In Britain and the United States, West Germany and Scandinavian countries, there had never been mass Communist parties to attract the same projections or hopes in the postwar period.'[1] While many French Marxists recanted in the mid-1970s, some academics, mostly British and American, built the foundations, notably around the *New Left Review*, of a rejuvenated Marxism confined to academia.

Translating their work was not always easy. In 1997 the director of a Gallimard history series refused to publish *The Age of Extremes*[2] by the British historian Eric Hobsbawm because Hobsbawm still showed 'an attachment, even though remote, to the revolutionary cause'.[3] But with the convulsions of capitalism and the international growth of the global justice movement, the ideological pendulum, which had swung to the right during the 1980s,[4] swung back. Once the directors of big publishing houses had been alerted to the commercial success of critical and demanding titles published by independent houses, they thought again of anti-Establishmentarianism as a profitable market niche, and produced series to attract the activist's eye and money. *Le Monde des livres*, which cleverly had kept quiet about the success of the first books in the activist series Raisons d'Agir, launched by Bourdieu, devoted its front page on 26 November 2010 to 'rebel literature' and feted insurrectionary style. It was a sign of the times – critiques of the media, of finance and the western world order, previously confined to the margins, have become a fought-over commercial genre.

Back in the 1930s, Paul Nizan depicted academia as conservative and filled with 'watchdogs'.[5] Then in the radical 1960s and 1970s, human sciences, social critiques and revolution seemed to go together. Their connection has enlivened an institution riven with tensions, designed to back the bourgeois regime but also capable of nurturing revolutionaries. This contradiction may explain why critical publishing is both fascinated and repulsed by academia and lecturers or researchers. The stereotype of the independent publisher suggests a 30–40-year-old who has begun, or even finished, a doctorate in human sciences but hasn't found a research or higher education post that allows him or her to combine academic work with anti-Establishment action. Though this picture fails to take account of the diversity of the new 'militant' publishers, it captures their conflicted environment, falling somewhere between the scholarly and the political.

Publishers look to academia for a robust scientific method and prestigious names, but are unhappy with the ever-smaller focus of academics' objects of study, their taste for hermeneutics and the demands of mandarins eager to sue over a misplaced comma. For safety and self-preservation, publishers put a lecturer-researcher or at least someone who straddles science and politics (production and consumption), in charge of their social critique series. With similar logic, directors of critical journals fill their reading panels with senior lecturers, doctoral students and established authors, sometimes to the detriment of intellectuals who belong to the industrial movement, being attached to trade unions, political groups or associations. Since the editorial boards of committed journals, which are responsible for selecting anti-Establishment texts for a mainstream audience, use the same names as the scientific committees of scholarly journals, we might ask if all types of critical thought have an equal chance being selected.

A doctoral degree ensures a solid analytical method, a corpus of knowledge and even, sometimes, critical sense. But it also teaches propriety and precedence, encourages a willingness to surrender strong opinions, highly values give and take, and (because of over-specialisation within disciplines) promotes the view that things are 'always more complicated' than they may actually be. It authorises criticism but rejects politics, and blurs the line between seriousness and pompousness. *Homo academicus*, when asked to decide the editorial fate of an article that challenges the established order, is not neutral; he uses both the knowledge and bias that go with his position.

ENTER THE STUDENT ACTIVISTS

Something similar happens with writers. In the 1960s, German, American, French, Italian and British universities were centres of political socialisation for young radicals. With the conservative backlash and the dissolution of small groups, many revolutionary activists withdrew into higher education and research in social sciences, which were recruiting heavily at the time. As their careers waned in the 1990s, a new generation of students radicalised by the 1995 strikes took their academic posts. They are a minority in academia. But 'today more than ever, critical thinkers are academics...which cannot fail to have an impact on the theories they produce,' wrote Razmig Keucheyan in his overview of contemporary critical theories. 'They are fully integrated into the university system and do not in any sense constitute an "intellectual counter-society", unlike the German school for Social Democrat cadres at the beginning of the 20th century, or the later equivalent for the French Communist Party.'[6] These institutions established a permanent link between political leaders, makers of ideas and social movements. At the end of the 19th century the anarcho-syndicalist movement tried to fuse these factors of change into a single force.

The influence of the French Communist Party spread via higher education after the Second World War. Those communist philosophers, historians and economists who managed to obtain academic positions brought with them Marxist concepts and terminology; in return they channelled new recruits towards a party that had powerful intellectual attraction. The weakening of political education within leftwing organisations and the decline of internal trade-union training centres meant that the homegrown intellectuals of the workers' movement had nowhere to go.

Foundations, permanent committees, round-table talks and think tanks were set up to maintain the link between intellectuals, politicians and activists, not just in moments of social upheaval but in ordinary daily life. They made no impact. And meanwhile, the force of attraction was reversed. The authority of scholars dazzles even cultured autodidacts (central to French political history), so much so that a libertarian journal has to use the knowledge of a senior lecturer to give its dossier on police repression credibility. Status legitimates content.

The intellectual mobilisations post-1995 rehabilitated the idea of a direct link between critical theory and industrial action. These supplied anyone who was interested with rigorous and accessible analytical tools and a way of seeing the world as it is, rather than as it ought to be. This, added to the success of the global justice movement, generated many books straddling activism and scholarship, whose authors, 'committed' academics, explored the new anti-Establishmentarianisms. Such works projected a grand vision of the social struggles and legitimated them for journalists, who could then ask experts to comment on them.

But they soon hit the limit of academic criticism: the issue of strategy. If Marxist theoretician and activist Rosa Luxemburg had had to submit her texts to a reading panel for approval, she would probably not have targeted the same audience or pursued the same goals. The problems of organising the masses, building a cross-class alliance, overthrowing the social order and taking power here and now are shared by 20th-century revolutionaries and the Bolivarian socialists of the 21st century; and none of them can be solved by academic research, if they ever feature in it. They need intellectuals armed with the most advanced state of knowledge but independent of the norms of academic success and disciplinary straitjackets.

MEDIA-CONSCIOUS ESSAYISTS

The divisions of criticism reflect the divisions of academic work: economists, historians, sociologists, philosophers, demographers, political scientists. Anti-Establishmentarianism is not short of experts who are capable of rebutting technocratic authority with their own specialised knowledge. But this logic of expertise and counter-expertise has gradually pushed from the public stage intellectuals who, like Chomsky or Edward Said,[7] founded their political action on the universal categories of rationality, equality and emancipation. Their near-disappearance, combined with the deaths of several great names in French thought (Pierre Bourdieu, Jacques Derrida, Pierre Vidal-Naquet, Jean-Pierre Vernant), has left the field open for media-conscious essayists and intellectual marketers.[8]

At first sight, the hold of higher education and research on critical thought seems to correspond to the aspirations of politicised students. But it is a challenge to reconcile scholarship and political commitment in an enduring way.

Student activists postpone having to choose by putting their commitment not so much on hold as between inverted commas: they analyse mobilisations, march while studying other marchers. When they write up their dissertations, they distance themselves from their convictions, now subjects of study. They have to show that they are less committed so as to appear more objective, and more moderate so as to seem more subtle, because in academia radicalism means oversimplification. Imperceptibly, they cross a line.

The novelist Annie Ernaux, who went from a working-class background to the world of letters, wrote: 'I slipped into that half of the world for whom the other half is only a backdrop.'[9] Others have joined her without necessarily being aware of it. They convince themselves they are helping to emancipate humanity by promoting a book on the sociology of social movements among fellow attenders of lectures. They join the editorial boards of critical journals beside well-known names who will one day examine their dissertations. At the end of this, activists turned theoreticians of activism are more inclined to write than demonstrate, and to elevate their research methods to the status of political causes that threaten the order of words, not things.

The idea that political combat and an academic career can be combined may not survive the transformations in a system split into a minority of elite institutions and a mass of establishments weakened by reforms. In the latter, the deterioration of teaching conditions adds to the marginalisation of students. The social sciences, which peaked in the 1960s and 1970s, have been brutally devalued. Newly graduated PhDs know that they learned a lot to get their doctorates, but they lost out too.

Many who did not get benefits were unemployed or had only part-time jobs; they paid their own travel expenses for conferences; did unpaid work for their laboratory or supervisor; inserted desperate footnotes into their dissertation typescript to hail the 'seminal', 'insightful', 'groundbreaking' works of members of the PhD committee. And what awaits them? A decrepit professional world with faded prestige and an email list that foreshadows the future: an internship ad for 'a graduate with five years of study in sociology/ethnography...the intern will draw up an overview of the main profiles (diameter, thickness, form, etc.), the fundamental differences, the associated practices (gestures, cosmetic routine, etc.) and the issues related to hair and skin in this country'. Potential Durkheims find themselves researching shampoo.

The clash between student aspirations and professional opportunities can lead to resignation – or revolt. In 2006, the student movement against job insecurity and France's notorious first-employment contract suggested, by its radical, determined nature, that the lines had shifted. Everything seemed to indicate that belief in salvation through higher degrees had evaporated. In a single winter, campuses rediscovered that they could be places of political socialisation. Some general meetings, uninfluenced by media pressure, used social science tools in making general demands together with trade union activists. These could have been the 'collective intellectual' Bourdieu had hoped for.

Translated by Tom Genrich

Pierre Rimbert is editor in chief of *Le Monde diplomatique*.

1. Perry Anderson, *In the Tracks of Historical Materialism*, Verso, London, 1983.
2. The book was finally translated and published by *Le Monde diplomatique* and Complexe in 1999.

3. Serge Halimi, 'Maccarthysme editorial', *Le Monde diplomatique*, March 1997.
4. François Cusset, *La Décennie: le grand cauchemar des années 1980*, La Découverte, Paris, 2006.
5. Paul Nizan, *Aden-Arabie*, Maspero, Paris, 1960 (in French only), and especially *The Watchdogs*, Monthly Review Press, New York, 1971.
6. Razmig Keucheyan, *Hémisphère gauche: une cartographie des nouvelles pensées critiques*, La Découverte, Zones collection, Paris, 2010, pp. 28–9.
7. Edward W. Said, *Representations of the Intellectual*, Vintage, London, 1994.
8. Bernard-Henri Lévy, Jacques Attali and Alain Minc alone published over 63 works between 1995 and 2010.
9. Annie Ernaux, *La Place*, Gallimard, Paris, 1983.

❖❖❖❖❖❖❖❖❖❖❖❖❖❖❖❖❖❖❖❖❖❖❖❖❖❖❖❖❖❖❖❖

MAY 2011

FRANCE'S THINKERS IN THE BUSINESS OF LIVING

Communism revisited

Alain Badiou, a philosopher who sympathises with communism, has been well received in France and elsewhere for his claims that a radical break with the democratic consensus is necessary.

Evelyne Pieiller

Philosophy has lately come down from its ivory tower and got back into the business of living, perhaps hoping to restore some sense there. It used to be crucial only to morality, now it's needed in politics. This is a sign of the times: people want to escape their sense of impotence in the face of market forces and the end of ideology. The issue of commitment is back, along with renewed interest in Jean-Paul Sartre and Albert Camus. But it would have been hard to foresee the impact of the latest works of French philosopher Alain Badiou, other than his short *De quoi Sarkozy est-il le nom?*[1] Badiou's critique of capitalism isn't the only recent one, but it is linked to praise for communism. History has made communism a synonym for failure and despotism, yet Badiou calls it 'that magnificent old word'. His popularity suggests it is not enough to demand that the system be moralised: the fight against resignation needs dreams, even weapons.

But what is this radical alternative, of which Badiou and Slavoj Žižek are the champions? Badiou's goal is not to set out a programme, but to use philosophy as a 'destabilising force against prevailing opinions' and assert its 'revolutionary relevance[2] by demonstrating the 'internal link between capitalism as we know it and representative democracy'.[3] Representative democracy permits 'adversaries but not enemies'. No one can 'take a different viewpoint or play by rules other than those that prevail',[4] such as respect for individual freedoms, including the freedom to set up a business or own property. Taking part in democratic debate means accepting the limits it sets, which prohibit thinking outside its values. (These happen to be the values of capitalism.) The only legitimate political programme is 'the administrative definition of what is possible'[5] – within the limits of private ownership. Parties and trade unions have to be collaborators with capitalist parliamentarianism. Badiou believes the freedom of thought and choice offered by liberalism (and by reformism) is illusory, up to and including universal suffrage. Because the individual is subject to influence, ego and ignorance, the 'recurrent stupidity of the many' (majority rule) must perforce be a tyranny of opinion.

There is nothing new in the arrogance of the 'elites', who are convinced they alone are intelligent, except that Badiou justifies this arrogance in the name of a revolutionary ideal. That ideal is true equality, which implies that 'others exist exactly as I do'. The obstacle to true equality is what Badiou calls 'animality': an attachment to self and identity that unthinkingly puts self first and thrives on material possessions.

This idea is a constant in rightwing thought, which defines human nature as greedy and egocentric in order to 'naturalise' capitalism. But Badiou rescues this poor 'animal species that is trying to overcome its own animality'[6] by maintaining that it has a capacity for transcendence, the ability to subordinate personal needs to universal principles and truths. This is the real foundation of democracy, which presumes that all humans are endowed with reason and that society has a duty to enable them to learn, through education, how to use that reason, so that they can emancipate themselves from chaotic impulses. But Badiou believes that leaving the 'cave' of ego can't be planned for, and can't happen gradually. It happens when a shock 'event' – historical, artistic or emotional – suddenly reveals 'a possibility that had previously been invisible or even unthinkable'.[7] It breaks through the consensus that puts the highest value on what sets an individual apart, rather than on the universal within us. This revelation makes it possible to detach oneself from 'the animal-like finiteness of personal identity' and recognise the fundamental equality of humans – to achieve transcendence.

This raises questions. How does one cast aside error and embrace the truth? How is one 'chosen'? Transcendence, when it occurs, seems close to religious grace, and the illuminating power of truth close to conversion. Žižek is right to emphasise that 'religious revelation is its secret paradigm'.[8] Could Badiou's 'communist hypothesis' be another name for love, that 'personal experience of a possible universality'[9] to which Badiou (a Platonist who has written about St Paul) has devoted a book of interviews?

This would explain why it is not the working class that matters most to Badiou, but the very poorest – immigrant workers and, even more, illegal immigrants – who 'are to be honoured because they express, in our name, a different way of looking at life'.[10] It would also explain why, in Badiou's logic, communism has to have the means of 'limiting the grip of identity' (a constant threat) if it is to maintain a truly egalitarian society. But who is qualified to decide what makes for inequality? Only an enlightened aristocracy of philosophers, the keepers of truth. 'Without an Idea the disorientation of the popular masses is unavoidable.'[11] Badiou admits that a day must come, 'in a thousand years, or two, when society will be educated, in Plato's sense of the word'[12] – when everyone will be a philosopher. Until this paradise is attained, what makes for the common good must be imposed. The notion of imposition doesn't worry Badiou. He has always believed that 'we owe a huge debt to the Cultural Revolution' and approves of Saint-Just, co-author of the Terror during the French Revolution, who asked: 'What do they want who want neither Virtue nor Terror?' – clearly a non-egalitarian democracy.

In the long term, Badiou's 'hypothesis' is terrifying. In the short term, though, his idea of communism scarcely disturbs the established order. His attack on 'populist' universal suffrage satisfies the proponents of 'governance', who are seldom revolutionaries. His rejection of action within the framework of a party or trade union delights supporters of the system. Above all, Badiou's affirmation of faith in a revealed absolute truth seems to offer little more than a communism divested of Marxism, so far removed from history that it has the poetic charm of a harmless utopia.

Translated by Tom Genrich

Evelyne Pieiller is a member of *Le Monde diplomatique*'s editorial team.

1. Alain Badiou, *De quoi Sarkozy est-il le nom?*, Circonstances series, vol. 4, Lignes, Paris, 2007.
2. Alain Badiou, *Second Manifeste pour la philosophie*, Fayard, Paris, 2009.
3. Alain Badiou and Alain Finkielkraut, *L'Explication: conversation avec Aude Lancelin*, Lignes, Paris, 2010.
4. France Culture radio, 27 February 2010.
5. Badiou, *De quoi Sarkozy est-il le nom?*, op. cit.
6. 'L'Hypothèse communiste: interview d'Alain Badiou par Pierre Gaultier', Le Grand Soir, 6 August 2009.
7. Alain Badiou, *L'Hypothèse communiste*, Circonstances series, vol. 5, Lignes, 2009.
8. Slavoj Žižek, *The Ticklish Subject: The Absent Centre of Political Ontology*, Verso, London, 1999.
9. Alain Badiou with Nicolas Truong, *Eloge de l'amour*, Flammarion, Paris, 2009.
10. Badiou, *De quoi Sarkozy est-il le nom?*, op. cit.
11. Badiou, *L'Hypothèse communiste*, op. cit.
12. Badiou and Finkielkraut, *L'Explication*, op. cit.

Part V: Roots of Conflict

❖❖❖❖❖❖❖❖❖❖❖❖❖❖❖❖❖❖❖❖❖❖❖❖❖❖❖❖❖❖❖❖❖❖

OCTOBER 2010

PROBLEMATIC PARTITION OF PALESTINE

One state, two dreams

Renewed Arab/Israeli negotiations, opened under the auspices of President Barack Obama in September, are undermined not just by settlement building but differing visions on other fundamental issues. The impasse has led to calls by some senior figures, including Israelis, for the creation of a single state from the Mediterranean to the Jordan.

Alain Gresh

'The lesser danger, the lesser evil, is a single state in which there are equal rights for all citizens,' said the Israeli parliament's speaker. Another politician, a former minister, added that the only remaining option for Israel is the declaration of a single state covering the whole of the historical territory of Palestine, from the Mediterranean to the Jordan. A young female member of parliament with strong religious convictions has also defended the same conclusions. These three politicians are not members of Hamas, or even Palestinians, or European anti-Zionists. They are prominent members of the Israeli right.

The Knesset speaker, Reuven Rivlin, has challenged the idea of an Arab demographic threat and said this attitude 'leads to thinking of transfer, or that they should be killed. I am appalled by this kind of talk. I go into schools, and when they hold mock elections, Lieberman [the foreign affairs minister and leader of the extreme right party, Yisrael Beitenu] gets 40 per cent of the vote and I hear kids saying that Arabs should be killed. It seems to me that many of the belligerent Jewish movements that were built upon hatred of Arabs, and I'm not only talking about Lieberman but within the Likud as well, grew out of the patronising, socialist attitude that said "They'll be there and we'll be here." I have never understood this. When Jabotinsky[1] says "Zion is all ours", he means a Jewish prime minister and an Arab deputy prime minister.'[2]

Moshe Arens first came to prominence as defence and foreign minister in the 1980s. Arens, who is Netanyahu's political godfather and regarded as a hawk, wrote in the daily *Haaretz*: 'What would happen if Israeli sovereignty were to be applied to Judea and Samaria [the West Bank], the Palestinian population there being offered Israeli citizenship? Those who, in Israel and abroad, consider the Israeli "occupation" of Judea and Samaria an unbearable evil should be greatly relieved by such a change that would free Israel of the burden of "occupation".'[3] But how would that population be absorbed? Israel, he replies, already includes well-integrated minorities such as the Druze and the Circassians. As for Muslim Arab difficulties with integration, they stem from 'successive Israeli governments that have not taken effective measures'. He believes that this is the primary task to be addressed.

Tzipi Hotovely is the youngest member of Knesset and a rising star in Likud, which she joined in response to a personal invitation from Netanyahu. She opposed the disengagement from Gaza in 2005, which she claimed demonstrated the failure of any sort of withdrawal. She is in favour of the idea of Israeli settlements: 'The Jews lived in Hebron, in Beit El. These are biblical places. Hebron is the place where King David began his kingdom. I don't think it's something we can let go, because what is Zionism all about? Zionism is really about going back to Zion, going back to Jerusalem, going back to all those biblical places. We need to start talking about the peace process without removing people from the settlements.'[4] In which case the only possibility is the extension of Israeli law to all of the West Bank and the granting of citizenship and the vote to the Palestinians: a single state which, for Hotovely as for Rivlin and Arens, could only be a Jewish state.

These proposals are an attempt to resolve one of the fundamental contradictions for the liberal wing of the Israeli right: how to reconcile its claims to sovereignty over the whole of 'Judea and Samaria' with democratic principles, and how to avoid establishing an apartheid system in which Palestinians are deprived of their political rights.

Menachem Begin, who led the right to victory for the first time in 1977, was the first to try to solve this dilemma. After welcoming Egypt's president Anwar Sadat to Jerusalem in November 1977, he put forward a plan which set out his idea of Palestinian autonomy and offered the residents of the West Bank and Gaza the choice of

Israeli or Jordanian nationality, and thus the right to vote in one of two states. This proposal was quickly dropped because it ran into the same obstacle that none of our three contemporary politicians has managed to overcome: could the claims of a Jewish state be reconciled with granting the Palestinians the right to vote? Arens claims that the Palestinians wouldn't represent more than 30 per cent of the total, but that underestimates the population of the West Bank and ignores Gaza. His plan failed to explain how it would prevent the Palestinian population from crossing the critical 50 per cent threshold. Even at 40 per cent, no government could be formed without Palestinian support, and it is hard to understand what interest they would have in supporting the government of a 'Jewish state'.

PEACE PROCESS ON LIFE SUPPORT

Whatever their limits and contradictions, these iconoclastic points of view reflect the general pessimism that characterises the 'peace process', on life support for years now. Despite the resumption of Israeli-Palestinian negotiations under the aegis of President Barack Obama on 2 September, few commentators would bet on the patient being resuscitated. The sense of discouragement is widespread and has perhaps affected most of all the US officials who have recently held the Middle East brief.

Aaron David Miller served as adviser to six secretaries of state under three presidents from 1988 to 2003. He took part in all the negotiations, public and secret. In a sensational article called 'The false religion of Mideast peace and why I am no longer a believer',[5] he explains that the Israeli-Palestinian conflict is no longer central to Washington now that Iraq, Afghanistan, Pakistan and especially Iran monopolise its attention, and even a great power such as the US cannot do everything at once, especially in a crisis.

'The believers need to re-examine their faith, especially at a moment when America is so stretched and overextended. The United States needs to do what it can, including working with Israelis and Palestinians on negotiating core final-status issues (particularly on borders, where the gaps are narrowest), helping Palestinians develop their institutions, getting the Israelis to assist by allowing Palestinians to breathe economically and expand their authority, and keeping Gaza calm, even as it tries to relieve the desperation and sense of siege through economic assistance. But America should also be aware of what it cannot do, as much as what it can.'

Robert Malley, who acted as adviser to President Bill Clinton during the Camp David negotiations in July 2000, also draws a pessimistic conclusion from his experience. He has developed a radical critique of the two-state solution: 'The problem with the two-state idea as it has been construed is that it does not truly address what it purports to resolve. It promises to close a conflict that began in 1948, perhaps earlier, yet virtually everything it worries about sprang from the 1967 war. Ending Israel's occupation of Palestinian territories is essential and the conflict will persist until this is addressed. But its roots are far deeper: for Israelis, Palestinian denial of the Jewish state's legitimacy; for Palestinians, Israel's responsibility for their large-scale dispossession and dispersal that came with the state's birth.'[6] The creation of a Palestinian state and debate over who will regain what territory will not pacify 'the two peoples' most visceral and deep-seated emotions, their longings and anger'. So what option does that leave if, like Malley, you reject the single-state solution?

NON-VIOLENT STATUS QUO

Like other US commentators, he supports the idea of a 'long-term interim solution'. The contours of this vary, but it would permit the postponement until some unspecified later date decisions on the most sensitive issues, such as Jerusalem and refugees.

Roger Cohen, a leader writer at *The New York Times*, has summed up such a vision:[7] 'Obama, who has his Nobel already, should ratchet expectations downward. Stop talking about peace. Banish the word. Start talking about détente. That's what Lieberman wants; that's what Hamas says it wants; that's the end point of Netanyahu's evasions. It's not what Abbas wants but he's powerless. Shlomo Avineri, a political scientist, told me, "A non-violent status quo is far from satisfactory but it's not bad. Cyprus is not bad." A peace of the brave must yield to a truce of the mediocre – at best.'

This pessimism is fed by a false symmetry which has characterised the actions of the great powers since 1993: two peoples live on this land, they must reach an accord, which presumes that the extremists are isolated and there is good will on both sides. It obscures the particular responsibilities of the occupier and puts the occupier on the same level as the occupied. It overlooks the fact that all Israeli governments, even after the Oslo Accords, have pursued a policy of territorial expansion: the number of settlers has gone from 100,000 in 1993 to 300,000 today, not including the 200,000 who have moved to East Jerusalem. Likewise, 'the addition of territories situated to the west of the wall of separation, land held by official and unofficial settlements, spaces used for bypasses and closed military zones in the valley of Jordan which the Israelis intend to retain in any event'[8] represent 45 per cent of the territory of the West Bank. Israeli political parties on the right and the left reject with impunity UN resolutions and international law.

The start of the second intifada in September 2000 enabled the then prime minister Ehud Barak to convince the majority of Israeli public opinion that there was no 'Palestinian partner'[9] and never had been. Even the historic decision of the summit of Arab nations in Beirut in March 2002, which accepted global peace with Israel in return for the creation of a Palestinian state within its 1967 borders, was contemptuously rejected. And the government paid no price for this rejection, since the major world powers – the EU, the US, China and Russia – dealt with Israel as though the occupation did not exist, even though the image of Israel in public opinion was being eroded.

More fundamentally, Israel's leaders refused to recognise Palestinian equality in their actions. Signing the Olso Accords didn't dent their arrogance or overturn the idea that the life of a Palestinian is worth less than the security of an Israeli. Citing the hostility of neighbours and drawing justification from the genocide of the Jews in the Second World War, Israel's leaders have constructed a concept of security as an absolute beyond the reach of any power, which drags the country into endless wars. Is a solution possible if the principle of equality between all human beings in this land is not recognised? 'Equality or nothing' used to be the watchword of the American-Palestinian Edward Said,[10] and it is an idea that has now been taken up by various parties, not least the Palestinians of Israel, who claim it vehemently.

This worries Ehud Yaari, a veteran Israeli journalist and author of one of the first books about Fatah.[11] In an article this spring, he explained his view that within the next few years, support for a two-state solution will crumble and new concepts take its place, that the disappearance of the Palestinian Authority will bring about the de facto annexation of the occupied territories and that the Palestinians will 'accomplish by stealth the sort of Arab demographic dominance that Israeli leaders have for decades sought to avoid by occupying, rather than annexing, the Palestinian territories. Such an annexation in reverse would leave no choice but to coexist alongside an Arab majority.'[12] He believes that an armistice is necessary and could be facilitated by an Israeli retreat to the line fixed by the 'security wall', which would mean dismantling some 60 settlements and repatriating 50,000 of Israel's half-million settlers.

OCCUPATION BY OTHER MEANS

All these plans for interim solutions in the context of current power relations will in fact only prolong the occupation in other forms; the Palestinians will be confined to reserves without territorial unity, control of their borders or economic or political power. As for the Palestinian Authority's threat to declare an independent Palestinian state, it is derisory.[13] Such a state was previously declared by the PLO in 1988 and recognised by more than 100 states. Even if the EU were to recognise such a state today, would it be prepared to treat Israel as an occupying power and subject it to sanctions to force it to withdraw?

The prospect of a single state covering all the historic territory of Palestine is equally problematic,[14] as demonstrated by the debate in the Palestinian camp after the proposals from Rivlin and Arens.

Uri Avnery, a veteran Israeli peace campaigner, has criticised the flaws in these plans.[15] They exclude Gaza; the single state would be Jewish; the annexation of the West Bank would allow settlement building to continue; the granting of citizenship to the Palestinians would happen at best over a decade, if not a generation. He concluded: 'In Roman Polanski's movie *Rosemary's Baby*, a nice young woman gives birth to a nice baby, which turns out to be the son of Satan. The attractive leftist vision of the one-state solution may grow up into a rightist monster.'

This viewpoint is contested by American-Palestinian Ali Abunimah, who runs the Electronic Intifada website and has written a book arguing for a single state.[16] Like Avnery, he enumerates the limits of the right's plans, but goes on: 'Once Israeli Jews concede that Palestinians must have equal rights, they will not be able to unilaterally impose any system that maintains undue privilege. A joint state should accommodate Israeli Jews' legitimate collective interests, but it would have to do so equally for everyone else.'[17] He draws a parallel with what happened in South Africa: 'By the mid-1980s, whites overwhelmingly understood that the apartheid status quo was untenable and they began to consider "reform" proposals that fell very far short of the African National Congress's demands for a universal franchise – one-person, one-vote in a non-racial South Africa…Until almost the end of the apartheid system, polls showed the vast majority of whites rejected a universal franchise, but were prepared to concede some form of power-sharing with the black majority as long as whites retained a veto over key decisions.'

HAMAS EQUIVOCATES

Hamas has remained on the sidelines, limiting itself to the acceptance of the creation of a Palestinian state in the West Bank and Gaza and to promising in these circumstances a *hudna* (truce) of unspecified duration with Israel, but without recognition of Israel. As for what would amount to 'the liberation of all Palestine' and the future of its Jewish population, Hamas confines itself to statements about Islam's acceptance of religious minorities. And Fatah has remained silent.

While the two most representative Palestinian organisations, Fatah and Hamas, remain absent from the debate about a single state – even though it is not a new debate – Edward Said and Tony Judt, some of the solidarity movement with Palestine, and a significant though minority part of Palestinian opinion have supported or do support the utopia of a single democratic state.[18] But like the Fatah proposal from the end of the 1960s, it still remains hampered by its ambiguities: are we talking about a state of all its citizens on the South African model? Or a state of two nations like the former Czechoslovakia? What would its constitution be, and what guarantees would it offer to its different national and religious communities? What stance would it take towards its neighbours? Would it be a member of the Arab League?

More problematic still, such a project could only come about through the Palestinians making common cause among themselves, and among some significant part of Israel's Jewish population. The example of South Africa is often mentioned. But beyond the question of whether Israel is or is not an apartheid state, the South African model was made possible because the African National Congress (ANC), through its alliance with the Communist party, had a 'white base'; it also adapted its language and combat methods to the will to build a rainbow nation to avoid the exodus of the white population experienced by Angola and Mozambique. It made only limited use of terrorism for fear of alienating support, especially among the white community.[19] The ANC, while uncompromising on the principle of 'one man, one woman, one vote', also knew how to take into account the fears of the white and mixed race communities and offered them firm guarantees.

This model requires new forms of organisation on both the Palestinian and Israeli sides, and it needs to overcome the fears, hatreds and prejudices that divide them. Describing the difficult pilgrimage back to his house in Jerusalem, the Palestinian poet Mahmoud Darwish wrote:[20]

Should I ask permission from strangers
sleeping in my own bed
to visit myself for five minutes?
Should I bow respectfully
to the inhabitants of my childish dreams?
Would they ask, Who is this inquisitive foreign visitor?
Would I be able to speak
of peace and war among victims?
and victims of victims?
Without contradiction? Would they say to me,
There is no room for two dreams in one bedroom?

Translated by George Miller

Alain Gresh is vice-chairman of *Le Monde diplomatique* responsible for the Middle East and Muslim world.

1. Vladimir Jabotinsky (1880–1940), leader of the Zionist right, whose ideas inspired rightwing parties which under Menachem Begin won the Israeli elections for the first time in 1977.
2. *Haaretz*, Tel Aviv, 15 July 2010.
3. 'Is there another option?', *Haaretz*, 2 June 2010.
4. TheJewishPress.com, 10 July 2010.
5. 'The false religion of Mideast peace and why I'm no longer a believer', *Foreign Policy*, Washington, May–June 2010.
6. Co-authored with Hussein Agha, 'Can they start over?', *New York Review of Books*, 3 December 2009.
7. 'A Mideast truce', *The New York Times*, 16 November 2009.
8. Denis Bauchard, 'L'Etat palestinien en question: la solution des deux Etats est-elle encore possible?', Institut Français des Relations Internationales, Paris, March 2010.
9. See 'Camp David's thwarted peace', *Le Monde diplomatique*, English edition, July 2002.
10. *Israël-Palestine, l'égalité ou rien*, La Fabrique, Paris, 1999.
11. *Strike Terror: The Story of Fatah*, Sabra Books, New York, 1970.
12. 'Armistice now: an interim agreement for Israel and Palestine', *Foreign Affairs*, New York, March–April 2010.
13. The scenarios are intelligently examined by Jean-François Legrain in *Palestine: un Etat? Quel Etat?*

14. See Dominique Vidal, 'Palestine: à propos de l'Etat binational', Association France-Palestine Solidarité, 23 November 2009.
15. Uri Avnery, 'Rosemary's Baby', Gush-shalom.org, 24 July 2010.
16. Ali Abunimah, *One Country: A Bold Proposal to End the Israeli-Palestinian Impasse*, Metropolitan Books, New York, 2006.
17. 'Israelis embrace one-state solution from unexpected direction', The Electronic Intifada, 21 July 2010.
18. See Leila Farsakh, 'Time for a bi-national state', *Le Monde diplomatique*, English edition, March 2007.
19. See Nelson Mandela, *Long Walk to Freedom: The Autobiography of Nelson Mandela*, Little, Brown & Co., New York, 1994.
20. From 'Counterpoint (for Edward W. Said)', *Almond Blossoms and Beyond*, translated by Mohammad Shaheen, Interlink Books, Northampton, Massachusetts, 2009.

❖❖❖❖❖❖❖❖❖❖❖❖❖❖❖❖❖❖❖❖❖❖❖❖❖❖❖❖❖❖❖❖❖❖❖❖

OCTOBER 2010

DIVIDED PASHTUN LANDS AND PROTECTION RACKETS

Afghanistan's future lies in its past

The September elections were marked by low participation and massive fraud, and an increase in attacks. This shows the impasse of NATO strategy, which fails to recognise the importance of the Pashtun people, torn between Afghanistan and Pakistan on account of a borderline inherited from the colonial past.

Georges Lefeuvre

In Afghanistan 2,412 civilians were killed in 2009,[1] while in the Pashtun northwest of Pakistan, the number of dead – civilians, military and insurgents – was close to 12,000.[2] The resolutions of this year's international conferences in London (28 January) and Kabul (21 August) are clearly inadequate to stop this, or prevent the implosion of two countries with a combined population of 200 million. Are there any approaches possible, besides extending a hand to the Taliban? The search for an alternative solution takes us into sensitive territory – since unresolved colonial history is at the heart of all that is unsaid between Kabul and Islamabad – and leaves behind the usual simplifications.

The strategic errors made in Afghanistan since 2001 have been discussed at length. But little is known about an initial misunderstanding that urgently needs to be analysed. In 1986 Osama bin

Laden settled in east Afghanistan, near Khost, a few kilometres from the Pakistani tribal zones of Waziristan. At the same time, Jalaluddin Haqqani, the great Pashtun figure of the Hezb-e Islami Khalis movement (who is from Khost), was organising his forces in Miranshah, in North Waziristan. From there Haqqani held the 4th Soviet army in check. This Khost-Miranshah axis intersects the Durand Line, which was drawn in 1893 by Sir Henry Mortimer Durand to separate British India from turbulent Afghanistan. It has become the vector of extreme Wahhabi terrorism.

None of this happened by chance. Wahhabi radicals have elevated the *umma* (community of believers) to the rank of an indivisible nation. Their holy war aims to break up nation states to create a great caliphate throughout Muslim territory. The strategy of global jihad is to use local nationalisms to weaken frontiers and destabilise central state power.

As early as the 1980s the Durand Line was a golden opportunity for Bin Laden. This frontier – unrecognised by the Afghan state, but inviolable for Pakistan – bisects the Pashtun community, animated by a powerful shared identity that intensified with the Soviet occupation. The sentiment was also sustained by secular frustration caused by an etymological misunderstanding and a demographic paradox. The term 'Afghan' has always been used by Persian speakers to designate Pashtuns, wherever they might live (and those who live in Pakistan continue to call themselves indiscriminately Afghans or Pashtuns). The 12–15 million Pashtuns living in Afghanistan make up half its population – Pakistan's Pashtuns, twice as numerous, are only 15 per cent of Pakistan's population.

So everything was in place for Bin Laden to turn the region into his base and destabilise both states. The jihad was at this time generously funded by the US and Saudi Arabia, with Bin Laden's protector, Haqqani, receiving much of the manna. Nowhere else has al-Qaida found a more suitable terrain to settle; Bin Laden officially declared global jihad from here in August 1996 by publishing his 'Declaration of war against the Americans occupying the land of the two holy places' (Mecca and Medina).

ENTER THE TALIBAN

In 1994 the Taliban entered the stage. Their leader, Mullah Mohammed Omar, was linked to Haqqani, under whom he had fought. This was another golden opportunity for Bin Laden: following the arrival of the Taliban, al-Qaida merely had to surge in and monitor their strict religious orthodoxy. The Taliban helped to end the civil war which rent Afghanistan after the fall of the Communists in 1992. They ensured that the Pashtuns re-conquered the country all the way to the banks of the Amu Darya – albeit under the banner of sharia law, not that of ethnicity.

But in so doing, they served US interests as well as Saudi and Pakistani: the Californian oil company Unocal (whose representative with the Taliban at the time was the current president, Hamid Karzai) needed the country to be made safe for its trans-Afghan gas pipeline. And as expected, Saudi Arabia supported the emergence of a puritan Sunni emirate on the eastern flank of Shia Iran. This strategy of confinement suited the US as much as Pakistan, which was worried about Iranian influence on the Shia, who are 20 per cent of Pakistan's population. The question of 'strategic depth' haunted every mind in Pakistan, even that of Benazir Bhutto, then prime minister.

This obsession with strategic depth has often been explained by the Pakistani army's 'need' to fall back to Afghanistan in case of an attack by India – absurd to anyone familiar with the topography of the region. In reality, it is a geopolitical preoccupation, linked to Afghanistan's official refusal to recognise the Durand Line as its frontier. Secular Pashtun nationalism, supported by the USSR, was virulent from the 1950s to the 1970s: the Afghan president, Mohammed Daoud (1973–78) claimed the entire Pashtun zone of Pakistan as an integral part of his country. Pakistan, already threatened in the east by the dispute in Kashmir,[3] dreaded a second threat in the west. It did its utmost to encourage the establishment of a predominantly Pashtun Islamic regime in Kabul, whose survival it intended to safeguard, to stifle any nationalist expansionism towards a 'Great Pashtunistan'.[4] In 1994 Pakistan believed the Taliban would be enough – being Muslims, Pashtun and possibly nationalists, too – provided that they were kept under control.

These combined interests were an explosive force, mobilising colossal resources to allow the Taliban to assert themselves. The Northern Alliance, led by Commander Ahmad Shah Massoud until his assassination in September 2001, maintained a permanent centre of resistance. But after 9/11 anyone would have had to be naive or amnesiac to believe that an alliance of Tajik, Hazara and Uzbek parties could reverse the momentum. Massoud, though an important piece on the chessboard, could not alone be the nation's keystone – you cannot reconcile a family if you have sidelined half its members. And yet the international community, horrified by Taliban obscurantism but mistaking the part for the whole, contributed to the sidelining.

The new Afghan government that emerged from the December 2001 Bonn accords had 23 ministers from the Northern Alliance, and only seven Pashtuns. President Hamid Karzai is Pashtun but he is seen as a White House pawn. Pashtun civil society has felt unrepresented and has nursed a deep grievance. Over eight years it created layers of activism: ordinary 'Pashtunism', not necessarily nationalist but strongly concerned with cultural identity; 'Talibanism', the internal armed wing; and al-Qaida, a foreign auxiliary force that established itself like a virus in a sick body.

The Taliban movement, after it was routed in October/November 2001, would have dissolved like sugar in tea if the Pashtun tribes had had a say in the matter. That is not to validate the idea that Afghanistan is the 'country of the Pashtuns'; yet because of their history and numbers, the Pashtuns themselves believe just that. This is an anthropological and political fact – disturbing yet incontestable – which should have been, and must be, taken into account. National reconciliation in Afghanistan will be credible when the northern ethnic groups are no longer just fellow countrymen of the historical 'Afghans', but countrymen in their own right. This will happen; there is no Afghan Tajik who would prefer to be under the jurisdiction of Dushanbe (the capital of Tajikistan), no Uzbek under that of Tashkent (Uzbekistan) and no Shia Hazara under that of Tehran (Iran). All Afghans share a sharpened, almost religious, sense of an indivisible territory that they have defended together for almost two centuries. Ethnic divisions are not insurmountable.

BIN LADEN'S CALCULATION

These misjudgments have only benefited al-Qaida. The organisation, unable to survive without territory of its own, had to cultivate the Taliban irredentism in which it had taken root, or else the national jihad would, without any doubt, have turned against the global jihad.[5] Bin Laden was not wrong: in 1996 he was already worrying that negotiations between the Taliban and Unocal might lead to a normalisation of Mullah Omar's regime. This risk ended in August 1998 when the US took on al-Qaida by bombing Afghan soil for the first time, in reprisal for the attacks on US embassies in Tanzania and Kenya.

Here was yet another opportunity for Bin Laden, who knew how to exploit Mullah Omar's rage. August 1998 marked the emergence of a dual leadership in Kandahar, which was not shaken even in the aftermath of 9/11. But al-Qaida fell back to its Khost-Miranshah axis, where Haqqani still ensured that global and national jihad were united. The Taliban under Mullah Omar controlled the Kandahar-Quetta axis – with greater ease in that they are generally from the Ghilzai tribe, as are 85 per cent of the population in northern Baluchistan. Did this alter the strategic depth that Afghanistan was to provide for Pakistan? Not really, according to Pakistan's 'strategists': while waiting for the Taliban to regain control of the situation in Afghanistan, Pakistan hunted only foreign militants and dismantled foreign terrorist networks, while the indigenous Taliban were almost pampered.

But al-Qaida did not take long to bounce back, thanks to Operation Hammer and Anvil. This was drawn up in 2004 by the US general David W. Barno to capture at the border any militants from the Islamic Movement of Uzbekistan that Pakistan had committed itself to flushing out of South Waziristan. It was Pakistan's first frontal military engagement. However, its army lost more than a thousand men in a month and had to negotiate with Nek Muhammad Wazir, a young rebel villager. Two months later, he was killed by a US drone. Nek, a nobody who had stood up to 80,000 soldiers, became an epic hero. A whole generation was ready to avenge him. His successor, the formidable Baitullah Mehsud, joined forces with al-Qaida to harass the Pakistani state, which he terrorised by attacking military convoys, barracks, courts, even the army's headquarters. President Pervez Musharraf escaped three assassination attempts; Benazir Bhutto was murdered in December 2007. Then Mehsud founded the Tehrik-i-Taliban Pakistan (TTP), which gathered together some 20 organisations and dominated the northwest of the country. There, he also started a new war of religious purification: 162 Shias were eliminated in a single operation in Orakzai on 10 October 2008.

Young thugs managed areas infested by this latest al-Qaida avatar. More than 300 tribal chiefs who were accused of spying had their throats cut. Mehsud organised links with terrorist networks in the Punjab, who got actively involved: the Wahhabi Lashkar-e-Taiba, as well as non-Wahhabi but resolutely anti-Shia groups such as Lashkar-e-Jhangvi and Jaish-e-Mohammed. Even Mullah Omar was worried. He had no interest in a destabilised Pakistan, since he organised his resistance from there. Until the summer of 2009, the army could count on those Taliban who were faithful to Omar to fight the TTP, seen as the only real menace. The results were not convincing, but Mehsud was finally killed in August 2009. He was succeeded by his cousin Hakimullah Mehsud. Mullah Omar tried his utmost to regain control with the help of the Haqqani network. In October the Pakistani army launched a new offensive in Waziristan. The TTP countered violently: 81 suicide bombings killed 1,680 people between October 2009 and September 2010.

TALKING TO THE TALIBAN

The extent to which the London and Kabul conferences merely followed barely changed recipes is becoming clear. NATO troops are now in serious difficulty, for development economics cannot work in insurrection zones, and the political branch is not up to the task. How could helping with 'good governance' in Kabul and Islamabad be enough to untie such knots?

What remains is President Karzai's solution: negotiating with the Taliban. President Barack Obama is dragging his feet, but has accepted the solution for lack of any better alternative. The situation has never been as serious as it is now. The TTP has closely linked Pakistani Taliban with al-Qaida and Punjabi terrorist groups. It has usurped traditional tribal authority, made civilian life a misery and pursues its terrorist activities without any sign of weakening. Where are the Taliban who might be bought? And if international strategists are to get involved in the negotiations as well, how can they be sure they will not be deceived by systems of kinship and allegiance they do not understand? Negotiating with the Taliban isn't the right strategy. It would be better to tackle the problem higher up. Al-Qaida cannot survive without territory, while a pacified Pashtun society would no longer need the armed wing of the Taliban. This is the population that must be approached.

Some might counter that the tribal system has been destroyed. Nothing is less certain, since the usurpation of power is not necessarily irreversible. Traditional chiefs have had their throats cut – but what is meant by 'traditional'? An ethnocentric view of feudalism confuses this word with 'hereditary', because in Europe feudal power was distributed by kings, who thought they had a divine right. This led to a timeless allegiance to God and the transmission of the sacred legacy by lineage. But in eastern feudalism, where the divine does not control access to power, any man can become chief if he proves his temporal power and is generous towards those who lend him their allegiance on this condition. Any influential

Pashtun is a potential interlocutor, whether or not he is a Taliban or sympathiser, out of conviction or opportunism.

Shocking though it might sound, the formidable Haqqani is Pashtun first, Taliban second and Bin Laden's strategic ally third. He protects his power and the riches of the cross-border fiefdom he has carved out between Khost and Miranshah by crossing the Durand Line. For Haqqani, al-Qaida and the TTP are the tools of this transgression; but planetary jihad is not really his focus. This was what the Pakistani chief of staff Ashfaq Parvez Kayani meant when he proposed on 2 February using his influence with Haqqani. He made the concept of 'strategic depth' official, while specifying that 'this is not about controlling Afghanistan, only about ensuring the security of Pakistan's western frontier' (meaning the Durand Line, without actually naming it).

He justified his concern by harshly criticising the strong Indian presence in Afghanistan, perceived as a hostile encirclement. This seems exaggerated, but not without foundation: during the cold war, the diplomatic US-China axis went through Islamabad and crossed the Russia-India axis. Secular Pashtun nationalism was supported by the USSR but also by India. This is the real (but unspoken) problem that poisons the Pakistani-Afghan relationship.

Since the creation of Pakistan in 1947, the Durand Line has been its legal frontier through the inheritance of treaties guaranteed by international law. Afghanistan rejects the line, arguing that no treaty ever gave it the status of an international frontier. How can something that has no legitimate foundation be legalised? The Durand Line is a permanent point of contention, an abscess made sensitive again by the effect produced by Pashtun marginalisation, and made purulent by the al-Qaida virus. Even leftwing secular parties once close to the USSR, such as the Awami National Party (ANP) currently in power in Peshawar, are ill at ease.

THE LINE ALIVE AND WELL

In April 2007 a crucial event went unnoticed. President Karzai travelled to Jalalabad, near the Pakistani border, to inaugurate a cultural centre named after Bacha Khan, the founder of the ANP, who had left Pakistan in 1948 for exile in Afghanistan, where he was buried in 1988. His grandson Asfandyar, President of the ANP, was the guest of honour. '*Lar aw bar, ya o Afghan!*' ('Here or on the other side, I am Afghan!') he exclaimed by way of conclusion to his speech, which was enthusiastically applauded by Karzai. There is another Bacha Khan Centre, on the Pakistani side, in Peshawar. The Durand Line poses problems that are as delicate as they are ambiguous. Peace in the region will remain beyond reach as long as no solution is found to give the line a real status. To talk of a line suggests a ceasefire, and therefore an unresolved conflict. (Such is the case for the Line of Control that cuts Kashmir in two.) But who still calls the Iranian-Pakistani frontier, recognised by both states, the Goldsmid Line?

Afghanistan has for so long resisted the existence of the Durand Line that President Karzai could obviously not do an about-turn without being shouted down or even risking his life. And yet, if this border were recognised by Kabul, the Pakistani concept of strategic depth would become meaningless, anti-terrorist alliances would become more efficient, and even 'Indian encirclement' would lose its edge. In August 2009 an exasperated Pakistani government threatened to fence off and mine the line. But that is impossible: it would be the best way of vastly increasing the strength of local insurrections and their recourse to the operational capacity of al-Qaida.

This line of division must be transformed into a peace line. Since the neighbouring states find it hard to effect a rapprochement because of ancient identity and border tensions, it is now up to the 'international community' to help them. After eight years of presence in the zone, that is the least it could do. But any recognition of a shared border can only take place under conditions negotiated with the tribal chiefs on both sides – the objective would be to define a modus operandi that would end the partition of the Pashtun people and reclaim a shared space without putting the states' sovereignty into question.

Perhaps a mini-Schengen area, as in the European Union? Such an area would be a trafficker's dream. But it already is; and would be infinitely less so in a pacified region, which would also be conducive to the opening up of Afghanistan. Besides, negotiating 'instructions for use' for this frontier is hardly shocking in principle, since the Durand Line has already been the subject of four treaties (in 1893, 1905, 1919 and 1921). In fact, it is this redundant rewriting that casts doubt over its permanence – or even its reality. Finally, there are many indications that the Pashtuns will round on the terrorist networks once they no longer need them.

This validates the belief that it is better to have the two states rethink the Pashtun question with tribal chiefs, whatever their past sympathies, rather than negotiate an improbable peace with the Taliban itself. For if negotiations with the Taliban did not yield results, should one then negotiate with al-Qaida? Khaled Aziz, the former Secretary-General of North-West Frontier Province in Pakistan, was right when he wrote: 'It is thus clear that the interests of the US and Pakistan will not converge without a solution of the Durand Line issue with Afghanistan.'[6]

He put into words what Islamabad and Kabul know, and what the head of the Pakistani army has hinted at in public. Putting out the fuse that the frontier represents is the prerequisite for attempting national reconciliation in Afghanistan and succeeding. Pashtun cultural identity, far from being just an opportunist tool in the hands of al-Qaida, is also dear to the hearts of the secular parties that are fiercely hostile to the Taliban. Thus, while pursuing different aims, leftwing nationalists, the Taliban and al-Qaida (even with Bin Laden gone) could be the ingredients for an uncontrollable chemical reaction.

Adapting western diplomacy to the complexity of conflicts requires going beyond the ordinary. If these ostracised populations were given a voice again, they would see it not as a glittering victory but as a well-won honour. And the most powerful armies in the world would have to suffer the inconvenience not of a bitter defeat, but of a withdrawal without glory.

Translated by Tom Genrich

Georges Lefeuvre is an anthropologist and diplomat, and former political adviser to the European Commission in Pakistan.

1. United Nations Assistance Mission in Afghanistan (Unama) Annual Report, January 2010.
2. South Asia Terrorism Portal.
3. Since 1947 India and Pakistan have been fighting for control of Kashmir; today it is divided in two.
4. This term is the more disturbing because it is synonymous with Afghanistan. In 1948, the flag of independent Pashtunistan flew over North Waziristan and the Tirah valley, supported by the Afghan king Zahir Shah. The rebel state held out for some 20 months.
5. Jean-Pierre Filiu, in an appearance before the French Senate Foreign Affairs Commission, 29 January 2010.
6. 'Aligning regional security policies', *The News*, Islamabad, 25 November 2008.

❖ ❖

October 2010

Divided Pashtun lands and protection rackets

The Taliban's secret weapon

The Taliban doesn't rely on drug money or Iranian bounty rewards for serious funding. It takes protection money from infrastructure and transport projects, and donations where it can get them.

Louis Imbert

Last year Hajji Mohammad Shah began to build a new road outside the city of Kunduz in northern Afghanistan, to allow farmers in the Chahar Dara district to take their products to market in the provincial capital. The 25 km road was funded by the Asian Development Bank at a cost of $82,000. But on the first day of construction, a member of the Taliban approached the district council of elders, who had commissioned the work, and demanded protection money. The elders paid $18,000 to make sure the road was not destroyed before it had even been completed. Then another Taliban turned up: they paid him too. When a third one arrived, the elders explained that they had no more money. So, one day in March 2010, Shah came back to the site from his lunch break to find that his workers had been taken hostage by armed men and most of his equipment had been destroyed, at a loss of $227,000.

The governor of Kunduz, Mohammad Omar, is not sure what went wrong: did the elders not pay enough, or just not to the right people? 'The Taliban do what they like around here,' he told me. 'They torture and kill, and run countless rackets.' (Omar was killed by a suicide bomber on 9 October 2010, the third government official to be assassinated in two months.) Omar's Taliban counterpart, the 'shadow governor' of Kunduz, takes a percentage of almost all construction work in the area, including roads, bridges, schools and clinics. The more Afghanistan is reconstructed, the richer the Taliban become.

It is generally believed that the Taliban get most of their money from opium, but drug money is only 10–15 per cent of their revenue, according to a 2009 report by the UN Office of Drugs and Crime.[1] 'Most money is raised at the local level,' said Kirk Meyer, director of the Afghan Threat Finance Cell at the US embassy in Kabul. 'We don't know to what extent profit from opium in Helmand province[2] is redistributed to the poorer provinces. Elsewhere the Taliban live on money donated by fake non-governmental organisations, and by kidnapping, and smuggling cedar wood and chromite ore to Pakistan.'

Abdul Kader Mojaddedi, 32, is an engineer, and nephew of Sibghatullah Mojaddedi, the leader of the Afghan Senate and the first president of Afghanistan after the fall of the communist regime in 1992. Mojaddedi is currently building 7 km of road beneath the mountains in Laghman province. He employs guards to look after his equipment; half are dressed in uniform, while the other half wear traditional tunics and beards. That is because they were provided by the local Taliban for the duration of the works, for a fee of $67,000. 'It's nothing,' Mojaddedi told me. 'If I had to pay 100 guards it would cost me $20,000 a month. With the Taliban, it costs me $10,000, and the construction site is safe.' There had been four or five attacks on the site, but for the last six months everything has been calm. The provincial governor is delighted, and the Americans, who are funding the project through their Provincial Reconstruction Teams, a military programme designed to 'win hearts and minds', turn a blind eye.

This small project is not an isolated case. The former deputy minister for public works, Wali Mohammad Rasuli, who retired four months ago, defends the system: 'I have talked to President Hamid Karzai about this on two occasions, for more than two hours. If we get the roads finished, vehicle traffic and business will automatically increase security. We already pay the Taliban, so we should end this hypocrisy.' But the current minister and international donors repeat the official line: we do not pay insurgents.

The main target of extortion is the US military, and more specifically its local contractors. Every month, 6,000–8,000 convoys deliver supplies to around 200 military bases: everything from ammunition and petrol to toilet paper and television sets.[3] Security for the convoys is provided by private companies, through the 'Host Nation Trucking' contract of March 2009, worth $2.16 billion (16.6 per cent of Afghanistan's 2009 GDP). A US official of the International Security Assistance Force (ISAF) told me: 'We don't know anything about the contractors' networks. We don't know if they pay the Taliban for safe passage. We put in billions, and it's possible that millions end up in the hands of the insurgents.'

(Pentagon officials hope that a new contract and new guidelines that went into effect in mid-September 2011 will decrease the level of corruption. This is worth about $1 billion over the next year.)

'OF COURSE WE PAY THE TALIBAN'

Zarghuna Walizada is the only woman running a freight transport company in Afghanistan. She understands the pressure the Americans are under, and knows they do not reimburse her for lorries attacked on the road: 'I don't care whether we pay the police, the insurgents, or the Taliban. What matters is that the lorries get through.' Sometimes they do not even use an escort: 'Why would we need one? The Taliban guarantee our security.'

'Of course we pay the Taliban,' said Ghulam Abas Ayen, head of the main freight transport union. 'It's a racket, pure and simple. Some security companies demand $2,000 per container, for just a few hundred kilometres of road. About half of that money could end up in the hands of the Taliban.'

Safe passage is not negotiated directly, of course. 'My boss wouldn't appreciate it if I went to negotiate face to face with the tribal leaders of Helmand,' said Juan Diego Gonzales, a former US soldier and head of the private security company White Eagle. 'We have intermediaries who recruit our security guards locally. Sometimes it's the tribal chief himself, or his son, who takes charge of the convoy. You just hope they're not linked too closely with the Taliban.' The balance of power on some of the roads he uses is volatile: one warlord alone cannot guarantee security, which gives Gonzales some scope to choose his partners. On other roads, 'If you go alone, you are going to have big problems. If you don't have authorisation from the local warlord, you're dead,' said an Afghan official with the Australian private security company Tacforce. He said Tacforce followed the recommendations of the Afghan interior ministry, to identify the 'right' warlords to deal with.

The most powerful of those at the moment is Ruhullah, a commander aged around 40 who has never been in contact with a US army official. He wears a Rolex watch and shalwar kamiz, speaks with an unusually high-pitched voice, and controls an important part of Highway 1, which links Kabul with Kandahar in the south. Ruhullah works with the Popal brothers, owners of the Watan Group and cousins of President Karzai. A typical convoy will have 300 lorries and 400–500 private guards. Safe passage for one container from Kabul to Kandahar can cost up to $1,500. According to a recent report by the US House of Representatives, a tribal chief who controls a route, and his English-speaking associates, can make tens of millions of dollars a year escorting US convoys. Ruhullah and the Popal brothers deny paying the Taliban to pass through the sections of the road the insurgents control. They say they lost 450 men last year. Transport and security companies have complained many times to the US army about the money they have to pay warlords, but the army does not know how to resolve the problem.

(In December 2010, the US command in Afghanistan announced that it had stopped working with Watan Risk Group, arguing that the firm had diverted funds and violated weapons regulations. In August, however, Watan and Ruhullah's ban were overturned. According to *The Washington Post* (16 September 2011), 'Ruhullah acknowledged making payoffs, but he was excused by the army's legal department on grounds that Watan had not explained contract rules to him and that his inability to speak English prevented him from reading the rules himself.')

DISCREET AND EFFICIENT BANKERS

The Taliban do not get all their money through threats and force, however. Discreet and efficient bankers transfer sizeable donations from the Gulf, Dubai and Pakistan. The key venue is the Sarai Shahzada money market in Kabul. Three floors of galleries look onto a central courtyard where wooden stalls are set up on the ground, piled with wads of dollars, rupees and yuan. A study by the Afghan Threat Finance Cell suggests that 96 per cent of Afghans prefer using the market to the bank. There are hundreds of brokers' offices – narrow shops, where, at the end of the day, employees sit slumped on hot leather sofas counting the day's takings. The system, called *hawala*, dates back to the eighth century. In a few hours hundreds of thousands of dollars can be transferred from the other side of the planet, with minimal commission. According to Hajji Najibullah Akhtary, head of the moneychangers' union in Kabul, $5 million passes through the market every day. The system relies on trust: each agent knows his clients and their guarantors.

The authorities have been trying since 2004 to register these agents and record their monthly transactions. Akhtary says dozens of security agents hang around the market every day, taking a look at the accounts. But no government inspectors dare go near the busy money market in Kandahar, even though a significant proportion of Taliban funds pass through it.

The Central Bank's financial intelligence unit has recorded the transfer of $1.3 billion worth of Saudi banknotes into Afghanistan since January 2007. According to the unit's director general, Mustafa

Massoudi, the money comes from the Pakistan tribal areas: 'Now can you tell me who needs Saudi riyals there? They are sent by *hawala* from Peshawar [in northwest Pakistan] to Kabul, where they are changed into dollars. The dollars then disappear into the mountains, while the riyals go back to Dubai, perfectly legally, by air.'

General Mohammad Asif Jabbar Kheel, head of security at Kabul airport, is furious about the law that allows any individual to fly with several million dollars in cash, as long as he declares it. Since the financial crisis hit Dubai in 2009, the authorities there are even less concerned about the sources of funds. According to a US official, more than $2 billion was transferred to the United Arab Emirates last year from Kabul airport. What is even more surprising is that the majority of these transfers, according to Massoudi, are made by only a few people, mostly *hawala* agents. General Jabbar gave me a list, with the names angrily underlined. The figures are impressive: one person took $464 million in 2009, another $89 million.

Not all of this money is linked to the Taliban. Some is legal, some represents international aid misappropriated by officials, and some is linked to drug trafficking, which is not only controlled by insurgents. The pallets of notes wrapped in plastic that fill the hold of Ariana Afghan Airlines planes are a symptom of the government's inability to control its finances. It collected only $819 million in customs revenue last year, half the potential sum. The deputy minister for customs and revenue, Said Mubin Shah, cannot go to some border posts because he has no protection against the police: many border policemen run customs for their own benefit. In the border town of Spin Boldak, in Kandahar province, Mubin Shah would rather be escorted by a warlord suspected of being involved in the drug trade than by the Afghan police.

Translated by Stephanie Irvine

Louis Imbert is a journalist.

1. 'Addiction, crime and insurgency: the transnational threat of Afghan opium', UNODC, Vienna, October 2010.
2. Province in southern Afghanistan where the majority of the opium is grown.
3. 'Warlord Inc. – extortion and corruption along the US supply chain in Afghanistan', US House of Representatives, Washington, 22 June 2010.

❖ ❖

June 2011

Pakistan after the death of Bin Laden

Now that he's gone

The assassination of Osama bin Laden in his compound in a city in Pakistan changed the placement of all the pieces on the board and focused attention on how Pakistan's military will react. The great game goes on, and several players have a keen eye on the future of Afghanistan and Pakistan.

Jean-Luc Racine

The US raid in Pakistan on the night of 1–2 May only partly revealed the shadow war which the Americans and Pakistanis are engaged in; some of its secrets remain hidden.

Under the Bush administration, Pakistan in 2004 joined the privileged category of major non-NATO allies (MNNA), a club with fewer than 15 members, including Australia, Israel and Japan. Now, after the killing of Osama bin Laden in Abbottabad, near Pakistan's most important military academy, there is a question mark over the real state of US-Pakistan relations. A week earlier in Abbottabad, General Ashfaq Parvez Kayani, Pakistan's chief of army staff, told a passing-out parade that they had 'broken the terrorists' back'.[1]

After Bin Laden's assassination, Leon Panetta, head of the CIA, made it clear that Washington did not tell the Pakistani authorities about the raid in advance because 'it was decided that any effort to work with the Pakistanis could jeopardise the mission. They might alert the targets.'[2] The US decided to conduct a military operation in a sovereign country without its permission.

For months, dialogue between the two countries has been fitful. The US military has been dissatisfied with their Pakistani counterparts' apparent inability to intervene in the tribal area of North Waziristan,[3] the region from which the Haqqani network, the descendants of the Afghan mujahideen, carry out missions against NATO troops in eastern Afghanistan.

Panetta's statement, in conjunction with the increased tension since 2 May between the Pakistani military and the CIA, contradicts the theory that there was a covert joint operation in which the Pakistani army played their Bin Laden card – under pressure or voluntarily – realising it would become worthless if secret contacts were established between the US and the Afghan Taliban.

Official statements from Pakistan suggest that the presence of Bin Laden, however long he had been there, was the result of a failure in the intelligence services of *all* the countries that had tracked him, not just of the directorate of Pakistan's army-controlled Inter-Services Intelligence (ISI). The head of the ISI, General Ahmad Shuja Pasha, expressed regret before parliament over the failure of Pakistan's entire security network, and also blamed the provincial government and the local police.[4] It is almost impossible to believe that an organisation as powerful as the ISI could have been unaware of the occupants of the incongruous compound building in a garrison town.

That does not necessarily mean that the CIA failed to cross-check its information with the ISI before the trail led to Abbottabad, especially to confirm that Abu Ahmed al-Kuwaiti, a Pakistani born in Kuwait who had been identified by a source in Guantanamo, was Bin Laden's intermediary. On 3 May Pakistan's president, Asif Ali Zardari, reminded readers of *The Washington Post* that terrorism has claimed tens of thousands of victims in Pakistan and said that 'we in Pakistan take some satisfaction that our early assistance in identifying an al-Qaida courier ultimately led to this day'.[5]

FAILED STATE OR ROGUE STATE?

Since then, the language has changed. Some brave journalists have risked asking about the army's version of events[6] or saying aloud what many think silently: 'If we didn't know, we are a failed state. And if we did, we are a rogue state.'[7] A few figures called for a rethink of Pakistan's whole strategy, but public rhetoric, expressed by the authorities as well as political leaders and the media, quickly focused on the issue of national sovereignty and denunciations of US interference. The question of possible complicity by the army and the special services was replaced by reactions to the security failures that allowed an airborne commando unit to operate deep within Pakistan and, having accomplished its mission, to leave without losses.

In an unusual departure, the army decided to explain itself to parliament. But the direct criticisms of a few MPs – such as Nisar Ali Khan, a member of the Pakistani Muslim League-Nawaz Wing and leader of the opposition in the National Assembly[8] – did not feature in the resolution passed unanimously on 13 May. This condemned the 'unilateral US action' and US drone attacks in the tribal areas. Parliament reiterated, again unanimously, its 'full confidence in Pakistan's defence forces.'[9]

The army is more preoccupied with denouncing the 'campaign of calumny launched against Pakistan' than the presence of the head of al-Qaida in a military town. The ISI leader offered to resign, but the president, prime minister and parliament did not think that necessary; though he may be replaced soon, as an exception had already been made to extend his contract. The independent investigative commission that was announced has not yet been set up nor its mandate defined, which raises doubts about the extent of its powers. Some sceptics have pointed out that previous inquiries into the assassinations of former prime ministers, Liaquat Ali Khan in 1951 and Benazir Bhutto in 2007, did not produce results.

Pakistan aims to soothe 'national honour' despite embarrassing questions and criticisms from abroad. Opposition leader, Nawaz Sharif[10] of the PML-N, which governs Punjab and won 66 out of 259 seats at the general election in 2008, has called for a review of relations between Islamabad and Washington, but he also asked for future military and secret service budgets to be discussed in parliament. He pointed out that it is up to the government, not the intelligence services, to determine foreign policy. The army, whose position is delicate, intends to use Pakistan's prevailing anti-Americanism, also found in the army, to its advantage.

CAREFULLY CHOSEN WORDS

US leaders have weighed their words carefully. Barack Obama spoke only of 'networks' that could have helped Bin Laden, without specifying his suspicions or making accusations. He intends to oppose the Republicans, and also a number of Democrats such as Dianne Feinstein, chair of the Senate Intelligence Committee, who want to cut the considerable funds to Pakistan ($20 billion in the past ten years and several billion more in the next budget).

The US's difficult relations with Pakistan are played out on different chessboards, both critical for its foreign policy. The US can neither break with Pakistan nor be certain of counting on it. The first chessboard is Afghanistan and Pakistan. Since the London conference in January 2010, the idea of national reconciliation launched by the Afghan president, Hamid Karzai, has been backed by the US and its allies. The US military surge approved by Obama is designed to increase the pressure on the Taliban.

US Secretary of State Hillary Clinton said this February that the three key points of a possible negotiation with the insurgents were objectives rather than preconditions: 'They must renounce violence;

they must abandon their alliance with al-Qaida; and they must abide by the constitution of Afghanistan.'[11] After the elimination of Bin Laden, she reiterated that central point: 'Our message to the Taliban remains the same, but today, it may have even greater resonance. You cannot wait us out. You cannot defeat us. But you can make the choice to abandon al-Qaida and participate in a peaceful political process.'[12]

That is the core of the strategy implemented by General David Petraeus, first in Iraq and then in Afghanistan, where he leads the NATO forces (though he is soon to take over the running of the CIA): decouple the insurgents, who pursue a national programme, from international terrorism. In theory the disappearance of al-Qaida's emblematic leader should make that task easier. It remains to be seen whether the current tension between the US and Pakistan will hinder the second plank of US strategy: leaning on the Pakistani services to influence the Afghan Taliban.

AMBIGUOUS RELATIONS

A 2010 study underlined the ambiguity of the links between the Taliban and their Pakistani protectors:[13] the links are close – ISI representatives attended council meetings of the Afghan Taliban held in Pakistan – but also awkward for some Taliban commanders, who are tired of Islamabad's dominance. Islamabad does not hesitate to manipulate the Taliban: 20 days after the London conference, the ISI arrested Mullah Abdul Ghani Baradar, the Taliban's number two, in Karachi. He had been in indirect contact with Kabul.[14] The message was clear: being cut out of the loop was not on, with a post-NATO Afghanistan in sight in 2014 or later. For Pakistani strategists, the major objective is to assure Pakistan's influence in the Afghanistan of the future. Such a scenario presumes that the Pashtuns (40 per cent of the Afghan population) are again predominant and that relations made with the Taliban via the Haqqani network and Gulbuddin Hekmatyar (the old warlord prominent in the anti-Soviet jihad) are sufficiently solid to avoid the revival of claims for Pashtun territory in Pakistan.

Influencing the future of Afghanistan also means limiting India's role. In cultivating links with Hamid Karzai and supporting the Tajiks of the Northern Alliance, India has been building up credits since 2002. It has set in motion economic and social development programmes with strong symbolism (such as the construction of the Afghan parliament); strategic infrastructure projects (the road to Iran and non-Pakistani access to the sea); and the training of the Afghan elite (bursaries for Afghan students at Indian universities). Visiting Kabul ten days after Bin Laden's death, the Indian prime minister Manmohan Singh announced an increase in the aid budget for Afghanistan (more than $1.5 billion over ten years). New Delhi has now accepted the principle of national reconciliation, he said, as long as it leads 'without interference and coercion...to a stable, independent Afghanistan at peace with its neighbours'.[15] Pakistan does not have to be mentioned for his meaning to be clear. Though this has not stopped the Indians from pursuing the dialogue they reopened recently with Pakistan.

THE GREAT GAME GOES ON

There is a second, much larger chessboard: emerging Asia. Two priorities meet in the conjunction of the boards. The first is the fight against terrorism, which has bogged down the US in an Afghan-Pakistani swamp. The US is trying to extricate itself with honour, and without cutting itself off from Pakistan. The concept of AfPak[16] is no longer part of official US discourse but it remains relevant: it indicates that Pakistan seems to be part of the solution *and* part of the problem. This is exacerbated by the worrying situation within Pakistan. There is no guarantee that parliament and the political class will manage to impose a new strategic model on the military: less disruptive, more favourable to the expected benefits of future regional stability, and taking advantage of the geopolitical benefits of a country that is both Himalayan and maritime, between the energy poles of the Middle East and Central Asia and the emergent nations of China and India.

The second priority, critical for the US, comes from the rise in Asia's power, driven by economic dynamism and opening up to world commercial, financial and energy networks: the opposite of the geopolitical tensions and internal crises that affect the AfPak dimension. It is there that the future will be played out. The US needs to find compromise among contradictory interests. It must not overlook India as a counterbalance to China. But in AfPak, Pakistan remains fixated on Kashmir and concerned to keep India out of any Afghan settlement. How far can Washington go along with that? The building blocks of the negotiations slot into place without New Delhi: the Afghanistan High Council of Peace, three-way meetings between the US, Afghanistan and Pakistan, and in the future possibly a Taliban diplomatic office in the Gulf. But there will come a time when progress, if any, will have to be guaranteed by an international conference, which will require the attendance of all Afghanistan's neighbours, including Iran, India and China. China has been discreet since 2 May. Beijing hailed the death of Bin Laden, while unambiguously siding with Pakistan, whose contribution to the war on terror it applauded 'based on its [own] national conditions'.[17] For some Pakistani analysts, the friendship of a powerful China permits the idea of revamped foreign policy in which Pakistan frees itself from the US embrace and plays the China card – or the Russian one. On an official visit to Moscow on 11 May, President Zardari mentioned the idea of Russian access to 'warm seas', the dream of the czars. China, the main supplier of arms to Pakistan, has economic interests in that country and in Afghanistan, as it does in Central Asia and the Middle East. China has promised Pakistan a gift of 50 advanced fighter planes, JF-17s.

On 16 May, before his departure for Beijing, Pakistan Prime Minister Yusuf Raza Gilani received US senator John Kerry in Islamabad. Their joint declaration underlined the importance of the partners' national interests and made clear Pakistan's desire to 'renew full cooperation with the United States'. Behind the obvious tensions, there is bilateral dialogue, while the defence secretary Robert Gates has said there is 'no proof' of high-level Pakistani complicity with Bin Laden.[18] Three days later, Marc Grossman, Obama's representative for AfPak was in Islamabad to prepare for Clinton's visit while the CIA's number two, Michael Morell, was mapping how future joint operations would be run with the head of the ISI.

So the great game goes on. Pakistan's political forces may not be able to alter the parameters established by the army leadership, which may have weathered another storm, its power intact.

Translated by George Miller

Jean-Luc Racine is a director of research at the Centre National de la Recherche Scientifique (CNRS) and teaches at the Centre d'Etudes de l'Inde et de l'Asie du Sud in the Ecole des Hautes Etudes en Sciences Sociales (EHESS); he is co-editor of *Pakistan: The Contours of State and Society*, Oxford University Press, Karachi, 2002.

1. 'General Kayani says militants' back broken', *Dawn*, Karachi, 23 April 2011.
2. See Massimo Calabresi, 'CIA Chief: Pakistan would have jeopardized operation', *Time*, 3 May 2011.
3. Pakistan's tribal areas are divided into seven zones.

4. Editorial, 'ISI's admission', *Daily Times*, Islamabad, 15 May 2011.
5. Asi Ali Zardari, 'Pakistan did its part', *The Washington Post*, 3 May 2011.
6. Shahid Saeed, 'Grab the reins of power', *Dawn*, 5 May 2011.
7. Cyril Almeida, 'The emperor's clothes', *Dawn*, 6 May 2011.
8. Jane Perlez, 'Denying links to militants, Pakistan's spy chief denounces US before parliament', *The New York Times*, 14 May 2011.
9. Resolution on the US forces' unilateral action, 2 May; resolution 44, joint session of parliament, 14 May 2011.
10. He was removed from power by a military coup in 1999.
11. Hillary Clinton, speech in memory of Richard Holbrooke, Asia Society, New York, 18 February 2011.
12. Hillary Clinton, 'Remarks on the killing of Usama bin Laden', State Department communiqué, 2 May 2011.
13. Matt Waldman, 'The Sun in the Sky: the relationship between Pakistan's ISI and Afghan insurgents' (PDF), Crisis States Research Centre, London School of Economics, June 2010.
14. Interview by Ahmed Rashid on National Public Radio, Washington DC, 17 February 2010.
15. Speech given by Indian prime minister Manmohan Singh to the Afghan parliament, Kabul, 13 May 2011.
16. The concept of AfPak, popularised by Richard Holbrooke in 2008, treats Afghanistan and Pakistan as a single theatre of war. After protests from Islamabad, the US authorities now rarely use this term.
17. Jiang Yu, spokesperson for the foreign ministry, 'China urges the world to back Pakistan in terror fight', *Dawn*, Islamabad, 5 May 2011.
18. 'Gates says no sign that top Pakistanis knew of Bin Laden', *The New York Times*, 18 May 2011.

❖ ❖

MARCH 2010

IRAQ: WINNERS AND LOSERS

Red line, green line

Before US combat troops leave Iraq, the most crucial policy question to be solved is settling the dividing line – and the possibilities for reconciliation – between the Kurds and the Arabs, especially those who have been forced to live together for decades.

Joost Hiltermann

The rift between Arab and Kurdish Iraq is not new; it stems from promises said to have been made and then betrayed in the immediate aftermath of the First World War and the demise of the Ottoman

Empire. However, longstanding Kurdish claims against central rule emerged strongly after the 2003 US invasion, and Kurdish leaders are pressing for advantage now that the Baghdad government is weak.

But the tide may be turning. The central state is slowly starting to reconstitute itself, financed by the prospect of greatly increased oil exports once the contracts just signed with foreign companies come to fruition. We may soon reach the moment at which Kurdish and federal leaders will have to make a critical decision: cut a deal or, failing that, face off in what could become Iraq's next bloody civil war.

Many Iraqis reject the term 'Sunni-Shia conflict' as a misnomer for what is at heart an effort by sectarian leaders to claim religious allegiances to advance their political agendas. And in the same way they object to the term 'Arab-Kurdish conflict'. They have a point. At the level of the street, neighbourhoods, families and communities, Iraq's Arabs and Kurds are not only intermingled but often intermarried, and go about their business primarily as Iraqis.

But this is an urban phenomenon. Beyond the cities, northward into the hills and up against the borders with Iran and Turkey, the mountains of Kurdistan, this Iraqi identity begins to fade and a strong Kurdish nationalism takes hold. It opposes what it views as ethnic Arab nationalism disguising itself as Iraqi unity. So it questions the legitimacy of the post-Ottoman order, which it never embraced, and rekindles the ideal, prevalent in centuries past, of a 'nation state' in which state-building and ethnicity converge.

SHIFTING THE LINE

The fight, for now, is over the location of the boundary between this Kurdish Iraq and the rest of the country, which is mostly Arab (with a host of minority groups). If it were up to the Kurds, this boundary would lie at the first chain of hills travelling from Baghdad toward the northeast, out of the Tigris valley. Though called the Hamrin Mountains, they seem a slight bump in the rising plains that stretch to the foot of the faraway Zagros Mountains.

But for the Arabs, or those representing them in Baghdad, the boundary lies where past political leaders agreed to put it: at the administrative line that demarcates the three Kurdish provinces of Dohuk, Irbil and Sulaimaniya from the rest of Iraq. This agreement derived from an earlier Kurdish attempt to exploit central weakness, in the late 1960s, when the Ba'ath Party's hold on power was tenuous and it needed allies. In 1970 the regime and the Kurdish leader Mullah Mustafa Barzani signed an agreement that promised a degree of self-rule in areas with a Kurdish majority. The deal fell apart four years later when Barzani rejected an autonomy law enacted by the Ba'ath regime. Nevertheless, the boundary of the new Kurdish autonomous region established by this law had a certain legitimacy, as did the idea that the Kurds were entitled to self-governance within Iraq.[1]

In 1991, the Iraqi army, which had re-conquered much of Kurdistan following the post-Gulf War mass uprising that ousted the regime's security apparatus, decided unilaterally to pull back to a defensible line that resembled, but in some areas departed from, the border of the autonomous region agreed to in the 1970s. This became known as the Green Line. And it held throughout the 1990s up until the US invasion. At that point, the Kurds crossed it to seize towns and areas they consider historically part of Kurdistan, although they did not go as far as the Hamrin hump. Still, the Green Line enjoyed a degree of consensus in post-2003 Iraq: it appeared as the legitimate border of Kurdistan in both the 2004 interim constitution (the Transitional Administrative Law) and the 2005 permanent constitution. What lay beyond the Green Line were considered 'disputed territories' whose status was to be resolved, the constitution prescribed, via a local referendum by the end of 2007.

This referendum has not taken place, and since its deadline passed, Kurdish leaders have begun to reject the legitimacy of the Green Line. They claim they don't know where it lies (although good maps from the 1990s that the Kurds handed out are readily available). And they have taken to calling a different line the Green Line in a successful effort to deceive US troops whose knowledge of the terrain and history is minimal. This other line (which deserves the name Red Line, and has also been called the Trigger Line) is the current de facto boundary separating Iraqi army troops from Kurdish regional guard forces formerly known as Peshmergas. It lies a good distance south from the proper Green Line and incorporates significant chunks of disputed territories, including part of the province that is central to the debate – Kirkuk.

WHY IT MATTERS

The demarcation of the boundary between Kurdistan and the rest of Iraq matters from the Kurdish perspective for historical and emotional reasons. But it also matters because of what lies beneath the ground. The disputed territories, Kirkuk in particular, are extremely rich in oil and gas that the Kurds covet in their quest for statehood and that the central government in Baghdad will never give up willingly, because it doesn't want to see a strong Kurdistan emerge, as either an autonomous or an independent entity. And just as Kurdish politicians have shifted the location of the Green Line in their public rhetoric, they now include Kirkuk's oil wealth in their public estimates of Kurdistan's oil reserves – multiplying it by several factors. This is in contrast to the limited oil and gas resources that have been proven to exist so far inside the Kurdistan region as delineated by the original Green Line.

Clashing nationalisms are rarely reconciled, though historically accommodations have been found that have endured for generations, despite grievances, border disputes and occasional conflict. Consider the boundary between Persian Iran and Arab Iraq, fought over bloodily in the 1980s, but relatively stable for centuries, even in the absence of a definitive settlement. There is no reason why Iraq's Arabs and Kurds could not find a workable accommodation that would have mutual benefits. If you talk to Kurds and Arabs and Turkmen in Kirkuk, it soon becomes clear that they agree on many things, and that they can even come to formal agreements between themselves. They have given every indication that they want and are ready to manage their own affairs, jointly, in some form of power-sharing arrangement.

However, outside actors, with inordinate control over local politicians, can and will thwart any efforts at reconciliation. For leaders in Baghdad and Irbil, the Arab-Kurdish ethnic dispute is a zero-sum game in which local actors are unimportant counters to be manipulated and deployed against each other. If you add the Turkmen, who have an uneasy sponsor in Turkey, the game becomes even more complex.

Baghdad and Irbil each have a national project, and their success in advancing it depends on their relative strength vis-à-vis each other. Today, the Kurds are pushing, sensing opportunity. They have a strong moral case, having suffered from decades of Arabisation (ta'rib), expulsion and, in the 1980s, even genocide, especially in the hills east of Kirkuk called Germian.[2] Deported Kurds who grew up in barebones resettlement projects in Kurdistan or in refugee camps in Iran are now returning, reclaiming their land and rebuilding their homes.

But the response to ethnic cleansing appears to be a reverse ethnic cleansing, an effort that many Arabs, eager to forget the past, refer to as Kurdification (*takrid*). This means that Arabs induced by the Ba'ath regime to settle in Kirkuk and other areas now disputed are being induced to depart, to return to their original areas. In both eras, the act of inducement suggests that these people are victims of greater powers that use them as pawns in their national projects. What is lost in the debate is that they have intrinsic rights as citizens, protected by the constitution, including the right to reside, and vote, anywhere in Iraq. It also elides the tricky problem of generations born in Kirkuk from Arab 'settlers', who have no other place they can call home.[3]

Older Kirkukis fondly remember earlier times, from the 1930s until the fall of the monarchy in 1958, during which the city of Kirkuk was a model of pluralism and ethnic coexistence (*ta'ayush*). Arabisation put a brutal end to that, but why should the response to a racist policy be to replace the domination of an area by one ethnic group with another when a more peaceful model of recent vintage is available?

The Kurds may point out, with some justification, that their approach toward Arabs and minority groups in the disputed territories lacks the violence of the Ba'ath, and that they resort only to the constitution and the law (which they were instrumental in drafting in their interest) in pressing their claims. Yet the overall effect is the same: disenfranchisement, even displacement, and profound alienation. This is a recipe for endemic conflict, not for a durable solution in which, somehow, magically, Kirkuk's non-Kurds accept the benign rule of their Kurdish compatriots.

TIME IS SHORT

In 2007 the UN Security Council empowered the United Nations Assistance Mission for Iraq (Unami) to find a solution to the question of what the UN terms Iraq's disputed internal boundaries. Unami has since produced an important report, yet to be made public but available to the principal stakeholders, which lays out various scenarios and makes tentative proposals toward a negotiated settlement. The Obama administration has backed this effort, and is waiting to learn from Iraq's legislative elections in March who the new leaders will be.

It will be incumbent on these leaders to tackle head-on the question of the disputed territories and formulate a solution that recognises all sides' grievances and narratives, with a compromise that crosses no red lines, but offers something important that all sides can present to their publics as a gain, even if it fails to meet their maximum demands. This is no mean task, and time is short. The imminent withdrawal of US combat troops will diminish US leverage, and the UN is in no position to fill the void: in the absence of a deal between Baghdad and Irbil, tantamount to a peace agreement, the UN will not send peacekeeping forces.

It is likely that the conflict over Kirkuk and other disputed territories – the conflict over the boundary that separates the Kurdistan region from the rest of Iraq – will continue to shake the fragile foundations of the new Iraqi state. Over time, the central state may grow stronger and try to impose its will on the Kurds, as past regimes have done: dominate their cities in the plains and push their fighters back into their mountain strongholds, from which they will relaunch their struggle for national liberation.

Alternatively, the Kurds may be able to hold on to their post-2003 gains, enjoy a large degree of autonomy within their region and exercise de facto control over those parts of the disputed territories that have a majority Kurdish population. Most importantly, they will seek to keep alive the hope that one day, perhaps not too far into the future, they will achieve statehood thanks to a game-changing event such as a war between the US and Iran – which allows international frontiers to be altered and presents new opportunities for non-state nations. Much as did the collapse of the Ottoman Empire almost a hundred years ago.

Original text in English

Joost Hiltermann is deputy programme director for the Middle East and North Africa at the International Crisis Group.

1. One of the best histories of the Kurds is David McDowall, *A Modern History of the Kurds*, I.B. Tauris, London, 2000. For a good journalistic account of Iraqi Kurds see Jonathan Randal, *After Such Knowledge, What Forgiveness? My Encounters with Kurdistan*, Farrar, Straus and Giroux, New York, 1997.
2. See Human Rights Watch, *Iraq's Crime of Genocide: The Anfal Campaign against the Kurds*, Yale University Press, New Haven, 1995.
3. For a discussion of the Kirkuk conundrum, *Iraq and the Kurds: Resolving the Kirkuk Crisis*, International Crisis Group, Brussels, April 2007.

Part VI: Revolution: The 'Arab Spring'

❖❖❖❖❖❖❖❖❖❖❖❖❖❖❖❖❖❖❖❖❖❖❖❖❖❖❖❖❖❖❖❖❖

MARCH 2011

THE NEW ARAB AWAKENING

The Muslim Brothers in Egypt's 'orderly transition'

After the revolution, a newly respectable Muslim Brotherhood, supportive of the army, is emerging. Could it become the best bet for the 'orderly transition' that Egypt, and the US, hope for?

Gilbert Achcar

Egypt's uprising, contrary to most predictions, was initiated and driven by coalitions – including political parties, associations and internet networks – which were dominated by secular and democratic forces. Islamic organisations or their individual members took part on an equal footing with groups of marginal importance before the uprising, and with groups closer to eastern European dissidents of 1989 than to the usual mass parties or revolutionary elites of social revolutions.

The discretion of Tunisia's Islamist movement can be explained to a large extent by the harshness of its suppression under Ben Ali, impeding the ability of the Islamic Nahda Party to act. However, the Muslim Brotherhood in Egypt was also discreet, but for the opposite reason: because it was a party tolerated by the military regime (although not legalised).

Anwar Sadat, when he came to power after Gamal Abdel Nasser's death in 1970, favoured the Brotherhood's return to the public stage and its enhanced position as a counterbalance to the Nasserist or radical left. The Brothers fully subscribed to the economic liberalisation (*infitah*) of Sadat when he embarked on dismantling Nasser's legacy. This led to increased influence of members of the new Egyptian bourgeoisie within the Brotherhood. Even so, it continued to assert its piety against rampant corruption;

this was a key argument for the petit bourgeois, the Brothers' favourite constituency.

The Brotherhood built itself as a reactionary religious political movement, whose main concern was – and still is – the Islamisation of Egypt's political and cultural institutions and the promotion of sharia as the basis for legislation. This programme is summed up by its main slogan: 'Islam is the solution'. At the same time, the Brotherhood has served as a political antidote to extreme and violent fundamentalist groups.

Sadat continued to play the religious card to legitimise his power ideologically in the face of social and nationalist opposition. He tried to compensate for the impact of the unpopular peace treaty he signed with Israel in March 1979 (less than six weeks after the Iranian revolution) by amending the constitution in 1980, making sharia the 'principal source of all legislation', even though Egypt has a sizeable Christian minority. The concession was not enough to win the Brothers' support for the peace treaty. So Sadat decided to deal them a stopping blow. In 1981, only months before his assassination by extreme Islamic fundamentalists, he launched a major wave of arrests against the Brothers.

Hosni Mubarak, succeeding Sadat as president, soon released them. At the beginning, Mubarak played it restrained and moderate, in contrast to Sadat's flamboyant style. He tried in his turn to come to terms with the Brothers in order to win popular support, while perpetuating the controlled freedom introduced by Sadat to check their development.

The Brotherhood's relations with the regime were strained in 1991 when Egypt joined the US-led coalition against Iraq in the first Gulf War. This was a turning point in relations between the US and its Saudi ally, on the one side, and the regional camp of moderate Sunni Islamic fundamentalism to which the popular Algerian, Egyptian and Tunisian Islamist parties belonged. To the great displeasure of the Saudi monarchy, which had been cultivating links with these parties, they joined the anti-war protest. Their rupture with Saudi Arabia accelerated the repression that struck them at various degrees during the 1990s, with the consent of the US and Europe.

ATTEMPTS TO PLEASE

Since the turn of the century, the Brotherhood has been torn between the conservative timidity of its older leaders and pressure from part of its younger members for active demands for political freedoms. It was thus careful not to antagonise the regime, while engaging in democratic and nationalist protest. Its members took part in the protest coalition Kefaya (Enough). This began out of solidarity with the second Palestinian intifada, developed in opposition to the 2003 war against Iraq and established itself as a force fighting against Egypt's dictatorial government and a likely dynastic succession.

Those Muslim Brothers favouring greater political boldness were encouraged in 2002 by the electoral rise to power in Turkey of the Justice and Development Party (AKP), a conservative Muslim party. Its success in government seemed to confirm the possibility of a model previously thought unworkable. The brutal end of the electoral process in January 1992 in Algeria, and the forced resignation of Necmettin Erbakan in 1997 in Turkey (removed by the army a year after becoming head of government), suggested that the parliamentary route was blocked to Islamic-inspired movements in countries where the military stood behind political power.

The new AKP Turkish experience was a change, as both the US and EU gave it their blessing. The Bush administration, after the collapse of the 'weapons of mass destruction' pretext that it had given for the invasion of Iraq, took up 'democracy promotion' as its prominent policy goal in the Middle East. Encouraged by developments in Turkey, voices in Washington extolled the virtues of a more open attitude to Egypt's Muslim Brotherhood. Under pressure from the US, Mubarak introduced greater pluralism in the 2005 elections and granted more seats to the opposition, mainly the Brothers. He hoped to demonstrate that free elections in Egypt would benefit the Brotherhood more than any others. A few months later, in January 2006, the electoral victory of Hamas in Palestine ultimately convinced the Bush administration to give up on democracy in the region, particularly in Egypt.

Barack Obama's accession to the US presidency, and his speech in Cairo on 4 June 2009 supporting the democratisation of the region (and his snubbing of Mubarak), galvanised Egyptian opposition. After some hesitation, the Brothers associated themselves with the National Association for Change, the predominantly liberal coalition created in February 2010 with Mohamed El Baradei as its figurehead. But several months later, ignoring the liberal opposition's calls to boycott the parliamentary elections, the Brotherhood participated in the first round, hoping to retain a good share of representation in parliament. The result meant that it had to boycott the second round. It was left with a single MP (expelled from the Brotherhood for failing to observe the boycott), against 88 in the outgoing parliament.

These elections exasperated Egypt, where 44 per cent live on less than $2 a day, where a greedy, self-serving bourgeoisie flaunt a luxurious lifestyle only matched locally by the rich from the Gulf's oil monarchies seeking a 'One Thousand and One Nights' experience on the Nile. Egypt was a powder keg. Tunisia was the spark. Networks and coalitions of young opposition called for demonstrations on 25 January. The Brotherhood decided not to associate itself with this for fear of the regime, and it wasn't until the third day that it joined the movement. Its leaders were careful to praise the army, knowing that this hard kernel of the regime would be called upon to resolve the situation.

When Mubarak appointed as vice-president the chief of the Egyptian General Intelligence Directorate, Omar Suleiman, and he in turn called the opposition to 'dialogue', the Brothers' leadership agreed to meet. This concession, after their refusal to join the initial phase of the protest, contributed to discrediting them in the eyes of the youth leadership (the *shabab*). When Mubarak finally stood down, the Brotherhood praised the military junta, while demanding the release of prisoners and lifting of the state of emergency, and announced a plan to establish a legal political party.

NO DOMINANT ROLE

The Brotherhood got in line to contribute to the 'orderly transition' that the US had advocated from the start of the Egyptian uprising. It declared it had no aspiration to take office, and wanted only democratic rights. Essam el-Errian, one of its leaders, explained in *The New York Times* on 9 February: 'We do not intend to take a dominant role in the forthcoming political transition. We are not putting forward a candidate for the presidential elections scheduled for September.' The Brothers 'envision the establishment of a democratic, civil state' but oppose the 'secular liberal democracy of the American and European variety, with its firm rejection of religion in public life'.[1]

During a press conference the same day in Cairo, el-Errian emphasised that the Brotherhood is 'against a religious state', that is, a state run by religious leaders as in Iran, but stands 'for a civil state with a religious reference'.[2] The Arab term used – *marja'iyya*

– can refer to a legal-theological authority responsible for verifying the compatibility of laws voted by parliament with Islam, and equipped with a legislative veto. This is what the Brotherhood's draft programme, made public in 2007, envisaged, but it was not formally adopted. It had been criticised in particular for declaring that women and non-Muslims would be barred from becoming president of Egypt.

To secure the Brotherhood's support, the military named a prominent member – the lawyer and former member of parliament (and author of an anti-secular book), Sobhi Saleh – to its constitutional revision committee. As head of this committee, the military chose Tariq al-Bishri, a judge who went from Nasserist-inspired nationalism to ideas that underlined Egypt's Islamic identity and the need to base its laws on sharia. In the sermon he gave in Cairo during the huge rallies on 18 February, the Brotherhood's spiritual leader, Sheikh Yusuf al-Qaradawi, urged workers on strike to desist and give the army time, while also calling for a change of government.

The 'orderly transition' is taking shape, as envisaged by the military with US backing: the course is set for transition to an electoral democracy under the army's control, as took place in Turkey between 1980 and 1983. Another facet of the 'Turkish model' looms on the horizon: the possibility of an Islamic-inspired political party eventually coming to power, running Egypt in cooperation with the military. This could prove easier in Egypt, since its army does not uphold secularism as the Turkish army claims to do. But such an arrangement will remain problematic if the Brothers do not carry out the type of makeover the Turkish AKP undertook, and for as long as they arouse the suspicion of the US and Israel's hostility for their attitude towards Palestine.

If the revolutionary potential of 25 January lasts and becomes radicalised (a wave of social struggles have followed Mubarak's resignation), Egypt might well see the growth of a leftwing mass opposition. Then the Muslim Brotherhood would seem the lesser of two evils, for the US as much as its Egyptian military clients.

Translated by Ursula Meany Scott

Gilbert Achcar is professor of development studies and international relations at the School of Oriental and African Studies, London, and author of *The Arabs and the Holocaust: The Arab-Israeli War of Narratives*, Metropolitan, New York, and Saqi, London, 2010.

1. Essam el-Errian, 'What the Muslim Brothers want', *The New York Times*, 9 February 2011.
2. 'Al-Ikhwan al-Muslimun: Narfud al-Dawla al-Diniyya li annaha dud al-Islam', Ikhwan online, 9 February 2011.

❖❖❖❖❖❖❖❖❖❖❖❖❖❖❖❖❖❖❖❖❖❖❖❖❖❖❖❖❖❖❖❖❖❖❖❖❖❖

MARCH 2011

THE NEW ARAB AWAKENING

To shoot, or not to shoot?

Each revolt has compelled the armed forces to choose between siding with the regime, or with the people. Will they be able to preserve their decades of privilege now the regimes are falling?

Salam Kawakibi and Bassma Kodmani

For 40 years now, the word 'army' in the Arab world has evoked military coups, states of emergency, secretiveness and surveillance. The armed forces have been the foundation of political systems, or served as their ultimate guarantors, but have rarely been visible. Several times they have served as protectors of the people and saviours of the state; although they are part of the state security apparatus, the last line of defence for the regime, they have been seen, in Tunisia and Egypt, to dissociate themselves from police forces, to recognise the demands of demonstrators as legitimate and, eventually, to abandon the leaders they had installed, and under whose command they were expected to operate.

What has happened over the last few decades to make people glad of military intervention, or even demand it, first in Tunisia, and then during the Egyptian revolution which swept away the Mubarak regime?

Most Arab leaders, whether they came from the armed forces or not, knew the historic importance of these forces in the establishment of nation states after independence, and were quick to see the threat they posed. They have all tried to marginalise and neutralise the forces, chiefly by granting them considerable economic privileges. In Egypt, much of the funding was provided by the US, which paid generous subsidies to the generals. The generals were allowed to build shopping malls, towns in the desert and seaside resorts, and were admitted to elite clubs formerly reserved for the Cairene aristocracy. They occupy all the regional governorships and head a number of major public enterprises and government ministries.

Heads of state have also developed complex security apparatuses led by high-ranking officers, who found their mission changed from protection of the state to protection of the regime. This trend can be seen in every country, but it was generally started by leaders who came from the forces.

The security services gather intelligence, maintain order and monitor the activities of people on a day-to-day basis. The number of security services always grows, because it allows them to watch each other. In Egypt, their staff numbers have grown to three times those of the armed forces (1.4 million compared with only 500,000). It is rare to find the two merged into a single cohesive body, as they are in Algeria.

The security services, though conceived as the coercive arm of political regimes, have become directly involved in administration. They deal directly with civil society, striking workers, the unemployed and demonstrators demanding housing or the right to buy the land they farm. They also manage relations between the different religious communities, apply censorship orders issued by the government or religious authorities and set the limits on free speech.

EVERYTHING IS A SECURITY ISSUE

The penetration of all institutions by the security services is not new, but the degree to which public life has been directly managed by the *mukhabarat* (intelligence agencies) has risen over the past decade. They now operate openly, and the language used by their heads suggests that they see themselves as omnipotent. A high-ranking official of Egypt's interior ministry told us: 'In this country, everything is a security issue. We are responsible for everything, from the birds in the Sinai desert to the elements of al-Qaida wandering around in it, via the mosques of Cairo and Alexandria.'[1] Their activities have even come to include mind control: in Saudi Arabia, in the context of the struggle against jihadism, the interior ministry has developed the concept of 'intellectual security'.

Leaders have been able to sleep easy in the knowledge that the security services were looking after things, which has led to more and more security and less and less politics. The term 'securitocracy', coined by the Sudanese political scientist Haydar

Ibrahim, characterises such regimes well.[2] The recent uprisings have revealed the dilapidated state of political institutions in country after country. In most cases, the armed forces have found themselves rescuing what are basically failed states.

The security systems of the Arab world resemble those of Latin American and eastern and southern European countries before the transition to democracy. They act as a buffer between the state and the people; they are made up of institutions of varying size and complexity, all operating in a closed loop, all with the same culture of impunity, and all geared to the systematic creation of terror. But although their primary task is to foster an atmosphere of fear and prevent citizens from banding together, they too are ruled by fear, at every level, a fear that is proportionate to the complexity of the hierarchy and its tendency to change in reflection of clan rivalries.

This year's uprisings, from North Africa to the Middle East, have broken the closed loop. The people, making a surprise appearance on the political scene, have revealed hidden differences and stirred up rivalries. They have brought the structures of the state face to face with a dilemma – to fire, or not to fire, on the demonstrators.

When something goes wrong in the security apparatus, dysfunction spreads to other pillars of the regime: the ruling party, the business oligarchy and the armed forces. Popular uprisings separate the institutions that serve the regime from those that present themselves as serving the state – first and foremost, the armed forces, having played no part in maintaining order, are able to act as guarantors of the transition to democracy.

There are many links between the armed forces and the security services, most often provided by the heads of the military intelligence services, such as General Omar Suleiman in Egypt or General Mohamed 'Toufik' Mediene in Algeria, who occupy the most important positions in the political system.

It should be noted that the contributions of the Tunisian and the Egyptian armed forces to the outcome of the revolts in their respective countries were different. Like most of the Arab leaders who moved from the barracks to the presidential palace, the Tunisian president Zine al-Abidine Ben Ali was fearful of the ambitions of the military. Shortly after he came to power in 1987, the armed forces suffered personnel and budget cuts, and several senior officers were fired. The still unexplained helicopter accident that killed General Abdelaziz Skik and other senior army officers heightened the suspicion between the president and the armed forces.[3] Having been kept out of the political decision-making process, even during the Bourguiba years (1957–87), the armed forces were not involved in the economic life of Tunisia and were therefore not involved in the regime's corruption.

IN POWER SINCE 1952

The Egyptian military, by contrast, have been in power since the Free Officers' revolution of 1952. Colonel Gamal Abdel Nasser, who died with only 85 Egyptian pounds to his name, initiated an ambitious social and economic development programme in Egypt, and throughout the Arab world. His nationalist ideology appealed to the people, who forgave his political mistakes and his systematic attack on freedom of speech. His successor Anwar Sadat, who also came from an army background, was the champion of an economic liberalism that benefited a new parasitical bourgeoisie. He introduced a culture of corruption and ensured the loyalty of the armed forces by giving them economic privileges to marginalise them, having robbed them of their 'victory' in the 1973 war against Israel, by signing the Camp David accords in 1978.

During the past decade, resentment towards Mubarak grew within the armed forces. They were dissatisfied with his refusal to appoint a vice-president, which created a dangerous uncertainty as to the future, and his obstinacy in promoting his son Gamal[4] as his successor – a man whom they did not recognise as having any legitimate claim and whose accession would deprive them of their traditional role of kingmaker. Mubarak also caused dissatisfaction by allowing a small circle of businessmen close to his heir apparent to acquire greater and greater wealth.

In the days before the fall of the regime, the differences of opinion became apparent: should the armed forces continue to support Mubarak or push him to step down? The consensus favouring non-support grew, but the armed forces seemed hesitant to assume responsibility for deposing the president. The US issued cautious, sometimes contradictory, statements, trying to preserve stability at all costs, even if that meant Mubarak had to go. Between 10 and 11 February, the armed forces allowed the demonstrations to achieve full force by facilitating access to the parliament building and the presidential palace, symbols of the regime's power, making the demonstrations look like the principal cause of the regime's fall. They have taken up the kingmaker role again but are now presenting themselves as rebuilders of the entire political order, promising a democratic system. Many people had hoped they would intervene, believing this was necessary to protect Egypt's internal transformation from regional and foreign interference (from Israel, the US, other Arab countries, or even Iran).

The major difference lies in the nature of the military intervention. In Tunisia, the armed forces intervened to protect the people; they forced Ben Ali to step down, with the approval of their US 'friends'. The Egyptian armed forces, on the other hand, stepped in at the beginning of the revolt to fill the security void in the street. Later on, they stood by while Mubarak's militia attacked the demonstrators in Tahrir Square. It is true that they did not fire at the demonstrators; but neither did they prevent others from doing so. Ultimately, they decided to abandon a regime in its death throes and preserve the system.

In Algeria, the political role of the military general staff was defined during the presidency of Houari Boumedienne (1965–78), by the establishment of the Military Security (MS). In Algeria, the MS was the kingmaker. At every election, the MS intervened to perpetuate an order that proved remarkably stable, except for the disastrous period after the failure of 1991. The armed forces got Bouteflika elected in 1999. But the first signs of a split between the MS and the armed forces appeared in 2004, when the MS organised Bouteflika's re-election, against the advice of the army chief of staff Mohamed Lamari. As Mustapha Mohamed notes: '2004 confirmed the autonomy of the MS and its supremacy over the armed forces.'[5] The re-election of Bouteflika removed the last faint hopes that Algerian politics could be rescued from the grasp of the MS, which strengthened its grip on the entire state apparatus. The situation seems to have reached a deadlock: the armed forces cannot withdraw from political affairs without leaving a void in the system, but are not doing anything that might encourage the emergence of a democratic process.

In Algeria, the interweaving of the military and the security services makes for total opacity and total control of politics. In this 'ideal' securitocracy, those in charge – the president and the government – do very little governing. The unpreparedness of the non-violent opposition suggests that change can only come from within the system, but it is hard to see those in power favouring changes that might threaten their own position. This is why hopes are emerging again today that people power will start a process that will lead to the overthrow of the regime, as in Tunisia and Egypt. It would force the security/military apparatus to make the same fateful choice – to fire, or not to fire, on the people.

In Libya, despite the opacity of the system, the armed forces have been marginalised over the last three decades in favour of the Revolutionary Committees. Army camps have been moved out into the desert, to prevent the military from fostering political ambition. In the first days of the repression ordered by Muammar Gaddafi, there were defections and the head of the army, General Abu Bakr Younes Jaber, was placed under house arrest. Gaddafi's reinforcement of the security system, which is based on special units loyal to him, and his use of African mercenaries are confirmation that dictators are wary not only of their people, but also of their armed forces.

After the revolutions, the armed forces in Egypt and Tunisia are in a position to set conditions for a return to civilian government. There is nothing to suggest that they have ambitions to take power for themselves. In Egypt, the decision to intervene was collegiate and prompted by the popular uprising, which should help the more authoritarian elements to resist the temptation to transgress the boundaries the armed forces have fixed.[6] In fact, the armed forces have been quick to establish a time frame for the process of return to civilian government.

This will probably take place, as elsewhere, on the basis of a pact between the civilian population and the military, sheltering the latter from possible reprisals. In Egypt, and all the more in Algeria, if things change in that country, the negotiations are likely to include the preservation of the armed forces' economic privileges.

Translated by Charles Goulden

Salam Kawakibi is research director of the Arab Reform Initiative, Paris; Bassma Kodmani is its executive director.

1. At a political conference organised by the Arab Reform Initiative in March 2008. The purpose of the conference was to discuss the reform of the security services; participants included members of both the security services and civil society.
2. Haydar Ibrahim, 'Al Amnocratiya fil Sudan' ('Securitocracy' in Sudan), to be published as part of a collective work on 'securitocracies' in Arabic and English by the Arab Reform Initiative in Amman, November 2011.
3. According to the 22 January 2011 edition of the Tunisian daily *Al-Sabah*, a new inquiry is to be opened.

4. See Virginie Collombier, 'Egypt: before and after', policy brief, Arab Reform Initiative, February 2011.

5. Mustapha Mohamed, 'Etat, sécurité et réforme en Algérie' (State, security and reform in Algeria), to be published by the Arab Reform Initiative in the collective work on 'securitocracies', op. cit.

6. Amr Abdel Rahman, 'Why fear the military?', *Al-Masry Al-Youm*, Cairo, 17 February 2011.

❖❖❖❖❖❖❖❖❖❖❖❖❖❖❖❖❖❖❖❖❖❖❖❖❖❖❖❖❖❖❖❖❖❖❖

APRIL 2011

A REVOLUTION IN POLITICAL ECONOMY

Follow the money

Those Arab states that have erupted this year – and others that may follow – want freedom and democracy, but also to end the way their countries have been run for the financial benefit of rulers and their friends.

Samir Aita

The reasons for the 'Arab Spring' go deeper than immediate demands for freedom and democracy. The protesters want to end the political economy and the authoritarian regimes in place since the 1970s.

Monarchies in the Arab world have been absolute, and life-long presidents (with hereditary office) ruled the republics, because they created a supreme power above both state and post-independence institutions.[1] They set up and controlled their own security services to ensure that their powers would endure; the services escaped parliamentary or government supervision, and their members could reprimand a minister and impose decisions. It costs money to run such services, and the clientelist networks of one-party states. The funds derive not from public budgets, as do those for the police and the army, but from different sources of revenue. (*The New York Times* recently reported that Muammar Gaddafi had demanded in 2009 that oil firms operating in Libya should contribute to the $1.5 billion he had promised to pay in compensation for the Lockerbie terrorist murders – or lose their licences. Many paid. And Gaddafi's immediate cash holdings of billions of dollars are thought to be funding his mercenaries and supporters to defend him.)

After the spectacular 1973 rise in crude oil prices, Middle Eastern revenues increased considerably. Through the distribution circuits, and in collusion with major multinationals, part of the revenue went direct to the coffers of the royal or 'republican' families instead of to the state. Nor was oil their only source of revenue. After there were no more commissions on major public contracts, civil and military, because of budget deficits and structural adjustments, new opportunities arose. In the 1990s there were mobile telephone network launches, and the first major privatisations of public services, with public/private partnerships and build-operate-transfer (BOT) contracts. Mobile networks had massive margins, especially at the start when better-off clients were prepared to pay high prices. The major multinational operators, influential businessmen and governments fought to capture the income. (There is evidence for this in the legal dispute over Djezzy, the Algerian branch of the Egyptian operator Orascom, and the Algerian military, and in a previous dispute between Orascom and Syria's Syriatel, which happened just as the first large Arab multinationals emerged.)

The globalisation of Arab economies and the demands of the International Monetary Fund – supported by the European Commission for the Mediterranean countries – tightened the regimes' hold on the economy, especially after the oil price crash of 1986. The ensuing decline in public investment and weakening of the governmental regulatory role ensured that the major multinationals held monopolies or oligopolies in exchange for sharing revenue with the powers-that-be. The senior management of the global corporations knew exactly where major decisions were taken and who the imposed local partners were for any new investment: the Trabelsi and Materi families in Tunisia, the Ezz and Sawires in Egypt, the Makhlouf in Syria, Hariri in Lebanon. The Sawires sold their shares in Orascom-Mobinil to France Telecom and offloaded their cement holdings before the Egyptian revolution. Najib Mikati, who had sold Investcom to the South African group MTN, is currently in charge of appointing the new government in Lebanon.

Enthralled by the Dubai miracle, all the Arab countries ventured into real estate transactions that allowed them to dissimulate a public/private interest mix. Land was expropriated and then sold cheaply to property developers. Historic city centres were neglected but the local *riad* (traditional palaces) were renovated by international investors, charmed by the exotic East, and property prices rose on a par with London, Paris or Tokyo. None of this would have been possible without banking, which facilitated the laundering of revenue and found ways to recycle it in real estate and commercial transactions. Banks were also the instruments of governments, providing credit to secure the lasting allegiance of local entrepreneurs.

EROSION OF PUBLIC SERVICES

But the state weakened and public services eroded. Where there was a need to send representatives abroad or to tap expertise at home, government members were co-opted; the good ones were technocrats from major international institutions such as the World Bank, but they lacked electoral legitimacy or programmes for which they would be accountable. The state ceased to be seen as a bureaucracy. Even the army weakened as well-equipped praetorian guards guaranteed the continuity of power.[2]

Arab governments bore no resemblance to those after independence, which had electrified the countryside and established universal public education. Public services deteriorated, as reports by the UN Development Programme (UNDP) observed, because of privatisations entirely for revenue raising. Even Jeddah in oil-rich Saudi Arabia only has running water one day a week; and a Saudi prince authorised construction work in a valley without planning drainage, resulting in lethal floods.

After every scandal there was an anti-corruption campaign, to little effect. The campaigns implied that corruption was a moral or religious issue rather than a systemic predation by leaders in alliance with business. Human dignity and work values were flouted. About a third of the working population in Arab countries is in the unofficial economy, in small jobs not included in unemployment statistics, which have been in double digits for a decade. Another third are self-employed, or employees without work contracts, social security, retirement or union rights. The concept of the employee is disappearing, outside the public sector and government. There, social rights have been maintained and so jobs are coveted, especially by women, but openings are rare, because of the 'structural adjustment' policies required by government spending cuts. The labour market is also fragmented by massive migration, both permanent (Palestinians, Iraqis or Somalis fleeing war) and temporary (mainly Asian), where migrants' economic and social rights are eroded, because the exploitation of migrant labour is now a source of revenue.

When the generation of the Arab demographic boom reached working age in the 2000s, connected by the new internet culture, the base toppled the summit in Tunisia and Egypt, and the entire social structure was shaken. People have been surprised by the many demands, social and otherwise, released by the revolution. Arab countries now have to rebuild the constitutional state, where power is finite and subject to institutions, instead of levitating above them. Government-dependent sources of revenue will have to be dismantled, as will monopolies, to release entrepreneurial energy. There will have to be states that guarantee public and social freedoms for all, so that workers have rights, and the states will have to be accountable, based on social consensus. It isn't going to be easy, because the world, including Europe, isn't going that way.

Translated by Krystyna Horko

Samir Aita is editor of the Arabic editions of *Le Monde diplomatique* and the author of *Les travailleurs arabes hors-la-loi*, L'Harmattan, Paris, 2011.

1. See Samir Radwan and Manuel Riesco, 'The changing role of the state', Economic Research Forum, 2007.
2. Read Salam Kawakibi and Bassma Kodmani, 'To shoot, or not to shoot?', *Le Monde diplomatique*, English edition, March 2011.

❖ ❖

JUNE 2011

A LONG HARD ROAD TO ARAB DEMOCRACY

Power of the word in the Syrian intifada

We can trace what's happening – and may yet happen – in Syria by what the protesters chant at their demonstrations: the slogans are already a history, a politics, a manifesto and a new identity.

Zénobie

'From now on, no more fear!' (*Ma fi khawf baad al-yawm!*) chanted the people of Deraa, in southern Syria, on 18 May. State repression intensified, but the protestors rejected the culture of fear, and in many towns declared they were ready to die: 'Martyrs are going to heaven in their millions'; 'There is only one God, and God loves martyrs'; 'Resist Banias, freedom is worth giving your life for' (Banias is the name of a port). Martyrdom was a theme in every region, expressed in a slogan currently popular in the Middle East: 'With our souls, with our blood, we sacrifice ourselves for you, oh martyr'. To express solidarity with a town where many people have died, they chant another version: 'With our souls, with our blood, we sacrifice ourselves for you, oh Deraa' (*Bi-ruh bi-damm, nafdîk ya shahîd*).

Every protest since March has called for freedom by twisting a slogan of the regime; so 'God, Syria, Bashar – that's all!' has become 'God, Syria, freedom – that's all!' Syria was under a state of emergency from 1963 until this April, so freedom is associated with democracy: 'We demand freedom and democratic elections.' This transcends sectarian divisions: 'Freedom, freedom, Muslims and Christians!'; 'We are the partisans of freedom and peace'.

The latest style, which is high-flown, is meant to mark the dignity of the individual citizen. And you can hear the growing rumble of anger in: 'Don't insult the Syrian people' (*Al-shaab al-suri ma byandhal*).

Martyrdom cleanses humiliation and restores an individual as a person and a believer (virtues traditionally reserved for nationalist heroes and saints): 'Better to die than be debased' (*Al-mawt wa lâ-l-madhalleh*). At the beginning of the intifada it was common to hear opposition supporters, at gatherings of friends or family, greet someone from Deraa or its region with: 'You have raised our heads high' (*Rafa'tu-l-na ra'sna*).

Ordinary people have tried to respond to accusations of division, violence and conspiracy. They proclaim their support for pacifism and unity, and reject sectarianism: 'One, one, the Syrian people are one!'; 'In peace, Muslims and Christians, in peace. No to sectarianism!'; 'No to violence, no to vandalism!'

'WE WANT NATIONAL UNITY'

In areas where there has been incitement to sectarian violence, the banners and slogans answer: 'Sunni, Kurd or Alawite, we want national unity' (*Sunni wa kurdi wa 'alawiyya, badna wahdah wataniyyah*). The authorities try to cause fear within Christian, Alawite and other minorities by claiming the uprising will be manipulated by Islamist extremists. But the protesters respond 'Neither Salafist nor Muslim Brotherhood, long live courageous people!'; 'Arabs and Kurds against Salafism'; 'Our revolt is the revolt of youth, no to Salafism and terrorism'; 'Neither America nor Iran, let us live in peace'. There are slogans that summarise it all: 'We are neither Muslim Brothers nor foreign agents, we are all Syrians, Muslims and Alawites, Druze and Christians' (*Nahna ma 'anna ikhwân wa lâ aydî kharijiyya, nahna kullna suriyya, islam wa 'alawiyya, durziyya wa masihiyya*).

In the first days, demonstrators had limited themselves to demands for reform and an end to the state of emergency. There was still some support for President Bashar al-Assad. The Syrians had seen the civil wars that ravaged neighbouring Lebanon for 15 years, and more recently Iraq, and were wary of a long confrontation with the risk of sectarian clashes. But then came Deraa, and violence by the regime. Then in Bashar's first, much anticipated, speech to the nation on 30 March, he scorned the protesters.

After that, the slogan of the Tunisian and Egyptian revolutions began to ring through the streets: 'The people want the downfall of the regime' (*Al-shaab yurid isqat al-nizam*). As state thugs spread terror and people were killed, the tone rose: 'We don't like you, get out, you and your party'. A new slogan became popular in April: 'Anyone who harms his people is a traitor'.

Even before his speech, there were slogans against Bashar from Deraa after the security forces' attack on the Omari mosque on 16 March, the murder of a mother and daughter, and the abduction of injured people who had taken refuge in a religious building. 'Lane by lane, house by house, we will get rid of you, Bashar' (*Zenga, zenga, dar, dar, badna nchîlak ya Bashâr*). 'Lane by lane, house by house' refers to a speech by Libya's Muammar Gadaffi broadcast on Al-Jazeera, which raced like wildfire through the Arab world.

Bashar's second speech on 16 April came far too late to decrease tension, and he said nothing about article 8 of the constitution (which establishes the Ba'ath as the ruling party) or about freeing political prisoners. Though he ended the state of emergency, that didn't stop thousands of arbitrary arrests and the deployment of tanks and soldiers against protesters: 'Oppression is such a habit for them, it has become a ritual'; 'They have not only stolen our dignity, they make us pay for their corruption'.

VIRTUE AND VIRILITY

Syrians are fiercely loyal to their homeland ('Long live Syria and down with Assad') and to their local roots. Every town commands its inhabitants; and in the tradition of the great Bedouin battles, it also demands their virility (*al-roujoula*) which, with virtue, is the key value of an Arab fighter. 'Where are you Deiri [inhabitant of Deir al-Zor]? Where are you? Stand up and paint your face.' (Tribesmen used to put kohl around their eyes before going to war.) Or 'Barzeh [an area of Damascus], we are your men, God knows who the traitors are'; and 'Here are your men, Daraya [a town southwest of Damascus]'. Any protester who braves death sacrifices himself for his homeland, and honours his town or village, which then measures its place in history by the number of its brave ones.

This uprising is not just about politics but a worsening social and economic situation, for the protesters come mainly from the underprivileged. They reject corruption and the regime's clientelist networks, and demand a fair distribution of wealth and jobs. These have been reserved for Ba'ath Party members and certain religious denominations, the Alawites, and to some extent the Christians. An unspoken truth, well known to the unprivileged, is: 'They ate the egg and the shell, and left us with nothing but straw' (*Akalu al-bayda wa-l-ta'shira wa khalluna 'ala al-hasira*).

Rami Makhlouf, Bashar's cousin, directly or indirectly controls every lucrative sector of the economy – the Syrian branch of the Lebanese bank Byblos, aviation, property and construction companies, hotels, duty free shops, Syriatel (mobile phones), a large part of MTN (another mobile phone company) and dozens of other businesses. That's why protesters in Deraa and Latakia set fire to the Syriatel offices.

The spontaneity of this intifada cannot disguise the disparities between town and country, and between Damascus, Aleppo and the rest of the country. The reluctance of the cities to join the revolt is nothing new: Aleppo did not erupt during the Franco-Syrian war of 1919–21, even though the Ottomans stored their weapons there. Nor did Damascus rise up during the great Syrian revolt started in 1925 against the French Mandate. So it is not surprising that the current uprising began in Deraa in the rural south.

The protesters hoped that the first unrest in Damascus on 15 and 16 March would become a large mobilisation at the heart of power. But as in 1925, it was the underprivileged suburbs of Damascus that saved the city's honour, while in Aleppo, after much dithering, a few hundred students put the city on the uprising's map.

Neighbouring Hama mocked on 29 April: 'Wake up, Aleppo!' (*Sah al-nawm yâ Halab*).

NEITHER ISLAMISM NOR ARAB NATIONALISM

All these slogans mark a major break from the ideology of Middle Eastern political parties of the 20th century: they don't refer to Arab nationalism or Islamism. Fear of the latter, more particularly of Salafism, is reinforced by the rumour that the political prisoners Bashar released on 30 March included the head of the Muslim Brotherhood, alongside common criminals. The regime has exploited this fear, and representatives of Christian institutions have been cautious, not even condemning the massacre of civilians.

The Syrian intifada has broken with the political past. Yet it reflects elements of 20th-century protests: the position of the mosque in the urban environment; the mosque as refuge (where the injured and those in flight should be able to take refuge); reference to Islam in slogans (*Allahu akbar*); the militant as a synthesis of the traditional figures of the hero and the martyr, based on virility and virtue, rooted in national identity and the land. The uprising is the outcome of the regional situation and of internal evolution. It is profoundly popular and patriotic, a patriotism instilled and cultivated by the Ba'ath state school system.

Since the uprising has no outside support from the region or internationally, its future depends on its ability to mobilise, and on uncertain factors such as divisions within the army, and the rallying of religious leaders, prominent figures or towns from minority communities. The protesters know this and appeal to the Druze, Christian and Alawite minorities in the name of national unity. Appeals to the army are less frequent: 'Syrian army, all powerful, protect Deraa from being surrounded' (*Al-jeish al-suri yâ jabbâr radduw 'an Der'â al-hisâr*).

The army, formerly in the political vanguard and glorious through the anti-colonial struggle, but since discredited (through the exercise of power rather than its defeats against Israel) could embody the main hope of the intifada in the absence of other realistic prospects.

Translated by Stephanie Irvine

Zénobie is a journalist in Damascus.

❖❖❖❖❖❖❖❖❖❖❖❖❖❖❖❖❖❖❖❖❖❖❖❖❖❖❖❖❖❖

JUNE 2011

A FREEDOM SQUARE IN EVERY VILLAGE AND TOWN

Yemen knows what it doesn't want

The impromptu coalition of revolution protesting regularly all over Yemen wants the president to leave office. Beyond that, it doesn't yet have a programme, although it does have an agenda.

Laurent Bonnefoy and Marine Poirier

The international community is paralysed by the fear that Yemen will fall into chaos after four months of demonstrations. Yemen's opposition shares that fear. The French foreign minister Alain Juppé said in March that it was not possible to avoid the question of President Ali Abdallah Saleh leaving office, but such statements do not change the situation any more than did the regional intervention of the Gulf Cooperation Council. What Yemen's allies want is the system preserved, even if it costs the president his job.

This seems paradoxical for, since the attack on the US warship USS *Cole* in Aden in 2000, the Yemeni regime has caused the displeasure of its allies, not least the US. Saleh's political and institutional system fuelled violence, repressing its own citizens, especially during the civil war in Sa'ada in the north – a conflict that has cost more than 10,000 lives since 2004 – and using the war against al-Qaida to its own ends without managing to limit its attacks.

The serious crisis in Saleh's regime dates back much further than 2011. Yemen was created in 1990 through the unification of the People's Democratic Republic of Yemen (South Yemen) and the Yemen Arab Republic (North Yemen). In the past decade, this unity has been challenged by Houthi rebels[1] around Sa'ada and by the separatist southern movement. Since 2007 armed Islamists have been directly targeting the authorities and security forces.

The legislative elections originally scheduled for April 2009 were postponed because of a political and institutional deadlock. The opposition – under the umbrella of the Joint Meeting Parties (*al-liqa al-mushtarak*) whose prominent members include the socialists (who ran former South Yemen) and the Muslim Brothers of al-Islah – has been criticising the regime for years and decided on a boycott.

Despite these political impasses, the regime continued to enjoy the support of the international community until the end of 2010.

Confident of its future, it was preparing to get parliamentary approval for a law allowing Saleh to be re-elected as head of state indefinitely, with his son, Ahmed Ali Saleh, a career soldier, to succeed him.

GALVANISING PROTEST

The Arab uprisings that began in Tunisia and Egypt galvanised Yemen's protest movements and precipitated the break-up of the machinery of state control. Yemen's youth, mostly unconnected to political parties, first revolted in the major cities: Sana'a, Ta'iz and Aden. Only in the second phase did opposition parties join and attempt to channel the *shabab al-thawra* (youth of the revolution). In March and April the protesters' demands and methods converged – whether they were Houthis or southern separatists, members of opposition parties or civil society, tribesmen, Islamists or liberals. They were united in demanding the overthrow of the regime and their favoured location for doing so was a crossroads outside Sana'a university, 'the square of change'.[2]

After 52 demonstrators were killed in Sana'a on 18 March, the regime was weakened by defections from the ruling party (the General People's Congress) but also, and more significantly, from within the government, state media and army. General Ali Muhsin, a relative of the president known for his links with the radical Islamists and hated by Yemeni youth, joined the protesters and promised them protection. He deployed his troops around the sit-in zone (*i'tisam*) in Sana'a. This alliance revealed the cracks within the regime and showed the uprising was at risk both of political hijacking and of turning into military conflict. Muhsin's support crystallised tensions among the demonstrators: it served as a reminder that the revolt could provide a springboard for Saleh's historical rivals and underlined the fragility of its peaceful option, which had held up until then.

WILY TACTICS

Saleh has lived up to his reputation as a wily tactician. He has blown hot and cold, first appearing to accept an agreement brokered through the mediation of the Gulf monarchies and then refusing to sign it. He has also demonstrated his capacity to organise mass mobilisations that reveal the great imbalance of resources between the sides. And by playing for time, he has created doubt and weariness among the demonstrators, foreign journalists and observers.

He has also tried to exploit obvious differences between the youths on the streets and the opposition parties. Immunity for Saleh and his circle was guaranteed under a draft agreement and accepted by the Joint Meeting Parties, but rejected by the *shabab*, who had been kept out of the negotiations. They were mistrustful of the coalition's strategies, especially that of Hamid al-Ahmar (the heir of a powerful tribal clan) and al-Islah party, whose influence has become dominating among the opposition forces.[3]

The slogan '*Irhal*' (Get out!) chanted by the demonstrators is hardly a programme and is unlikely to solve all Yemen's crises, especially the identity issue raised by the secessionist movement in former South Yemen since 2007. Neither will it overcome the social inequalities, nor provide an immediate answer to economic problems or dwindling natural resources.

The security issue will also have to be faced. The international community has taken a cautious stance, afraid that armed groups, particularly al-Qaida in the Arabian Peninsula (AQAP), might take advantage of a political vacuum and that certain benefits of 'war on terror' cooperation might vanish with the collapse of the Saleh clan.

Since the end of 2009, many US bombings targeting AQAP have undermined the Yemeni regime's legitimacy, while only marginally affecting AQAP's operational effectiveness. Within AQAP, figures have emerged capable of assuming the international leadership of al-Qaida, left vacant by the assassination of Osama bin Laden. Among them is Anwar al-Awlaki, an American of Yemeni origin. Less than a week after the death of Bin Laden in Pakistan, he was the target of a failed drone attack in the Shabwa region.

THE BALANCE OF FEAR

The break-up of Yemen is a risk given the diversity of sources of legitimacy (political, tribal, religious, generational) and the multiplication of opposition fronts in the past few years. Beneath the unity on the street, the movement opposing Saleh is fragmented. Competition between the regime and the opposition, but also within the opposition or within the army, could come at a high price. Despite the defection of military men and tribal chiefs, the president still has control of much of the army and security forces directed by his allies. In April intermittent clashes pitted the first armoured division commanded by Ali Muhsin against loyalist forces. An all-out confrontation would be extremely violent. Yemenis are aware of the risk of the conflict escalating. However, a balance of fear has prevailed, limiting the level of violence and repression since the beginning of the uprising, but also delaying change indefinitely. For four months, large pro-Saleh demonstrations have been organised in Sana'a each Friday, giving the president the chance to declare his constitutional legitimacy. Highly dependent on the regime's patronage networks, they cannot be compared with the huge spontaneous and daily demonstrations of the opposition all over the country. In cities and villages, in squares now named 'change' or 'freedom', the actors of this revolution, the *shabab* most of all, have transformed the rules of the political game. Their protests have been structured around spaces, actors and practices which, although inspired by old habits, are still very new.

Tawakkul Karman, a human rights activist close to the Islamists (and a woman), has become a symbol of the nascent revolution. The political emergence of a new generation, socialised by January's protests, was accompanied by a profound change in politics and the logic of collective action, and by a transformation in society. However risky it is to interpret the revolutionary process in the short term, Yemen's unprecedented protests suggest its revolution has strong political potential and may be able to overcome some of the divisions in Yemeni society.

PROTEST TRANSFORMED

The early protests, morning or evening marches and demonstrations, gave way to continuous sit-ins. On 20 February a few dozen people decided to pitch tents outside Sana'a University. Their example was followed, and squares, streets and whole neighbourhoods across the country were occupied as the number of 'campers' rose. These spaces were adapted and revitalised with hawkers and organisation committees.

These protests have taken many different forms: slogans, photo displays, revolutionary songs, theatre, poetry, exhibitions and artists' workshops, festive and family gatherings, newspapers, websites and community groups, debates and civil disobedience training. Unexpectedly, thousands of tribesmen laid down their arms in favour of peaceful protest and joined the sit-ins. This new form of resistance has shaken received ideas about tribal behaviour (conservatism, backwardness and violence). A new facet of Yemen's youth has emerged, politicised without being partisan, plural and autonomous. The national flag and anthem have replaced the sectarian and regional symbols of previous protest movements. Many participants and observers wonder whether they should fear Yemeni unity unravelling or whether it is being strengthened. The growing mobilisations and collaboration of different movements have made credible the idea of convergence. Exchanges and encounters between different regional groups have drawn attention to a regional readjustment of protest and underlined the key role of the city of Ta'iz in promoting this project.

Nothing can hide the strength of the hopes of the popular uprising or the transformations it has already brought about. This represents a success which the Yemenis will have to nurture.

Translated by George Miller

Laurent Bonnefoy is a researcher at the French Institute of the Middle East; Marine Poirier is a doctoral student at the Institute of Political Studies at Aix-en-Provence.

1. The name derives from their former leader, Hussein al-Houthi, a former member of parliament who was killed in 2004. He was replaced by his brother, Abdul-Malik al-Houthi.
2. During the events in Tahrir Square in Cairo, the square in Sana'a with the same name (freedom) was occupied en masse by supporters of Saleh's regime.
3. Fikri Qassem, *Hadith al Madina*, Ta'iz, 20 February 2011.

❖ ❖

JULY 2011

'IF WE STOP DREAMING IT WILL BE BETTER TO DIE'

Egypt's revolution is only beginning

Dazzled by events in Tahrir Square, the media overlooked the role of the workers in Egypt's revolution, whose 6 April movement was named after the struggles of the workers at the Misr textile factory at Mahallah al-Kubra. Similar protests continue across the country.

Alain Gresh

Youssef Chahine would not have recognised Cairo's central station, the backdrop to one of his finest films, shot in 1958,[1] which tells of the love of Kanawi, a crippled newspaper seller, for the beautiful Hanuma. The colossal statue of Ramses II that used to stand outside the station was moved to the Giza plateau in 2006, and the newly renovated façade gleams in the sun. But inside there was chaos: to reach the platforms, passengers had to pick their way across a construction site, between scaffolding, heaps of rubble and puddles, without any signs to help them. The train for Mahallah al-Kubra was due to leave at 1:15. People forced their way into sordid carriages, their windows opaque with dirt. Only two, at the back, offered reserved seats and air conditioning although the temperature was close to 40°C.

It took more than two hours to reach Mahallah, just 100 km north of Cairo across the Nile delta; nothing could explain why the train had to move so slowly as we crossed some of the world's most fertile farmland, being nibbled away by urbanisation. With half a million people (two million counting the surrounding province), Mahallah is typical of the middle-sized cities that have absorbed much of Egypt's population growth since the megacities of Cairo and Alexandria reached saturation. In the early 19th century it had a monopoly in silk. Later it became one of the centres of the Egyptian textile industry, whose reputation was founded on high-quality, long-staple cotton, introduced by the French in 1817. When the American civil war of 1861–65 cut off Europe's American imports, Egypt became a leading cotton exporter.

The Misr spinning and weaving factory is only a few hundred metres from the station, but you have to find your way along unpaved roads, crowded with traffic, vendors' carts and young female factory workers in headscarves, all trying to catch a bus, train, shared taxi or motorised rickshaw. The factory operates 24 hours a day, in three shifts, but women work only a day shift that finishes at 4:00 pm.

A sign proclaimed 'Welcome to the capital of Egyptian industry'. Misr's history reflects that of Egypt, and its development policy. The company was established in 1927 by Talaat Harb, the founder of Egypt's first national bank, who aimed to promote industry, and was floated on the stock market. British investors bought up the shares; though officially independent since 1922, Egypt was then under British occupation. Misr was Egyptianised between 1954 and 1956, then nationalised in 1962 by Gamal Abdel Nasser under a programme of socialist reform and rapid industrialisation supported by the Soviet Union that also led to the building of the Helwan iron and steel works and the Aswan High Dam. Anwar Sadat's accession to the presidency in 1970 brought *infitah* (economic opening), which encouraged private sector investment and the privatisation of the public sector. This policy accelerated in the 1990s and 2000s under Hosni Mubarak.

Only a few public enterprises held out, notably the Misr factory. The huge complex, surrounded by fences, contains Misr's headquarters, offices and workshops, housing for workers and managers and a sports stadium, hospital, theatre and swimming pool, open to all. Cooperative stores offer food, furniture and clothing at low prices. But some of the buildings, including the canteen, have been abandoned – a sign that the government has lost interest.

One is unsure whether Misr was inspired by paternalistic capitalism borrowed from the British or real socialism, descended from Nasserism; it certainly evokes nostalgia throughout Egypt. Besides the establishment of a minimum wage of 1,200 Egyptian pounds ($192)[2] there are frequent calls for the renationalisation of factories privatised in the 2000s, often under doubtful circumstances. These demands have already brought reactions from the US; in May the outgoing US ambassador Margaret Scobey said: 'A return to nationalisation will be a huge disincentive to investment...History proves privatisation has been very healthy, helpful and successful in helping many countries transform to democracy.'[3]

Scobey seems to have seen and heard nothing during her three-year posting: the press reports daily that the Egyptians have doubts about the benefits of privatisation: the courts have just stopped the privatisation of the Egyptian retail chain Omar Effendi; some 30,000 fishermen on Lake Bourlos, separated from the Mediterranean by a narrow strip of land, are fighting the illegal grant of vast areas of their waters to industrial concerns; the millionaire Saudi prince Al-Walid Bin Talal, who bought 420 sq km of farmland close to the Sudanese border in 1998, has had to agree to 'donate' three-quarters of it to the Egyptian people.

Egypt's prime minister, Issam Sharaf, described this agreement as 'an encouragement to Arab and foreign investment through amicable negotiation'. The government and the Supreme Council of the Armed Forces (SCAF) are still pursuing the same liberal economic policy. They have abandoned the idea of a progressive income tax (the rate is currently a uniform 20 per cent) and a tax on corporate earnings. On 5 June they reached agreement with the International Monetary Fund on a loan of $3 billion, subject to the usual conditions of macroeconomic and financial 'stability'.

(Note that in April 2010 the IMF had commended 'the authorities' sound macroeconomic management and the reforms implemented since 2004'.)

The privatisations of the 2000s were also hard on the workers, made redundant in tens of thousands or forced to accept ever harsher working conditions. In the Mahallah region, 225,000 people work in the textile industry, but only 25,000 of these in the public sector. Some 23,000 are employed by Misr, the rest by hundreds of smaller companies, of which only 36 have more than 1,000 workers. In the public sector the working day is eight hours; in the private sector it is twelve hours, without holidays or profit-sharing, and most of the pay consists of bonuses. Children under 16 are paid a pittance.

'ALL EYES ON MAHALLAH'

Afak Ishtiraki (Socialist Horizons), an organisation with links to the Egyptian Communist Party, has offices in a working-class area of Mahallah. These serve as a gathering place for trade unionists in the city, where leftwing politics are still strong. On the day I visited, a dozen militant workers, including two women, were meeting. The room was decorated with Palestinian flags and portraits of Nasser, Khaled Mohieddin (one of Nasser's Free Officers) and Nabil al-Hilali, a lawyer who fights for workers' rights. A slogan on the wall voiced anxiety over inflation: 'Prices are on fire! Take our wages and give us food!'

Some of the militants had been fired in recent years for taking strike action or trying to establish an independent trade union (the Egyptian Trade Union Federation is allied to the regime). Widdad Dimirdash has worked for Misr since 1984. Despite frequent interruptions from the men, she explained her difficulties in reconciling the demands of work, family life and her union campaigning. Her first campaign was in 2006, to persuade her employers to pay profit-sharing bonuses. The men were hesitant, she said, but 'we [the women] went down into the yard and challenged them: "Where are the men? The women are here!" And they joined us. Since then, all eyes are on Mahallah. Everyone believes the future rests on our shoulders.'

During the past five years, Misr – the workers' stronghold – seemed to embody hope for the future. But the media (national and international), dazzled by the events in Tahrir Square, lost sight of the working-class origins of the revolution.[4] 'They stole 6 April from us!' said Dimirdash. On 6 April 2008 the people of Mahallah had rioted in protest at the cost of living.[5] The movement that called for the 25 January 2011 demonstration adopted the name '6 April', but forgot its origins.

Mohammed Attar, 45, had taken part in the workers' struggles and had suffered violence at the hands of the state security service, which interfered in union elections and daily life in the factory – a practice that extended to all companies and the lives of all Egyptians. 'All the protest tactics people have copied elsewhere were invented here in Mahallah: occupying the space in front of the factory gates and pitching tents there; calling on everybody, including the people in the high-rises in Cairo; forming broad alliances with all opposition forces, from the left to the Muslim Brotherhood.' It was here too, in April 2008, that portraits of Mubarak were slashed for the first time. To break the movement, the authorities cut off access to the internet throughout the region. In October 2010 they conducted an exercise that simulated shutting down the net across the whole of Egypt. All the telecommunications companies (including Mobinil, an Orange subsidiary) obligingly took part.[6]

THREE EGYPTS

Perhaps the workers are the real heroes. In the Cairo offices of the daily *Al-Tahrir*, Mustafa Bassiouni, an expert on union and workers' affairs, asked: 'Why is it that the uprisings in Libya, Yemen and Bahrain have not yet succeeded? In Tunisia, it was the General Union of Tunisian Workers (UGTT)'s call for a general strike that struck the fatal blow to the government. In Egypt, the country was at a standstill; public transport was no longer running. In the last few days there were calls for political strikes, and these mobilised the population. In Suez, a strike at a fertiliser factory where workers had already been out in January 2009, to prevent exports to Israel during Operation Cast Lead, triggered a political strike.'[7]

Does this mean there are two Egypts: the middle-class Egypt of Tahrir Square, and the rest? 'No, three,' said Alaa al-Din Arafat,[8] a researcher at the French Centre for Legal Studies and Documentation (CEDEJ) who has been travelling the country for two years. 'First you have Cairo, Alexandria and the big cities, where most of the slogans were about democracy and liberty. Then you have the middle-sized cities and the countryside, especially the Delta, where the emphasis was on unemployment, education and prices, and where there was criticism of the US and Israel. And finally you have the "peripheral" regions (Sinai, parts of Upper

Egypt, Marsa Matrouh), where the questions focused on the status of those regions, which are neglected, and on the identity of their populations, which are often ignored by central government.' Had anything changed since the revolution? 'The uprising got rid of the top tier of politicians,' said Arafat. 'But the second and third tiers are still in place, and they still have the same culture.'

Thirty young lawyers were picketing the Court of Cassation in Cairo. Among their slogans was 'We have got rid of Gamal [Mubarak's son] but there are a thousand Gamals among the judges' – a reference to nepotism among the magistrates. Not a day goes by without a group calling for the firing of a corrupt company boss or the resignation of a university president. In June, for the first time in recent history, Cairo University's arts faculty elected a new dean without interference from the state security service. Neither the al-Azhar hierarchy nor the Coptic Church, which both worked closely with the Mubarak regime, has gone unchallenged. At Nag Hammadi in Upper Egypt, workers in an aluminium factory organised a sit-in, demanding bonuses and jobs for their children. In June, workers of a number of subsidiaries of the Suez Canal Authority went on strike, calling for existing agreements to be honoured and the director appointed by Mubarak to be removed. A demonstration by hundreds of doctors recently called for health spending to rise from 3.5 per cent of the budget to 15 per cent.

These countless protests reflect the magnitude of Egypt's problems, as do the subjects discussed by the SCAF, the government, the political parties and the media. The list is enough to dissuade any rational person from aspiring to lead the country: the organisation of the elections; a new law on places of worship; the future of the state media; the trials of senior figures from the former regime; the regeneration of the economy; the reorganisation of the police and the state security service; the dissolution and re-election of hundreds of municipal councils; the role of the armed forces in a democratic Egypt; the status of the universities; the establishment of a minimum wage; the replacement of all senior officials; a law on trade unions. The scale of the changes needed suggests that struggles will go on for years.

A DIVIDED LEFT

Egypt's left, weakened by years of repression, has yet to organise itself. The Egyptian Federation of Independent Unions (FIU) occupies a modest apartment on Qasr al-Aini Street, which leads to Tahrir Square. The rooms were filled with people talking earnestly; mobile phones rang. The walls were decorated with posters showing a fist grasping a wrench. Galal Shukri found a free corner in which we could talk: 'I was first elected as a trade union rep in 1979, in a public sector telecoms company. In 1987 I joined the board. We used public service regulations to secure improvements, but the company was privatised in 2006, the year I retired. The workforce had already been reduced to 700, compared with the 2,800 we'd had 20 years earlier.'

Shukri got involved with pensioners who had been watching their pensions stagnate since 2004 and had nobody to defend their rights. In 2008 he founded an independent trade union, which the government only recognised after 25 January 2011 and which now claims to have 200,000 members. He is a co-founder of the FIU, which also includes a telecommunications union, a union of tax authority employees, and the teachers' union. Their greatest challenge has been organising the millions who work in the private sector: 'We go into new towns, into free zones. We set up local organisations and train their militants. We want to hold a congress between now and October. We are trying to get recognition for these independent unions, but we are encountering resistance from local government, although the Ministry of Labour supports us.'

Two days earlier he had attended a meeting with businessmen to discuss raising the minimum wage. The businessmen had attacked Shukri, accusing him of mistaking Egypt for Switzerland and threatening their profits at a time when, amidst general instability, 'investors need a 50 per cent return on their investment'. Egypt's minister of labour and immigration Ahmed Borai, one of Egypt's few experts on employment law – he has worked for the International Labour Organisation and taught at the Sorbonne in Paris – replied: 'Do you know what will happen if we fail to set a minimum wage? People will go back to Tahrir Square and they will burn everything.'

Borai wants to change the wage structure, in which fixed pay accounts for only 20 per cent and the rest is bonuses. 'We want to invert the proportions, restore unemployment benefit, which was abolished in 1991, and reduce the range of wages.' The figure of EGP 700 ($112) that he is proposing as a minimum wage in the public sector – wages in the private sector are to be decided by a tripartite commission – is well below the inflation-linked EGP 1,200

($192) demanded by the trade unions. 'Seven hundred pounds is reasonable. We have economic constraints too.'

In June the SCAF announced that it would go ahead with the decision, taken soon after it acceded to power, to ban strikes, and several have been harshly repressed. Yet these movements are of limited scope and have not contributed to Egypt's economic problems, which are due to the decline in tourism, the return of 500,000 expatriate workers from Libya and the neoliberal policies pursued in Egypt for decades. What the military, some of the Islamists and the 'neoliberal' forces want is a return to order.

Khaled Khamissi, author of *Taxi*,[9] which describes imaginary conversations in this popular forum for the exchange of world views, said: 'We are seeing the clash of two opposing forces: on one side the army, which "speaks in the name of the revolution, the better to kill it off"; on the other, the revolution.' In spite of the pessimism of the small minority who are disappointed[10] because they believed the revolution would be 'as smooth as the pavement of Nevski Prospect' (Lenin, quoting Chernyshevski) and had forgotten that revolutions take years, hope is not dead in Egypt. In the words of a placard in Tahrir Square: 'If we stop dreaming, it will be better to die, die, die.'

Translated by Charles Goulden

Alain Gresh is vice-president of Le Monde diplomatique.

1. *Bab el-Hadid*; English title: *Cairo Station*.
2. One Egyptian pound (EGP) = US 0.16 cents; EGP 1,200 is considered to be the subsistence income for a family of four.
3. Ahram Online, 21 May 2001.
4. See Raphaël Kempf, 'Egypt: first democracy, then a pay rise', *Le Monde diplomatique*, English edition, March 2011.
5. See Joel Beinin, 'Egypt: bread riots and mill strikes', *Le Monde diplomatique*, English edition, May 2008. For more on Egypt's working class, see the Solidarity Centre report, 'Justice for All: the Struggle for Worker Rights in Egypt', Washington, February 2010.
6. 'Outrage over exoneration of Egypt telecom giants in communications shutdowns', Ahram Online, 1 June 2011.
7. In an article on the triggers of the Tunisian uprising ('Tunisie, quelle gifle?', *Libération*, 11–12 June 2011), Christophe Ayad refers to a demonstration in the Monastir area following Israel's deadly assault on the Gaza flotilla (31 May 2010). The slogans in this demonstration evolved from 'Down with Israel!' to 'Down with the 7 November System!' (when Ben Ali came to power).
8. Author of *The Mubarak Leadership and Future of Democracy in Egypt*, Palgrave Macmillan, London, 2009.

9. Aflame Books, London, 2008.
10. An opinion poll by the International Republican Institute (Salem Massachusetts), 'Egyptian Public Opinion Survey (April 14–April 27)', found that 89 per cent of respondents thought the country was headed in the right direction, while 81 per cent felt the economic situation was bad or very bad.

❖❖

SEPTEMBER 2011

TRADITIONAL NEGOTIATING SYSTEMS

How to make Libya work after Gaddafi

Gaddafi was defeated, as he had been sustained, by tribal affiliations and alliances as much as by the impromptu rebel uprising. Now he's gone, tribal politics will be crucial to establishing a viable state.

Patrick Haimzadeh

After the revolutions in Tunisia and Egypt, which toppled two tyrants in the space of a few weeks, many observers wanted to believe that the Libyan uprising of 17 February 2011 would produce the same result. It was hard to remain unmoved by the images on all the satellite channels of the rebels in the eastern province of Cyrenaica heading west on the desert road in their pick-up trucks, especially given the enthusiasm and courage of these young fighters, who proudly claimed they could 'liberate' Tripoli in two days.

And yet, after more than six months of civil war and 8,000 NATO bombing missions, the Brega and Misrata fronts remained little changed. What proved militarily decisive and led to the fall of Tripoli within days were not the actions of Libyans from the east of the country but those of people from western towns, members of a major Arab tribe from the western mountains (Jebel Nafusa), the Zintan.

To understand the resilience of Gaddafi's regime and the huge challenges of the post-Gaddafi era, we need to know how the system worked. Gaddafi, who was strongly influenced by Nasserism, always cited the Franco-British intervention in Suez in 1956 and the Algerian war of independence as the key events that shaped his political consciousness. But after 1976, the former anti-imperialist turned dictator and, at the head of a system that appropriated oil revenues, based his power on a vote-catching system that embraced the whole of Libyan society.[1] Yet he saw himself as a revolutionary fighter.

It is in this context that his speech of 21 February 2011[2] must be judged – as the first step in regaining control of the situation in Tripoli and surrounding towns where the people had risen up. This speech – in which he declared his determination to fight to the end – reassured the faithful and persuaded demonstrators to go home and those who were sitting on the fence to stay put. The western military intervention, which began on 19 March in support of the revolt, gave credibility to his rhetoric of a North-South clash ('Crusader' forces, colonialists and so on).

THREE LEVERS OF POWER

The Jamahiriya ('state of the masses') system of power drew its legitimacy from three sources: revolutionary, military and tribal. Since 1975 these three levers ensured its longevity. And they continued to function, albeit at reduced power, in the six months following the outbreak of the insurrection.

There were the revolutionary committees, which had affinities with the Ba'ath parties of Saddam's Iraq and Assad's Syria. They were represented in all state organisations and large companies and served as guarantors of the Jamahiriya doctrine and of mass mobilisations, similar to the Red Guard in China or the Revolutionary Guard in Iran. Their 30,000 co-opted members received promotions and bonuses. They intervened in Benghazi to repress the first demonstration on 15 February 2011, which led two days later to the start of the uprising. The revolutionary committees were supported by militias known as the 'revolutionary guards' – armed, plain-clothes men who played a dissuasive, repressive role from the start of the insurrection.

There was also the Praetorian Guard, charged with the protection of Gaddafi and his family. Before the uprising, it was reckoned to number 15,000 men, organised into three large 'security' battalions (the Benghazi one was disbanded soon after the revolt began, but many of its officers and men withdrew to Tripolitania) and three combined brigades. The members of these units were recruited mainly from the two large tribes from central and southern Libya, Qadadfa and Magariha, which were considered loyal to the regime. They were rewarded through bonuses, in cash or in kind, such as cars or foreign travel. These units fought for nearly six months on three fronts: Marsa Brega, Misrata and Jebel Nafusa, and intervened swiftly in Tripolitanian towns (Zawiya, Sabrata, Zwara) to suppress the first signs of rebellion in February and March. Gaddafi's youngest son, Khamis, commanded one of the three brigades on the Misrata front; his older brother Mu'tassim led another.

In the early years after the revolution (1969–75), the regime did not draw power from the tribes in any way. But in 1975 the *Green Book* devoted a whole chapter to them[3] and they then became an essential component of the vote catching that was central to the system. Oil income was shared out carefully between tribes and regions, in order not to threaten social peace, and indeed the unity of the country.

CARROT AND STICK

Gaddafi knew how to deal with the tribes by a mixture of duress, threats, payments and negotiation. Far from a monolithic or pyramidal structure, Libyan tribes, in peacetime, are above all a flexible solidarity network that allows access to jobs or resources and enables personal or collective strategies. Depending on members' relations with the leader, belonging to a tribe can bring advantages or disadvantages. The important families of Misrata[4] – even if they were not a tribe in the strict sense[5] – were in favour with Gaddafi until 1975. Then, because of personal and ideological differences with Colonel Omar al-Mheichi, one of Gaddafi's original companions who came from Misrata, Gaddafi ended his alliance with them and turned to their traditional enemies, the Warfalla from Bani Walid. From then on, people from Misrata were kept out of sensitive positions (Praetorian Guard, security services) and relegated to administrative roles.

In times of conflict, the tribes provide an effective means of mobilisation in countryside and town (people who originate from the same region tend to live in the same district). Here too they are segmented in dozens of subgroups, each with its own sheikh. This explains why, at the start of the conflict, both sides claimed to have the allegiance of sheikhs from the same tribe. Members of the Qadadfa tribe in Benghazi pledged allegiance to the rebel National Transitional Council (NTC) but abstained from military action on its side. So the lists of tribes supporting the NTC or Gaddafi in the newspapers at the start of the conflict do not mean much.

In central, southern and western regions of the country, in the countryside and towns mainly inhabited by members of the large tribes who were deeply involved with the Gaddafi regime, there were few signs of rebellion. Some provided the regime with fighters or militias. This was especially the case in the Bani Walid region, stronghold of the Warfalla; in Tarhuna, fiefdom of the important Tarhuna tribal confederation, which represents more than half the population of Tripoli; in Sirte (Qadadfa); in Fezzan (Qadadfa, Magariha, Hassawna and Tuareg, who were long paid and recruited by the regime); in Tawurgha, whose inhabitants have an ancient animosity against those of nearby Misrata; and in Ghadames on the Algerian border, whose sizeable Jaramna population had remained loyal to Gaddafi.

Other regions, while sympathetic to the regime, remained neutral, waiting to see who would gain the upper hand: the towns of Mizda, stronghold of the Machachiya and the Awlad Bu Sayf; of Al Ujeylat, Waddan, Hun, Sukna and Zliten, whose Awlad Sheikh inhabitants distrust those of Misrata – which explains in part the fact that, despite repeated assaults and numerous NATO bombardments, the rebels from Misrata had failed to occupy it.

From one village to another there were different strategies, rooted in old enmities sometimes dating back to the Italian colonial period. One such is the rivalry between the Zintans and the Machachiya, who coexisted peacefully before the uprising in Mizda (though intermarriage was forbidden). When the town of Zintan, stronghold of the Zintan tribe, rebelled, the Zintan in Mizda joined their comrades in the insurrection, but did not attack Mizda, where the Machachiya had stayed neutral (unlike Machachiya in other villages, who joined Gaddafi's supporters). There are many such examples. The key fact is that traditional negotiation mechanisms made it possible to limit the violence and avoid irreversible situations which would make the reconstruction of a national community at the end of the conflict more difficult.

ATTEMPTS AT UPRISING QUASHED

The capital, Tripoli, saw no general uprising until the arrival of contingents from 'liberated' Tripolitanian towns for two reasons: the repressive security apparatus, with its Revolutionary Guards, security battalions and 'popular guards' (freed non-political prisoners organised in militias under the control of revolutionary committees); and the city's demographics. Unlike Benghazi, where the cohesion of the large tribes of Cyrenaica, united by the same rejection of the regime, made possible united action, half of Tripoli's population is made up of people from the large tribes that originate in the Bani Walid, Tarhuna and Fezzan regions, whose fate was closely linked to that of the regime; and the other half are members of small tribes or town dwellers, who do not constitute large enough groups to turn into fighting forces. So attempts at uprising in certain districts were rapidly quashed.

The tactical breakthrough on the Brega and Misrata fronts, which had been described as imminent for five months by NTC and NATO spokesmen, was finally accomplished by the powerful Arab Zintan tribe from Jebel Nafusa, who had only around 3,000 fighters at the start of May. One of the keys to its success was incorporating the Libyan tradition of according primacy to the local over the regional or national in its strategy: it was down to the inhabitants of each town or region to 'liberate' it. The Zintan, spearheading and unifying the rebellion in the west, were careful to recruit, train and equip battalions who come from the towns to be liberated (Zawiya, Sorman and Gharian). Those battalions then went on to conduct simultaneous assaults on those three towns.

So it was the ingenuity, respect for local conditions and the fighting spirit of a tribe which proved decisive – a tribe which is not represented in a significant way in the NTC executive committee. That shows how unrepresentative of the real insurrection this committee is, and how unconnected to core realities and to the 'Libyan people', whose representative it claims to be.

This shift to the west in the military focus of the rebellion, which had its first successes in the east, raises the issue of just how representative the National Transitional Council is. Currently it does not include any representatives of the victorious uprising in the west. In other words, if the NTC wants to continue to claim to be the legitimate representative of the Libyan people (which France and Britain recognised in March), it must quickly grant political representation to the western rebels proportionate to their critical role in the final military victory – or risk the rapid establishment of autonomous institutions in the west of the country.

The other challenge will be to incorporate in new institutions representatives of the regions and tribes which were long Gaddafi's major supporters: the regions of Sirte, Tarhuna, Bani Walid, Sebha, Ghat and Ghadames.

GUARANTEES NEEDED

Ending the current mindset of civil war will therefore depend on the NTC giving guarantees about the future to these people, and also to the least compromised military leaders and members of the revolutionary committees. If the insurgents, bolstered by their victory, try to impose their will by force of arms on the tribes which long supported Gaddafi and possess territorial strongholds, the logic of war will persist.

If the war is to end, the traditional Bedouin mechanisms of mediation and negotiation will have to play a key role. For although some tribes long supported Gaddafi, nothing is set in stone in the Bedouin tradition: pragmatism and group interest often prevail over the mindset of honour, highlighted in caricatured descriptions of these societies in the West. A general desire to get oil exports flowing quickly and to share the revenue between the regions in a fair and transparent manner may also have a stabilising effect, as long as the new powers leave the regions and towns a significant degree of autonomy in the running of their day-to-day affairs.

The exit strategy from civil war will be a real challenge for a country where arms are now widely available, which has no political culture and where local interests still predominate over national ones. At what point will NATO decide that the Libyan people no longer need its 'protection'?

Translated by George Miller

Patrick Haimzadeh was a diplomat at the French embassy in Tripoli from 2001 to 2004. He is the author of *Au cœur de la Libye de Kadhafi* (Inside Gaddafi's Libya), Jean-Claude Lattès, Paris, 2011.

1. See Jean-Pierre Séréni, 'The subtleties of Libyan crude' and Rachid Khechana, 'Libya: only revolution was possible', *Le Monde diplomatique*, English edition, April 2011.
2. This speech was remixed by an Israeli DJ, who turned it into a techno hit.
3. The short book setting out Gaddafi's political philosophy.
4. Residents of Misrata took up arms against the regime immediately after those of Cyrenaica. There are close historical and demographic ties between the people of Misrata and Benghazi, half of whose population is descended from immigrants from Misrata.
5. 'Tribe' is here taken to mean a group sharing an eponymous ancestor linked through paternal descent.

Part VII: The Question of Islam

❖ ❖

AUGUST 2010

SALAFISM MUST BE ENGAGED WITH RESPECT AND COURAGE

The Arab world's cultural challenge

To many, the Arab world is just a place of conflict and lack of democracy. But what is really at play are ever-changing, tacit alliances between three unequal forces: Islamists, secular intellectuals and the regimes themselves.

Hicham Ben Abdallah El Alaoui

For the last two centuries, the *ulema* (Islamic scholars) have always been suspicious of modern forms of cultural production and expression, which carve out spaces that engage social subjects in ways of understanding their lives and their world that are implicitly autonomous from religion. For the most part, whatever the *ulema* said, artistic and cultural practices have operated in a sphere that constituted a continuum, even if certain activities (modern art and painting) were more westernised and consumed mainly in *effendi* (westernised bourgeois) ghettos.

Underlying this wary tolerance was a theological mode of thought (*kalam*) in which religion encompasses more than sharia: it accommodates a pluralist notion of society as a vast ensemble where culture develops alongside religion. In this conception, a wide array of profane literary and artistic activity (poetry, calligraphy, plastic arts, music) can be understood as being in continuity with religion. In this way, diversity and creativity have remained an integral and treasured part of our history.

Part of the grandeur of Islam was its ability to absorb a myriad of cultural influences. The Muslim world protected, studied and developed the great traditions of classical literature and philosophy. It was not a place for burning books, but for building libraries to preserve them. It was, for some time, the guardian of the founding documents of what became known as 'western civilisation'. It understood that these were a part of the intellectual legacy of all mankind.

With the rise of Islamist movements, however, a new public norm took root, often characterised as Salafist, since it is based on a narrow version of a 'return' to religious orthodoxy. This new social norm is, for the most part, implicit – an unofficial ethos or ideology, only rarely enforced by legal or administrative sanction. But it is even *more* powerful as a result. The authority and centrality of the new Salafist norm derives not from the power of a regime, but from the fact that an unapologetic Islam has installed itself at the heart of Arab identity; it has become the central signifier of resistance to westernisation and neo-colonialism.

In earlier decades, Arab nationalism fought off any such overbearing religiosity; today, 'moderate' secular voices refrain from challenging it. They are caught in an identity trap, constantly limiting their discourse, in fear of being accused by religious conservatives or regimes of undermining Arab authenticity and independence – even Arab nationalism itself.

There was a striking example of this last summer, when a group of young Moroccans decided to break the Ramadan fast with a picnic in a public park. Along with the predictable reactions from religious quarters, the USFP, Morocco's main social-democrat party, also demanded punishment for the fast-breakers. This leftwing 'religiosity' was couched in nationalist terms: it was an insult to national culture, and a disruption of the consensus on Moroccan identity. The government charged the youths under a secular statute for an offence against 'public order', in a way that had never been done before. This simple challenge to the Salafist norm turned out to be too radical for all the politicians.

THE CULTURAL SEEN AS PAGAN

The public space is increasingly dominated by a cultural norm based on elaborating a set of strict rules, a series of dos and don'ts, read off from a strict construction of religious texts. As religion is becoming a more dominant element of public ideology, it is contracting around Salafism, creating a context in which the cultural is now more easily perceived by believers as not just profane, but pagan. A capacious understanding of Islam as a partner with culture has been shrunk into a narrow version of sharia that excludes the cultural. The passages between the sacred spaces of religion and the secular discourses of profane culture are being barricaded.

This dynamic of Salafisation occurs even as people continue to consume a proliferation of profane and secular cultural products via television, videos, the internet and popular literature. It is easy to identify the 'western' and global forces driving secular culture, and denounce it as 'foreign'; but this would be to ignore the creativity with which Arabs have appropriated and transformed the contemporary means of cultural production.

At the level of elite culture, there is a burgeoning patronage system for artistic modernisation, financed by western foundations and transnational NGOs – but also by foundations of the Gulf. At the popular level, there is the dissemination of western media conglomerates. But there is also the growing presence of indigenous media outlets – from news sources like Al-Jazeera and Al-Arabiya, through popular soap operas and the popular literature of self-help and romantic advice, to the explosion of musical and artistic creativity, which the internet has made possible and Arab youth have seized upon enthusiastically. In the Arab world as everywhere else, it is a prodigious cultural mash-up, whose commercialised version is the 'festivalisation' of modern Arabic culture – a phenomenon in which Arab businesses, promoters and middlemen are entirely complicit.

Most of these cultural practices are without religious intent, saturated with global influences and, to all intents and purposes, completely secular. Despite the growth of political Islam, attempts to Islamicise art and culture in the Arab world have been relatively weak and ineffective. Still, caught between the pressure for modernisation from secularised global culture and the pressure for solidarity and authenticity from the Salafised indigenous public norm, artists and cultural producers in the Arab world have taken to calling themselves 'Muslim' (but not 'Islamic') – even though their artistic practice has nothing to do with religion, and may be implicitly contributing to the secularisation of Arab societies. By calling themselves Muslim, they are affirming an identity, not a religious practice.

ADVANCING SCHIZOPHRENIA

What is occurring in the Arab and Muslim world is a kind of schizophrenia: in private, one regularly consumes the cultural profane (via television, videos, the internet and popular literature, or in carefully segmented semi-public spaces); in public, one proclaims one's Muslim identity, avoids going to a movie theatre, and perhaps makes a show of religiosity by attending the mosque, sporting a beard or a veil. The two forms of cultural experience unfold in parallel, but it is the religious norm that maintains hegemony in the public space. In the Arab and Muslim world today, cultural practices produce a process of secularisation, but no one may acknowledge or accept it.

This is not simply because of the social division between elites and masses. Well into the 20th century, there was a simple working compromise: westernised elites could traffic with profane culture while ordinary people stayed in the traditional cultural sphere dominated by Islam. But over the last few decades, education, literacy and the exponential growth in communication have brought profound changes. Contact with other languages and cultures has spread beyond the elite.

Today, we have increasing diversity in the Arab world: the young read novels, watch movies and videos, listen to music, read blogs – and *create* all of these things – in many different languages. They are not just consuming, but mastering, modern cultures that are intertwined with linguistic and cultural influences from the East, North, South – and, yes, the West.

It would be naive to presume that this diversification of mass culture will inevitably feed into movements for secularisation or democratisation. The same person reads novels or astrology books one day, and the next reads mass-produced religious tracts, bought in the same bookstore; or watches Ikraa (the Islamic TV chain) at lunchtime and Rotana (Saudi) after dinner.

The Salafists have adapted well to the new means of mass cultural diffusion: paperback devotional and inspirational tracts and internet blogs replace theological texts. What is important for the Salafists, as for the region's regimes, is that mass profane cultural consumption is seen as a distraction – not entirely respectable and with no implications for social or political change. One must show respect for the Salafist norm even if one does not practise it. Transgression is individual; the public norm is Salafist. This is a form of ideological 'soft' power that is far more effective than any bureaucratically enforced censorship.

There is schizophrenia in the attitude to language, too. The *ulema* always deemed a scholar's written work to hold the highest intellectual and social importance. The consequence, today, is a constriction in writing: an Arab intellectual does not write in the language he or she speaks. On this point, pan-Arab nationalism and Islamism agree: both insist that classical Arabic (*fosha*) is the only legitimate language for cultural expression. For pan-Arabists, *fosha* is the glue of the Arab nation; for Islamists, of the *umma* (community of believers). This ignores the profound divergences between actual usage (and even modern standard Arabic, the language of journalism, television, academic discourse and fiction) and *fosha*, which is rarely used outside of religious schools. It makes the novel a particularly suspicious genre, since it explores 'existential' questions of life and its meaning; the novel is not just independent of religion, it reinvents the Arabic language far beyond the limits of *fosha*.

The same ambivalence governs law. Each Arab state has its own legal code, but almost all refer to sharia as the ultimate source of law. Each state defines its own version of legality and 'Islamicity', and does so for the most part by incorporating some secular principles of rights and justice; but none can refuse to acknowledge the primacy of sharia. The primacy of the Islamic norm governs the Arab polity at the moment. This norm maintains itself as the public standard of judgment, yet it does not always define or determine the real practices of courts and the law.

POLICING PIETY

By accepting Salafisation in everyday mores (requiring or encouraging the Islamic headscarf, suppressing cinema, etc.), the modern authoritarian state can renew its alliance with the *ulema* – the official, state-sanctioned guardians of Islam, who are more interested in exchanging favours with regimes than reforming them. It can tolerate (while officially keeping at arm's length) quietest Islamist currents whose sharia programme consists mainly of mobilising religious ideologues (not agents of the state) who will obsessively police piety within the community. A modern state can act against the harshest sharia penalties (for example, stoning women who have been raped), but let the primacy of Salafism remain unchallenged.

Yet many secular intellectuals, who would otherwise pursue democratic reforms, end up relying on protection from the authoritarian state against the *ulema* or the fundamentalists; and find themselves having to defend it in return. To them, the state is the lesser evil to Islamism, protecting present spaces of cultural autonomy and the possibility of future liberalisation. For example, many secular intellectuals reluctantly supported the Algerian state during its struggle with the Islamists in the 1990s. Conversely, today in Egypt, the state protected the writer Sayyid al-Qemni after a fatwa against him (and in June 2009 gave him a medal).

The state can even enter into implicit covenants with some militant Islamist currents judged less of a threat than the Muslim Brotherhood. It may even grant such groups parliamentary status as tolerated opposition. This enables the regime to crack down more harshly on jihadists or other Islamists contesting state power.

BRAIN DRAIN

The precarious equilibrium among these contending social actors works to the advantage of the state, free to maintain a programme of harsh, but now more finely targeted, repression – all while reinforcing the Salafist norm.

Among intellectuals, this frustrating situation can produce various forms of political withdrawal. There is a real and virtual brain drain: many Arab artists and intellectuals live and work outside of their home countries. They might identify themselves as Arab and Muslim, rather than Egyptian or Tunisian, as they assert an identity whose founding elements are very close to those of Salafism: the Arabic language is *fosha* and to be Arab is inseparable from being Muslim. Intellectuals in geographic or ideological diaspora lose touch with their specific national and social base and become generic 'Arab' intellectuals.

This withdrawal to the abstract unity of a virtual international community is exacerbated by the poor support intellectuals often receive from their state economies. The lack of support has led to a cultural milieu that is individualistic and depoliticised, looking for foreign audiences and funding. This external patronage has been forthcoming from western organisations like the Ford Foundation, as well as the philanthropy of Gulf personalities. As a result, we now see an increasing number of cultural artefacts, representing an abstract Arab/Muslim identity, produced for, and appearing in, western galleries and Gulf showcases.

In the realm of fiction alone, we now have multiple competitions for the best examples of 'Arab' culture: the Emirates Foundation International Prize for Arabic Fiction (known as the 'Arabic Booker'), the Blue Metropolis Al Majidi Ibn Dhaher Arab Literary Prize (Lebanon), and the International Prize for Arabic Fiction (managed with the Booker Prize Foundation in London).

There is nothing wrong with this, or with the potential for the greater integration of artists in our region into cultural developments throughout the world. But it is troubling that, as the status of the 'Arab' artist rises among international audiences, he or she can become more disconnected from people at home, and less valuable to them.

INTERNET GENERATION

The internet has fostered new spaces of cultural production and consumption. But while it can contribute to the growth and efficacy of a politicised protest movement, it does not in itself create political awareness. As we have seen in Egypt and Iran, it is an effective new tool in mobilising, but cannot substitute for the kind of grassroots organising required for serious struggle.

Jihadis use the internet most inventively and effectively for organisation and propaganda. Their Salafism has no problem with the *technological* aspects of modern culture – perhaps because they distinguish between the praiseworthy 'thinker' (*moufakir*) versus the reviled 'intellectual' (*mouthakkaf*).

The internet also contributes to isolation and segmentation. Users tend to form discrete groups who communicate exclusively – and often anonymously – through their screens, continually reinforcing a closed discursive loop. Anonymity allows dissenters to ratchet up their radicalism, while avoiding open confrontation and escaping any harsh consequences. Through the internet, it is easy to mock power, and avoid the real world.

Artists and intellectuals no longer (except in places like Iran and Turkey) spearhead movements for social, political and cultural change. They have become, rather, a kind of 'court' faction, protected and tolerated by the state or by powerful and wealthy patrons, international and indigenous. The earlier contestatory figure of the artist, like the Egyptian writer, Sonallah Ibrahim, or the Moroccan musical group, Nass El Ghiwane, has largely disappeared. For example, the avant-garde Egyptian painter, Farouk Hosni, is now President Mubarak's minister of culture. Hannane Kessab Hassan, translator of Jean Genet, was chosen by Syria's prime minister in 2008 to direct the Unesco-sponsored programme 'Damascus, Arab Capital of Culture'. Artists like Wael Chawqi (featured in the Alexandria Biennial) and Hala El Koussy (winner of the Abraaj Capital Art Prize from the Gulf) are not engaged in political contestation, however modern their ideas on culture and society.

Modernising cultural movements in the Arab world have real progressive potential. Those involved in them gain a symbolic transnational capital. They can try to influence trends within their own society, using this capital. Since regime manipulation is not perfect, in ceding new spaces of cultural autonomy and experimentation a process is unfolding that, in the long term, could foster a new type of opposition to authoritarian rule in the Arab world.

One thing is certain. If artistic and intellectual practice is to have an effect on democratisation, it will be necessary to engage the Salafist paradigm on its home ground, and present a credible and consistent alternative. This is not a matter of adopting anyone else's prefabricated model. We must first of all reconnect with the Arab and Islamic tradition that built spaces for cultural autonomy over centuries. A new cultural norm, appropriate to the contemporary world as well as our own traditions, means engaging the Salafist model with respect, but also with courage.

Original text in English

Hicham Ben Abdallah El Alaoui is a board member of the Freeman Spogli Institute for International Studies; scholar at the Center on Democracy, Development and the Rule of Law, Stanford University; chairman of the board of the Center on Climate Change and the Challenge to Human Security, University of California; and adviser to Human Rights Watch.

❖❖❖❖❖❖❖❖❖❖❖❖❖❖❖❖❖❖❖❖❖❖❖❖❖❖❖❖❖❖❖❖❖❖❖

JULY 2011

RIFT DEEPENS BETWEEN SUPREME LEADER AND PRESIDENT

Iran can't reform itself

Since Ayatollah Khomeini's era, all Iranian presidents have acted as the executive of the Supreme Leader. But lately Mahmoud Ahmadinejad has failed to comply. Where will the confrontation lead?

Farhang Jahanpour

President Mahmoud Ahmadinejad sacked his intelligence minister, Heydar Moslehi, in April, but was forced to reinstate him a few days later under pressure from the Supreme Leader, Ayatollah Ali Khamenei. What began as an incident has led to an open rift within the leadership of the Islamic Republic.

Iran's constitution has many contradictory concepts. The system is called a republic, yet it is based on the concept of Velayat-e Faqih: the guardianship of the leading religious authority that is supposed to rule on behalf of the Hidden Imam.[1] The constitution gives the Supreme Leader enormous powers: his word is regarded as that of God and any opposition to him is seen as opposition to God, liable to the severest punishment. Iran is a republic founded on universal suffrage and its constitution allows presidential and parliamentary elections; yet the Guardian Council has to approve the credentials of all the candidates. The system has a parliament, but it can only legislate on the basis of sharia and all its resolutions must be approved by the Guardian Council, to ensure compatibility with sharia and the constitution.

In 1997 Mohammad Khatami was elected president. He tried to reform the system from within and introduce a degree of democracy, calling for the establishment of civil society and advocating the rule of law, not the rule of sharia. He opened up Iran's foreign policy, called for a dialogue of civilisations and took tentative steps towards the West.

After Khatami's two terms as president, Khamenei was determined not to repeat the mistake of allowing another reformist government, and in 2005, with the backing of hardliners, the Revolutionary Guards and the Basij (paramilitary groups of young men from disadvantaged backgrounds), supported the election of the relatively unknown Ahmadinejad, former mayor of Tehran and member of the Revolutionary Guards.

He launched a populist programme of distributing oil wealth among the poorer classes, promising to return the society to the purity of its earlier days under Ayatollah Ruhollah Khomeini. There was a concerted campaign against reformers: many of their leaders and intellectuals were arrested and imprisoned, and what was left of the reformist media was shut down. Female activists, artists, musicians, filmmakers and human rights advocates were repressed, many were arrested and their activities curtailed.

Before the last presidential election in June 2009, the reformers tried to reorganise themselves, and turned to Mir-Hossein Mousavi, who had been a popular prime minister during the Iran-Iraq war. Mousavi revived many of Khatami's slogans, appealed to the educated and reformist classes, and according to all independent accounts, won a resounding victory. Yet overnight everything changed, and the following day it was announced that Ahmadinejad had won by a large margin.[2] Ayatollah Khamenei appeared on the scene and even before the election results had been confirmed, put his full support behind Ahmadinejad, describing his election as a 'divine blessing'.

Millions of Iranians poured into the streets demanding 'Where is my vote?' The Green Movement was born and Iranian streets witnessed the biggest demonstrations since the 1979 revolution. The security forces, Basij militia and plainclothes thugs attacked, killing 70 demonstrators, wounding hundreds and detaining 4,000. When the Iranian regime claimed this spring that the uprisings in the Arab world had been inspired by the Islamic revolution, Mousavi and his reformist ally, Mehdi Karrubi, called on the Iranian people to demonstrate on 12 February to honour the uprisings in Tunisia and Egypt. According to some reports, more than 350,000 people did so, in spite of the regime's ban, facing bullets and beatings. Two were killed, scores injured and hundreds arrested. The following day the regime arrested both Mousavi and Karrubi and their wives. (Mousavi was not even allowed to attend the funeral of his father, who died while he was in detention.)

'IRANIAN' ISLAM

Ahmadinejad thought he could profit from all this and steer a more independent course, but had forgotten that he governed at Khamenei's behest. To win back some of the people who had lost faith in the regime after the election, Ahmadinejad and his friend Esfandiar Rahim Mashaei, who had been appointed first as vice-president and later as chief of staff in the president's office, began praising Iran's ancient history and spoke of an 'Iranian Islam'. Mashaei has spoken of the 'Iranian school of Islam', saying that Shiism is the most perfect interpretation of Islam, as it is based on the guidance of the imams; that Iranians have always been monotheistic and so enriched Islam; that Iranians have a 'pure understanding of the truth of faith', and that 'Iran is the very manifestation of faith'.

Ahmadinejad has supported these views. When the British Museum lent Cyrus's Cylinder[3] to Iran, Ahmadinejad gave a speech at the Iranian Archaeological Museum, praising Cyrus both as the founder of the Iranian empire and as a great moral guide of mankind. In a one-hour interview, he used the word 'Iran' 45 times. This emphasis on Iran angered conservatives who described his comments as heresy.

His former mentor and supporter, Ayatollah Mesbah Yasdi, spoke openly against the idea of Iranian Islam: he described Ahmadinejad's ideas as shameless, and referred to the affair as the second 'sedition', after the sedition of the reformist movement.

Conservatives were also angered by predictions by Mashaei and Ahmadinejad about the imminent return of the Hidden Imam; this year a series of documentary films, *The Reappearance is Imminent*, were released, suggesting that world events – natural disasters, wars, uprisings in Muslim countries, the recession – were the signs of the Imam's imminent return. The concept is similar to millenarian views in Judaism and Christianity, but the widely distributed films referred to Ahmadinejad by name as the embodiment of Shu'aib bin Salih, a saintly figure who would accompany the Hidden Imam.

The president and Mashaei could not compete with Ayatollah Khamenei and senior clerics in Islamic credentials. But with the coming of the Hidden Imam, the clerical establishment would be useless, and the president would help establish an era of peace and justice throughout the world. Ahmadinejad has always made a great show of his devotion to the Hidden Imam: he always starts all his public speeches with a prayer about his return, and has taken his cabinet to a well in Jamkaran Mosque near Qom, from where the Hidden Imam is supposed to emerge.

This presumption was even more unpalatable to the clerics than the concept of Iranian Islam. Ayatollah Mesbah Yazdi said ordinary people should not interpret the traditions concerning the Hidden Imam or predict his reappearance. The interpretation of holy writ was the exclusive right of leading clerics. Another senior cleric, Gholam Reza Mesbahi-Moqaddam, objected: 'If, God forbid, Ahmadinejad means that Imam Zaman [the Hidden Imam] supports the government's actions, this is wrong. Certainly Imam Zaman would not accept 20 per cent inflation rates, nor would he support this and many other mistakes that exist in the country today.'

LAY VERSUS CLERICAL ISLAM

Ahmadinejad and Mashaei have started to undermine clerics by laughing at them as out of touch with the modern world. In 2008 Mashaei hosted a ceremony in Tehran in which women played tambourines while another carried the Qur'an to a podium to recite verses. The clerics thought the festive mood, especially the use of music, disrespectful to the Qur'an, and even forbidden according to sharia. Mashaei called the clerics unfeeling, and said that music enhances spiritual qualities and purifies the soul; those who cannot appreciate this are worse than animals.

Ahmadinejad and Mashaei imply that people do not need clerics to teach them about Islam. While all previous presidents had close relations with the grand ayatollahs in Qom, Ahmadinejad and his allies have deliberately kept their distance. The president has taken his cabinet on provincial visits, but his visit to Qom province was postponed and when he did visit, on 25 May, he took only a few ministers and did not meet any leading cleric.

There is a struggle for power between Ahmadinejad and his supporters, and Ayatollah Khamenei and senior clerics, backed by the main commanders of the Revolutionary Guards. The attacks on Ahmadinejad by Khamenei's supporters have been vicious and had a religious dimension. Mashaei has been accused of sorcery, 'spiritualism' and associating with the *jinns* (genies). More than 20 presidential aides and advisers have been arrested on charges of sorcery.

The confrontation is not entirely based on religion, though. The Majlis (parliament) had called for the merging of ministries to reduce bureaucracy. Ahmadinejad merged the ministry of roads and transportation with housing and urban development, energy with oil, industries and mines with commerce, welfare and social security with labour, without the prior approval of the Majlis. He declared himself the caretaker minister of oil, just as Iran gained the chairmanship of OPEC for the first time after 36 years. The Guardian Council declared his action illegal, but he did not accept the ruling. A meeting was held between the leaders of the three powers in the presence of the Supreme Leader who said that the Guardian Council's ruling was final and the government had to obey it; the president remained obstinate. In June, the Majlis took the unprecedented step of referring him to the judiciary to be prosecuted for violation of the law. The next day, Ahmadinejad was forced to appoint a new head for the oil ministry.

The tug of war between Ahmadinejad and Khamenei continues. Ahmadinejad might resign, or he might be impeached, or at best he might be allowed to continue as an enfeebled president.

Mohammad Reza Bahonar, the first deputy speaker, said on 2 June: 'Earlier on, we came to the conclusion that the Master [Khamenei] was prepared to incur many costs and put an end to the life of the government, but we saw that the Master still would like the present government to continue its work calmly to the end of its legal term and the life of the tenth government may end naturally.' But he called on the government to distance itself from the 'deviationist movement', those who joined the June 2009 demonstrations. How will Ahmadinejad respond?

Original text in English

Farhang Jahanpour is former Dean of the Faculty of Languages at the University of Isfahan and senior Fulbright Research Scholar at Harvard; he teaches at the University of Oxford.

1. According to most Shia, the Twelfth Imam (descended from the line of Ali, the Prophet's son-in-law), who disappeared in 874, is not dead but 'hidden'. Ayatollah Khomeini held that the Supreme Leader was his representative on earth and held unlimited power; other ayatollahs disagree.
2. See 'Iran's Stolen Revolution', Open Democracy, 18 June 2009.
3. Clay cylinder from 539 BC bearing a proclamation by King Cyrus II.

❖ ❖

JULY 2011

AN OFFICIAL UNOFFICIAL CULTURE

Islamic Republic uncensored

Censorship did not work, so now the Iranian authorities encourage a twin-track culture, producing their own versions of popular media (which they can easily deny).

Shervin Ahmadi

On a weekday in March the streets of Tehran were deserted, as many of its 14 million inhabitants had gone away for Norouz – the Iranian New Year, marking the beginning of spring. In the Tajrish bazaar in the north of the city, a hand-written notice on card stood out: the latest DVD of Bitter Coffee was in stock. This comedy series, co-written, directed and produced by its star, Mehran Modiri, is available everywhere, in grocery shops and newspaper stands. Modiri has been appearing on Iranian television for 20 years, and his act has evolved with society. He uses gentle humour and farce, and never criticises the regime; although he occasionally pokes fun at television presenters based abroad, his material is not usually political.

Each Bitter Coffee DVD covers three episodes, and sells 1.5 million copies, at $2 (easily affordable by the middle classes) to discourage pirating, which is widespread. The series has its own website, Facebook page and Twitter account, and entries on Wikipedia in Persian and English. It is set in a medieval royal court, ridiculing courtiers and despotism. Viewers can draw parallels between the characters and historical personalities, from members of the former regime (including Reza Shah) to those currently in power.

On 2 April the daily newspaper *Shargh* reported that the ministry of culture and Islamic guidance would block release of the 20th DVD, because it wanted to 'make some modifications for administrative reasons'. The online site Aftab revealed the real reason: one of the characters resembled a senior member of government. In the end the DVD appeared without modifications.

Apart from such occasional, hesitant attempts at censorship, the authorities tolerate, and even encourage, a parallel network disseminating material including pirated and locally subtitled US action films, and Iranian films that have not been given a distribution licence, such as *Ali Santoori* by Dariush Mehrjui, about drug-taking teenagers with no prospects. People can also buy DVDs of programmes already broadcast on official channels. The tight control of the media during the first decade of the revolution, which was a failure, has given way to a less strict policy towards popular and youth culture. The authorities now saturate it with material they regard as 'less dangerous', while maintaining complete control over politics.

Two arenas are developing in parallel: the first is the official voice of the Islamic Republic; the second, less controlled, is allowed to deviate from the political and moral principles of the regime because the authorities can deny responsibility. It started out as a counter to the influence of imported western culture. Several singers emerged, copying the pop music style of Los Angeles (home to the largest Iranian community abroad), and mimicking, timidly at first, their Californian competitors. Some sounded the same as famous exiled singers, but performed poems with a mystic content. Then a second wave of more talented artists arrived. After a while their music and lyrics sounded exactly the same as those produced abroad, which the regime says spread corruption (*Mofsedin fil arz*, the expression the authorities use to describe 'westernised' people). Pop and rock music, until recently illegal and produced underground, are also distributed through this semi-official network, although less widely.[1]

HOLLYWOOD-STYLE SERIES

The official media scene has also become more diverse. There are now more state TV channels, and their content is more varied. There are locally produced series, often with big budgets, including a Hollywood-style history of the religious/historical characters Yusuf (Joseph) and Zuleika, political histories and comedies. Mehran Modiri has helped this transformation.

In the 1990s radio stations such as Payam, which originally just broadcast Tehran traffic reports, began playing music previously banned. Pop, which disappeared after the revolution, has made a comeback, and since it has been played on official channels it has become more acceptable to conservatives. In the 2000s, some music even incorporated *nohe* elements (Islamic liturgy commemorating the death of Imam Hussein in 690).

The media war intensified with satellite channels. Despite an official ban on dishes, many people have them, even in the countryside, and the government has given up trying to get rid of them. The government makes it clear that state channels could never have the same freedom as satellite channels to voice opinions and criticism in political news programmes. But political news in Iran (as elsewhere) does not attract a large audience, so the regime has concentrated on other areas. It has decided to turn a blind eye to programmes that are not directly political, which it judges 'less dangerous', even if they go against the moral principles of the regime. Today there are officially banned channels broadcasting non-stop music videos which do not correspond to 'Islamic values', with adverts that include Iranian mobile phone numbers.

The decision as to what material is 'less dangerous' is arbitrary. A film could be non-political, but arouse desire for western consumer lifestyles. Most of the urban middle class already has this desire – sometimes to excess. Iran has become the second biggest importer of cosmetics in the Middle East, seventh biggest in the world. And some commercial festivals, such as St Valentine's Day, unheard of 30 years ago, are now celebrated in the cities.

For the last three years the authorities have been confronted with the success of Farsi 1, a mass-audience television station owned by Rupert Murdoch's News Corporation, showing Latin American soap operas. The US journalist Dexter Filkins wrote that Farsi 1 had become so popular it was a threat to the government.[2]

Translated by Stephanie Irvine

Shervin Ahmadi is a journalist and editor of the Persian edition of *Le Monde diplomatique*.

1. See Wendy Kristianasen, 'The view from Tehran Avenue', *Le Monde diplomatique*, English edition, February 2004.
2. *The New York Times*, 21 November 2010.

❖ ❖

JANUARY 2010

LESS THREATENING THAN EUROPE IMAGINES

The myth of Islamic conquest

The Swiss vote to ban minaret building reflects concerns about Islamic expansionism. The reality is less threatening. Those in Europe who lay claim to political Islam have failed to influence the third generation of Muslim immigrants, who just want to express their faith in individual ways.

Patrick Haenni and Samir Amghar

A question worries Europe: is Islam inherently expansionist and out to conquer the world? Yes, say those Swiss who voted against the construction of minarets. They see this expansionism underpinned by a desire for political control, sometimes imputed to the nature of Islamic ideology (pro-birth, proselytising, invasive), sometimes to the tactics of its main players (the Islamists and their agendas). Yussuf al-Qaradawi, a well-known moderate Sunni cleric, seemed to endorse this in his Al-Jazeera broadcast of 6 December, 'Sharia and life', on the Swiss referendum. He confirmed that conquest would happen and that all humans would be united by the word of God.

Questions about the nature of Islam are fair: like Christianity, Islam sets out to save humanity, a message implicit in the history of its prophecies. But what does religious expansionism mean in concrete terms? From a sociological point of view it can involve an aggressive move (political, propagandist, armed), increased religiosity (conversion or revivalism), or demographics.

In continental Europe the Muslim Brotherhood and the Turkish Milli Gorus[1] are groups with a political agenda. They seek the creation of an Islamic state, built not on universalist beliefs (Islam represents a religion for everyone) but aiming at domination, following the goal of guiding the world assumed by Hassan al-Banna, founder of the Muslim Brotherhood. They did not settle in Europe in the 1950s for those reasons, but because it provided a base for their fight in North Africa and the Middle East. That Muslim populations made their homes in Europe took them by surprise and caused them problems.

Being a minority community in Europe counters all the strategic plans of the agents of political Islam, trapping them in a dilemma: should they preach or lobby? The first option would put them in territory already occupied by the Salafist movement and the Tabligh organisation,[2] both groups that the political scientist Olivier Roy calls neo-fundamentalist. The second option would put the onus on them to find enough activists in a European context; pushing to become figures of authority can reduce their appeal to fellow Muslims suspicious of compromise with the powers that be.

The Brotherhood's predicament illustrates this well: by playing the institutional card they have, over time, lost their revolutionary verve, abandoned major causes and turned their backs on sensitive issues such as Palestine or, in France, wearing the hijab. Young Muslims criticise them and sometimes distance themselves from the Brothers because of their middle-class ways and their accommodation with the authorities. Even the charismatic Tariq Ramadan (whose appeal to young French Muslims was high) was disowned by former supporters when, in 2005, he put together a working party commissioned by the UK's government (under Tony Blair) to investigate religious extremism.

That the proponents of political Islam find it hard to adopt credible strategies in the West benefits neo-fundamentalist movements, which reject conventional political involvement. These form a nebulous grouping of which the most important is Wahhabi or 'scientific' Salafism (salafiyya ilmiyya); originating in Saudi Arabia, its characteristics are sectarian rigour and dogmatic radicalism – although remote from any idea of jihad or holy war. This variety of Salafism recruits from people disappointed in political Islam and in long-established neo-fundamentalist groups such as the Tablighis.

Far from proposing a fresh programme aimed at political control, this type of Salafism offers the bitter fruit of a depoliticised Islam and an ideological narrative that argues for withdrawing from western society, avoiding it: a community based on faith replaces one based on culture (Tunisian, Moroccan) and is very critical of the traditional Islam practised by ordinary families. In this way Salafism builds its own sectarian logic. Silent on the issue of the hijab, its protagonists offer no help when imams are expelled and they do not take part in demonstrations of solidarity with Palestine.

This call for withdrawal operates less in normal family or community life than among the numbers of newly Islamised young (known as the *firqa najiyya*). Salafism challenges the role of traditional imams, setting itself up in opposition to the real-life Muslim world and successful with those in distress, particularly the young. It does very little recruiting in strongly nationalistic communities like those from the Comoros or the Turks.

PARTING DESIRES

Its aim is not to conquer the West or establish Islamic ghettoes, but *hijra* (exodus), a return to Islamic countries – or failing that, to countries like the UK or Canada that are thought to be more tolerant to Muslims. So the young whom it attracts find themselves stuck, simply waiting, as their parents before them, instead of becoming involved in western society. But where their parents lived with the myth of returning to their land of origin, these young Salafists desire to leave their country of birth.

The formulation of any credible political project is blocked because they are a minority and because evangelical initiatives (the call for da'wa and the desire to return to Islam) are not part of an 'Islamic reconquest'. Nor is armed jihad. In Europe, jihadism is lived as a quest for sacrifice, not as politics by other means. Militant groups, like al-Qaida or the Metin Kaplan movement,[3] share the same sectarian mindset as non-combatant Salafists. Jihadists accuse of apostasy (*takfir*) all those adversaries they would like to fight: Jews and Christians, Muslims claimed not to practise properly – even the Muslim Brotherhood. There is no attempt to create a West of ghetto counter-cultures. On the contrary, the radical nature of jihadism, and Salafism drives them to break ties with the community and local area where people live,[4] and with the mosque – which it sees as too easily controlled by the authorities, compromised because it is a place for community dialogue. Jihadist recruiting takes place in internet cafés, sports clubs, prisons.

The new jihadists have pushed hatred to the limits. They have no precise objective (a land or state to liberate or win over, or political party to reform, or regime to bring down); their aim is restricted to armed struggle and its media impact, along with the destruction of the symbols of political imperialism (the US and its allies).

If the militant dynamic of the Islamists no longer pushes for conquest, can it still use the back door of religious renewal and so tip European societies' political balance or create Islamised spaces within them?

It's easy to mistake the high visibility of Islam in the West for a massive return to piety in Muslim communities. But for the last 20 years religious observance has stagnated, even slightly waned. Its reappearance is at an individual level, not as part of a shared project, even if it stems from a desire for communal solidarity, and corresponds most of all to the need to rediscover identity and roots.

Two wide currents are found in the present religious revival. First, marketplace Islam:[5] religiosity freed from the Islamist obsession with politics, and distinguished by a search for cultural normalisation of the Muslim identity. Fashionable Islamic streetwear (combining jeans, trainers and the hijab), halal pop and Muslim Up (a French soft drink like cola) all express an affirmation of Islam rooted in mass culture. Religion does not offer a complete solution but it does represent a concern for ethics in a globally accepted western culture. (Whereas neo-fundamentalism seeks to break with the western way but has no expansionist aims because its followers are waiting to leave.)

CHOICES ARE INDIVIDUAL

As for converts, they exist only in small numbers and work both ways, though the balance favours Islam. In France, according to the interior ministry, about 800 Muslims become Christians each year (usually evangelical), against 4,000 converts to Islam. Religious returnees are very visible, particularly in the physical appearance and clothes of born again Muslims and converts – men with beards, veiled women – but they are hardly institutionalised. Choices are individual, not those of organisations, and they have no wider meaning.

So this new kind of religiosity is both more public and less political. It poses an ideological problem in a country as strongly secular as France but it does not constitute a political threat or a security risk – except when jihadists are involved.

The fairy stories about ghettos being Muslim enclaves about to be hijacked by Islamist agents hatching plans of collective rupture with society are equally wrong. Even if the concentration of Muslim population in some areas may show signs of social control, it doesn't amount to a politically driven, communitarian strategy. It seems, rather, the consequence of complex economic, social and political processes, combined with the attitude of the powers that be – not only in countries like Holland and the UK where multiculturalism is encouraged, but also in France. The race for the Muslim vote, the occasional allocation of social housing on ethnic criteria, the search for local community figures to keep an eye on the deprived French suburbs, and the desire to control Islam through the French Council of the Muslim Faith (CFCM) created in 2003 – all smack of multicultural behaviour.

However, the Muslim Brotherhood, whose power base lies in the middle classes, has not made its mark in the French suburbs. The complete failure of the fatwa calling for calm issued by the Union of Islamic Organisations in France (UOIF, an organisation with links to the Brotherhood) during the 2005 riots in France proved that, and not for the first time. And if the Salafists are present in the suburbs, they are not in control either. Their influence remains limited; they have no experience of structuring a strong social movement in such a way as to acquire a leadership role; and their objective remains not to create Islamised or rebel urban spaces but a return to the *dar al-Islam* (lands of Islam).

In the areas where most Muslims live, individual values are emerging today in a strong way alongside consumer society. Witness the growth of mixed marriages,[6] including those of immigrant women, the problems of the Muslim associations, weakened parental authority and the very few religion-based schools. There are also the setbacks suffered when activists have tried to put together multicultural lists for local elections.

Twenty years ago, when there was no such thing as a Muslim part of town, any return to religion always took place within the context of an organisation. In contrast, today, a Muslim environment – with all its social and religious customs, bookshops, places of worship, halal butchers – has made for re-Islamisation on a highly individualistic basis, even for the first generation of immigrants.

MINORITY STATUS

The European context of a modern nation state and democracy, and Islam's minority status, are not conducive to establishing a dialogue between religion and politics. And within the Islamist circles authorised to take part in the political game, there is a desire to separate the *da'wa* (preaching) from the politics. Meanwhile, because the Islamists have proved unable to formulate a coherent project, forms of neo-fundamentalism such as Salafism have emerged, banishing politics to the distant realms of millennial dreams.

However, many Muslims who seek to play a public role now see this in terms of pure (secular) politics. Some Muslim Brothers make themselves heard within traditional political parties, both on the left and right. And Muslims[7] are presenting their demand for rights for a population of immigrant origin as a matter of cultural, and secular, identity.

These diverse processes of rupture between religion and politics reveal an implicit recognition that the idea of conquest is illusory. Whether old dreams of expansionism linger on is immaterial. What is important is that such a possibility has been ruled out by the transformations that have taken place at the heart of Muslim society.

Translated by Robert Waterhouse

Patrick Haenni is senior researcher at the Fondation Religioscope and co-author, with Stéphane Lathion, of *Les Minarets de la discorde. Eclairage sur un débat suisse et européen*, Infolio, Paris, 2009; Samir Amghar is a sociologist at the Ecole des hautes etudes en sciences sociales, Paris.

1. Founded in the 1970s by a former Turkish prime minister, Necmettin Erbakan, the movement is strong among Europe's Turkish population.
2. Salafism is a reformist branch of Islam which grew up during the 19th century and bases itself on the prophet Muhammad's teachings and the first generation of Muslims (the word *salaf* means ancestor). The Tablighi organisation, created in India during the 1920s but now scattered round the world, believes its principal task is to proclaim Islam's message through proselytising to other Muslims.
3. A radical movement founded in Germany in 1984, accused of many terrorist attempts.
4. See Olivier Roy, *Globalized Islam: The Search for a New Ummah* (The Ceri Series in Comparative Politics and International Studies), Columbia University Press, New York, 2004.
5. Patrick Haenni, *L'Islam du marché, l'autre revolution conservatrice*, Seuil, Paris, 2005.

6. Emmanuel Todd also shows in *Le destin des immigrés* that the rate of mixed marriages for Algerian women grew from 6.2 per cent to 27.5 per cent between 1975 and 1990. For Moroccan women it increased from 4 per cent to 13 per cent.

7. For instance, the Muslim Brothers who dominated the scene in the 1990s, and the Indigenes de la République (a French movement calling for an end to discrimination) in the 2000s.

❖ ❖

NOVEMBER 2010

ISLAM IN THE PANCASILA STATE

Indonesia, a democracy full stop

Indonesia's disasters get more media attention than its elections. Yet last year these marked, with the direct re-election of the president, a cautious step away from Islamising agendas, reaffirming the country's historic balance of secularism with Islam.

Wendy Kristianasen

The compromise almost didn't happen. Just seven words in the preamble to the Indonesian constitution would have made Indonesia an Islamic state: 'Muslims are bound to follow Islamic law.' They were withdrawn at the very last moment, on 18 August 1945. And Indonesia became the Pancasila state, based on five principles – belief in one God, humanitarianism, national unity, representative democracy, social justice – a historic compromise between secularism and Islam.

'Indonesia is the seat of a moderate, smiling Islam,' said Shafi Anwar, director of the International Centre for Islam and Pluralism. 'But with 9/11, the spread of radicalisation and conservatism, and the 2002 Bali bombings, suddenly we were frowned upon. My purpose is to convey the message that democracy is compatible with Islam.'

The country's democratic opening began in 1998 after two long periods of authoritarian rule, first under Sukarno, the founding president (1945–67) who juggled the three great forces: nationalism, Islam and communism (Indonesia then had the world's third biggest communist party). Then under Suharto (1967–98) who seized power on the pretext of a communist threat. Half a million or more died[1] and the country remains traumatised by these events.

Indonesia is now the world's third biggest democracy. 'That's something the West always overlooks,' said Anies Baswedan, rector of Jakarta's Paramadina University. 'They always refer to us as the world's biggest Muslim population. We say we are a democracy full stop. We have a free press, a dynamic political process, a vibrant civil society. Yes, there is corruption, there always was, but now there's transparency and it gets reported. The economy is resilient in this current world crisis, compared with that of our neighbours and with what is was ten years ago.' The Asian financial crisis of the late 1990s hit Indonesia hard. 'And yes, we have our Islamists and fundamentalists, but they have mostly been absorbed into the political process.'

Indonesia has a population of more than 240 million, 200 million of them Muslim, mostly Sunni.[2] Java is at the heart of this far-flung archipelago, now home to two-thirds of all Indonesians. The two main Muslim organisations, which divide along 'traditionalist' and 'modernist' lines (though both staunchly support Pancasila), began in Java long before the departure of the Dutch and independence.

The 'traditionalists' are mainly represented by Nahdlatul Ulama (NU), established in 1926, which has over 40 million followers, many of them rural, and accommodates local cultures that predate Islam. As Endy Bayuni of the *Jakarta Post* said: 'There is no single NU voice; they are led by a bunch of charismatic but independent *ulema* who often contradict one another, even when the NU chair speaks out; it's what makes them dynamic and interesting.'

The second biggest organisation, Muhammadiyah, represents the 'modernists' (in the sense of purist) and has 30 million followers. Founded in 1912, they are more urban, builders of schools, hospitals and universities, and more puritanical than NU. Abdul Muti, secretary-general, said: 'We are like Salafists in that we have the Qur'an as our first source, but our conclusions are different. Like Salafists, we're puritanical, but even so we're tolerant; our reference is Muhammad Abduh, not the Muslim Brothers or Maududi.[3] We also strongly believe in cooperation with ordinary people, and here we're closer to NU than to the Salafists. Indonesia isn't an Islamic state, it's a secular one. And this isn't the Middle East.'

'The organisation is like your family,' said Arifah Rahmawati, a researcher at Gadjah Mada University in Yogyakarta, central Java. She is a progressive: for years she lived alone in the house she owns, does not wear a headscarf and drinks wine. 'That annoys them. Yet even if I'm against their puritanical ways, I'm from a Muhammadiyah family, and still feel a sense of belonging and count myself one of them.' Her colleague Eric Hiarietj, a sociologist, added: 'After ethnicity, religion is what identifies you. When you meet someone in Java, first you ask if they are *santri* [devout] or *abangan* [nominal Muslim]. If they're *santri*, the next question is are they NU or Muhammadiyah?'

AN ISLAM THAT DRAWS FROM MANY ROOTS

Yogyakarta and nearby Surakarta (Solo), with their sultans, are the heart of *abangan*. The sultan of Yogyakarta, Hamengkubuwono X, has real power as regional governor; he is also the 'axis of the world', united with the spirit serpent-queen of the Southern Ocean in a mystical union. The local, the Hindu-Javanese and the Islamic meet in his person, and his palace or *kraton* reflects an astonishing fusion of religions and cultures, Hindu, Buddhist, Muslim, Christian, as do his family members, though he himself is Muslim. The Muhammadiyah movement with its Salafist teachings started here in reaction to that syncretic Javanism: Ahmad Dahlan, its founder, was born in the Muslim quarter behind the sultan's palace.

Toha Rudin, public relations director of Muhammadiyah University in Solo, like most Javanese, admires Java's courtly values: 'They are about tradition, benevolence and the wisdom that comes from an ancient way of ruling. I think Muhammadiyah should be more open to all this.'

NU's core home is in Jombang in east Java. The simple grave of its long-serving president Abdurrahman Wahid – known affectionately as Gus Dur, and Indonesia's president from 1999 to 2001 – draws hundreds of men and women freely mingling in prayer close to the *pesantren* (Islamic boarding school) founded by his grandfather. Gus Dur is often called 'the tenth saint', a reference to the nine Sufi saints or *sunan* who brought Islam to Java. As Ahmad Suaedy pointed out, 'Gus Dur felt close to indigenous beliefs and wanted an Islam which drew from these many roots. Our imams are not like ayatollahs, they have normal jobs, go to market. People consult them on farming, money, all sorts of things. They don't wear formal clothes. It's all part of our informal network, cultural and religious.'

NU and Muhammadiyah, from the beginning, both played an important role in the development of the country. Now they have chosen to put religious and social issues to the fore and downplay their political roles.[4] Both assimilate a broad range of personal views and have produced younger offshoots representing students, etc., some of them very progressive (known as 'liberal'), such as the Liberal Islam Network (JIL). The elders are wary of these 'too liberal' voices, wishing that those who express uncomfortably progressive views would not do so in the name of Islam. In a 2005 fatwa, the Indonesia Ulema Council (MUI) condemned liberals for trying to define Islam as they choose.

But liberal Muslims refuse to be silent in controversies over religiously inspired reforms, and there were more of these as Indonesia took an Islamic turn in the late 1990s. This resurgence had begun in the 1980s under Suharto, and in the 1990s a new Muslim middle class developed, which had been educated in *pesantrens*. Funding from the Middle East, and mosque building, helped. Dress is a key marker: a majority of women now wear pretty, pastel-coloured headscarves (known in Indonesia as *jilbab*), though downtown, outside the Islamic beltways, plenty of women go bareheaded. I saw no *niqabs* or black robes: the rarely seen ultra-devout dress in white from head to toe. In *pesantrens* and Islamic universities classes are mixed, but with girls on one side, boys the other. The mainstream organisations favour modest dress and scarves, but not the face veil. Abdul Muti said: 'Women should show their faces, it's important for social reactions.'

Eric Hiariej recalled: 'In the early 1990s when I was a student, only one out of 60 girls wore the *jilbab*. Now it's a fashion. On campus it's just your peer group that counts, so people are open to new trends and to radical movements.' Among these, Hizbut Tahrir Indonesia (HTI), founded in 1998, is in particular seen as an agent of radicalisation. As elsewhere in the world, it is vocal and well organised, and targets university students with its persuasive call for a return to the Caliphate. Ismail Yusanto, HTI's spokesman, claimed to condemn violence: 'Indonesia is not a suitable place for jihad. But,' he added, 'in Iraq, Afghanistan or Palestine it's different; there we don't consider violence as terrorism.'

FEAR OF FUNDAMENTALISM

Indonesia's *pesantrens* have been accused of fostering fundamentalism. Yet almost all follow NU or Muhammadiyah. Parents pay to have their children schooled from primary level up in a tough double curriculum, secular and religious, and nurtured in a safe religious environment. Graduates may go on to either secular or Islamic universities.

The few radical clerics linked to *pesantrens* have captured dispro-portionate media attention, especially since the 2002 Bali bombings. The best-known example is the Al-Mukmin *pesantren* at Ngruki near Solo where the firebrand preacher, Abu Bakar Bashir (72), leader of Jema'ah Islamiyah (JI) and its jihadist offshoots, has done much of his teaching. Bashir is now in prison. Ustad Wahyuddin, the *pesantren* director, spoke in his place: 'Every Muslim has a vision of an Islamic state; we want to *fight* for sharia, not watch and wait. This *pesantren* is a resource for propagating new values of Islamic law. And if one or two of our graduates have become radical [jihadis], it's because they went to Afghanistan or Pakistan and got involved in politics.'

Bashir was arrested on 9 August, for the third time since the original Bali bombings in 2002, accused of funding a terrorist training camp in Aceh. Its discovery was followed by that of a coalition led by Dulmatin, one of the region's most wanted terrorists, suspected of helping to plot and execute the 2002 Bali bombings. Dulmatin was killed, with seven others. Previously, in 2009, Noordin Top, the Malaysian mastermind of bombings in Jakarta in 2003, 2004 and 2009 and Bali in 2005, had been also killed.

These police successes suggest that terrorist violence in Indonesia may be a force in decline. Crisis Group's Indonesia specialist Sidney Jones says that successive internal rifts are weakening militant groups, composed of a changing mix of local thugs (such as the Islamic Defenders Front, FPI), ideological movements and pan-regional terror networks (Indonesia, Malaysia, the Philippines). In Indonesia, resort to violence loses Bashir popular support for his latest mass anti-democracy movement, Jama'h Ansharut Tauhid.[5]

Though the jihadist threat cannot be dismissed, its likely wane is a relief to mainstream Muslim groups. Abdul Muti said: 'For Muhammadiyah, terrorism is particularly worrying: some of the culprits came from our background, and radicals could infiltrate us because we're open, and therefore vulnerable.'

Extremists, in particular the FPI and Laskar Jihad, continue to provoke violence against religious minorities; this year there have been 28 incidents in west Java and around Jakarta, leading up to a violent attack on Christians at Bekasi on 12 September. The Ahmadiyah (a sect many do not consider Muslim) have suffered particular persecution. A fatwa by the MUI, for which HTI had lobbied hard, led to their suspension on 9 June 2008.

A GREATER ROLE FOR ISLAM

Democratisation after the fall of Suharto in 1998 inadvertently opened the way to demands for a greater role for Islam. Two new Muslim parties appeared, the Crescent Star Party (PBB) and the Prosperous Justice Party (PKS). There were also renewed attempts to introduce Islamic law nationally, which failed. But with decentralisation in 2000 – one of Indonesia's most far-reaching reforms – efforts turned to the introduction of sharia at district (*kabupaten*) or municipal (*walikota*) level, using local regulations (*peraturan daerah*, known as *perda*). Such regulations have since been introduced in some 50 out of 470 districts/municipalities.[6]

Aceh, after 30 years of separatist struggle, acquired 'special autonomy' status and, as a concession, gained full province-wide sharia – with a criminal court – on 15 August 2005. However, Aceh's sharia is not seen as representative of the rest of Indonesia (no other province is likely to win it). It has provoked considerable debate among Muslims. Ahmad Suaedy, of the liberal NU-linked Wahid Institute (named after Abdurrahman Wahid), said: 'We at Wahid are very critical. We think sharia in Aceh is artificial: it's transporting medieval Arab rules to the 21st century without re-assessing them through *ijtihad* [independent legal reasoning].' Abdul Muti of Muhammadiyah (with its Salafist leanings) also expressed concern: 'It's problematic. After five years there's been no significant progress in Aceh; their problems were economic. And people go to nearby North Sumatra to watch movies, so why ban them in Aceh? In any case, sharia means a uniformity of religious understanding which is contradictory to the spirit of Islam.'

Some mainstream Muslims disagree. Professor Masykuri Abdillah, vice-chairman of NU, said: 'We support sharia in Aceh because it is the democratic wish, although we have an internal debate at NU on stoning and flogging, and on whether that goes against Pancasila.' In reference to *perda* sharia, he said: 'Provided it doesn't discriminate, we support sharia in personal law.' Others in NU do not. The concept of sharia is vague to most Indonesians, since Islamic law has not been codified. Asked what sharia means, a typical answer is 'goodness'. As 'God-given', it is hard to oppose, at least in simple personal matters such as marriage, inheritance, dress, tax. But opposition to criminal sanctions is near universal. Moreover, liberals insist that *ijtihad* is necessary, as a means to determine whether Qur'anic precepts are suitable to modern times.

Perda sharia means that in Tangerang, outside Jakarta, women may not walk alone at night for fear of being charged with prostitution (as happened in 2006). In Padang in West Sumatra, all state-educated girls, Muslim or not, must wear a headscarf at school. Curiously though, a professor at Padang's Andalus State University, and father of a teenage girl, said that 'outside school, when my daughter goes out shopping or anywhere else, she doesn't wear *jilbab*' – an illustration of the many contradictions surrounding *perda* sharia.

In Makassar in South Sulawesi, known for its rigid interpretation of Islam, there have been attempts to introduce sharia. Dr HM Siradjudden is secretary-general of the Committee for the Implementation of Islamic Sharia (KPPSI), founded in 2000 by the head of the local Muhammadiyah branch. He said the goal was 'not to create an Islamic state but establish an Islamic society. When Aceh got autonomy and sharia, it gave the people of Sulawesi hope that we could have them too.' After their first Congress in 2000, a local poll at the end of 2002 'found 91.11 per cent in favour of sharia,' said Siradjudden. In that same year the district of Bulukumba banned alcohol, and a year later introduced *zakat* and imposed Islamic dress on all women, Muslim or not, asking for government services. In 2006 it introduced compulsory courses in Arabic writing. 'My vision is a charter as in the time of the Prophet,' said Siradjudden. 'The greatest moments of glory of our past Islamic kingdoms were when they implemented sharia.'

Professor Abu Hamid, rector of Makassar's University of 45 and also a member of the KPPSI, is trying to moderate this vision. He seemed pleased to tell me that 'Bulukumba, under a new regent, has now downscaled its reforms, from mandatory to optional'. This is in line with what is happening countrywide. The number of *perda* regulations were at their height in 2003, but had dropped dramatically by 2007,[7] and there have been virtually no new regulations since the legislative election in 2009.

Liberal Muslims have helped to rouse public awareness, and debate, on other issues. They oppose bans on pornography and prostitution – as do others closer to the Muslim mainstream. Anies Baswedan says of the anti-pornography law, backed by Muslim political parties and upheld by the Constitutional Court this March: 'The law was unnecessary; it was already provided for in criminal law.' He also opposes a ban on prostitution that hardliners seek to impose as 'morally wrong'.

Polygamy, a widely accepted practice, is also being debated by liberal Muslims. 'Some liberals even question whether it is Islamically authorised,' said Abdel Kadir Riyadi, a lecturer at Sunan Ampel University in Surabaya. 'It is widespread among rich and poor, even academics, and especially politicians; there are no statistics but I rate it at about one or two men in five.[8] But polygamy isn't mentioned in the constitution so there can be no official debate; NU and Muhammadiyah take no formal position.'

The legislative election on 9 April 2009, followed on 8 July by Indonesia's second direct presidential election, went nearly unreported in the West.[9] Yet they revealed that Islamist agendas, including sharia, no longer sold: support for Muslim parties dropped to 25 per cent – from 40 per cent in 1999 and 2004. Instead, Indonesians voted for secular parties that took account of Muslim concerns. Only the PKS, which with its professionals and cadres has features in common with Turkey's ruling AKP Party (although many suspect it of Muslim Brotherhood leanings), increased its votes – by taking them from other Muslim parties. And at its congress this June, the PKS decided to discard its Islamic image. Its deputy secretary-general Fahri Hamzah said: 'It is only a matter of time before we open up the party to non-Muslims; our values are democratic and universal.' Some observers believe that even the fashion for Islamic dress may now be waning among ordinary Indonesians.

As Indonesians make their choices, Kamala Chandrakirana, a secular activist and feminist, was hopeful: 'After a decade of crisis, with terrorism, tsunami, economic crisis, avian flu, perhaps we are now emerging. We have an amazing civil society, and there are signs that people who defend Pancasila may present an alternative to Islamisation that captures the imagination of the young. These could be exciting times for Indonesia.'

Original text in English

Wendy Kristianasen is a journalist and editorial director of the English edition of *Le Monde diplomatique*.

1. For an account of Indonesia since statehood, read Adam Schwarz, *A Nation in Waiting: Indonesia's Search for Stability* (3rd edn), Talisman, Singapore, 2008; and Benedict Anderson, 'Exit Suharto: obituary for a mediocre tyrant', *New Left Review*, London, vol. 50, March–April 2008.
2. According to the 2000 census, 88.2 per cent of the population described themselves as Muslim, 5.9 per cent Protestant, 3.1 per cent Roman Catholic, 1.8 per cent Hindu, 0.8 per cent Buddhist, and 0.2 per cent 'other' including traditional indigenous religions, other Christian groups and Jewish.

3. Muhammad Abduh was a 19th-century Egyptian reformer; Abul Ala Maududi founded the Islamist movement Jamaat-i-Islami in India in 1941.

4. See Robin Bush, *Nahdlatul Ulama and the Struggle for Power within Islam and Politics in Indonesia*, Institute of Southeast Asian Studies, Singapore, 2009, and Greg Barton and Greg Fealy (eds), *Nahdlatul Ulama, Traditional Islam and Modernity in Indonesia*, Monash Asia Institute, Clayton, Australia, 1996.

5. See 'Indonesia: jihadi surprise in Aceh', Asia Report no. 189, Crisis Group, 20 April 2010, and 'Indonesia: the dark side of Jama'ah Ansharut', Asia Briefing no. 107, Crisis Group, 6 July 2010.

6. For a detailed account read Robin Bush, 'Regional sharia regulations in Indonesia: anomaly or symptom?' in *Expressing Islam: Religious Life and Politics in Indonesia* (Greg Fealy and Sally White, eds), Institute of Southeast Asian Studies, Singapore, 2008; asiafoundation.org

7. See Robin Bush, op. cit.

8. In Indonesia, there is full marriage with civil and religious legality; paid 'contract' marriage, for an agreed length of time, not recognised in law or Islam; 'secret' marriage (*nika sirri*), admitted in Islam but not in civil law; and polygamy.

9. The well-respected Susilo Bambang Yudhoyono was re-elected at the first round with more than 60 per cent of the vote.

Part VIII:
On the Move: People and Cities

❖❖❖❖❖❖❖❖❖❖❖❖❖❖❖❖❖❖❖❖❖❖❖❖❖❖❖❖❖❖❖❖

MAY 2010

WHERE THE LION RIDES THE DRAGON

Africa does business in China

One zone of Guangzhou, China's workshop-of-the-world province, is home to perhaps 100,000 Africans, here to buy for the export market. Some of them are already considering moving on to India.

Tristan Coloma

This place is not really China, nor is it Africa; it lies between the thoroughfares of Xiaobei Lu and Guangyuan Xi Lu in Guangzhou, southern China, two hours by train from Hong Kong. Officially 20,000 Africans – and more like 100,000 according to a researcher at Hong Kong University[1] – live in or pass through 'Africa Town', between dual carriageways, elevated motorways and railway tracks, 10 square kilometres entirely given over to commerce, where Igbo, Wolof and Lingala mingle with Mandarin and Cantonese. The locals call it 'Chocolate Town'.

China has attracted former colonial countries ever since it arrived on the international trade scene. As Mark Leonard, executive director of the European Council on Foreign Relations, writes, 'Green tea, Jackie Chan and Confucius…[were] no match for McDonald's, Hollywood and the Gettysburg address. However, China has managed to associate itself with…big ideas that are potentially very attractive to middle-income and developing countries, particularly those which have been subject to western colonialism.'[2]

Africans are in this part of China less for its culture than its frenetic growth and wholesale consumer goods markets. Abou Kabba, a Guinean PhD in organic chemistry who has worked as a wholesaler in Asia for 15 years, is amazed at the numbers of young people here who believe Guangzhou is a staging post on the way to Europe, or a few metro stops from Tokyo.

In this roaring city of 18 million inhabitants and tens of thousands of micro factories, the commercial activity is very different from the oil deals and huge public works contracts the Chinese have secured in Africa. Here, the lion is riding the dragon to profit from China's export fever. 'I don't care if they're black or any other colour, as long as it's good business,' said the female manager of an electronics shop in a Donfeng business centre between two phone calls and a mouthful of tea. In Guandong, the workshop of the world whose shop window is Guangzhou, money has no colour. The Africans want to buy into the Chinese miracle. The list of goods they ship back is long: generators, shoes, cotton buds, mopeds, construction materials, human hair and toys. 'You can get anything you want in China,' quipped Joseph, a pedlar from Cameroon, 'even blacks'.

This hidden side of Sino-African relations has reached surprising proportions. Each year thousands of containers are shipped to Dakar, Mombasa, Abidjan and Doula, growing by 294 per cent between 2003 and 2007. At the fourth ministerial conference of the Forum on China-Africa Cooperation in November 2009, China's prime minister Wen Jiabao estimated bilateral trade in 2008 at $106.8 billion, up 45.1 per cent on 2007.[3] Forsaking traditional markets in Asia and Dubai, African traders have lost no time in exploiting the opportunities offered by China.

The foundations were laid in 1955 at the Bandung conference of Asian and African countries, which brought together non-aligned countries to resist Soviet influence as much as western imperialism and colonialism. Beijing supported independence movements in Algeria, Angola and Southern Rhodesia. Their support enabled China to take over in 1971 the Chinese permanent seat on the UN Security Council, until then occupied by Taiwan. Not until the 1980s did the first African traders arrive in Hong Kong, at that time still under British rule. China joined the World Trade Organisation in September 2001 and, since then, they have preferred to go directly to the low-cost production source.

LET'S MAKE LOTS OF MONEY

'Almost 90 per cent of goods on African markets come from China, Thailand and Indonesia,' said Sultane Barry, president of Guangzhou's Guinean community. 'Here in China you can mix different categories of goods in a single container. It's more flexible.' Like nine out of ten Africans in Guangzhou,[4] Barry is a businessman, who started his career in pursuit of the American dream as a dealer in precious stones, and is now proud to be a part of Yellow River capitalism. From his office wedged between a prayer hall and a meeting room, he runs an entire floor of Tianxiu Dasha, a 35-storey Tower of Babel crammed with businesses: shops bursting with samples from the region's factories, representative offices, freight forwarding companies, legal and illegal African restaurants, hairdressers and furnished apartments let by the week.

Ibrahim Kader Traore, an entrepreneur from Ivory Coast, explained how he and others live here: 'We're not here for fun. We work hard and do well. In Abidjan people still swear by France, where you might be able to save $13,000 over 25 years; in China you can have $130,000 in just five years.'

It is not surprising that more people are turning their backs on the old slave-trade routes, and on hard-to-penetrate Europe, to try their luck in the Far East. Between 2003 and 2007 the number of African immigrants grew by 30–40 per cent a year.[5] 'Increasing contact between the less-developed countries and China can only strengthen the presence of African businessmen in the home of the world's greatest exporter,' said Barry Sautman, a researcher at Hong Kong University.

The scale of immigration worries the Chinese government, which has never faced this kind of problem before. In 2006 President Hu Jintao invited 48 African heads of state to a lavish conference in Beijing, promising eternal friendship. But in 2007, would-be immigrants were shocked when the authorities revived an old slogan first pronounced by Hao Chiyong, a spokesman for the public security ministry on 20 August 2004: 'China is not a migration-targeted country and the new regulations are aimed at attracting high-level foreign personnel. There will not be many foreigners applying for Green Cards.'[6] This announced that there would be fewer visas for the Africans.

'The African population shrank,' said Barry. 'We were used to being granted one-year visas allowing multiple entry and unlimited length of stay. In 2008, just before the Beijing Olympics, the authorities decided to tidy up. They stopped renewing visas here. You had to return to your own country to get another work permit.' Since then, the constant quest for precious visas can become absurd. Ladji, an Ivorian whose visa status is irregular, sells pirated T-shirts. He showed me the dozens of visa stamps he had collected, mostly in Macao. 'At present visas are only valid for 30 days. So you have to leave mainland China once a month.'

50 YOUNG MEN WITH MACHETES

During the Beijing Olympics the authorities increased identity checks. The prospect of Guangzhou staging the Asian Games next November worries both the Africans and their Chinese neighbours: 'I sell more than 50 per cent of the output of my brother-in-law's TV factory to Africans,' said one saleswoman. 'We need them and I'm worried there are going to be fewer of them.'

A police raid in July 2009 almost ended in disaster. Two Nigerians, desperate to escape arrest, threw themselves through a window. One was seriously cut by broken glass, the other fell on his head and was in a coma for several days. Both recovered but the rumour of their deaths spread rapidly around the streets, provoking China's first-ever immigrant riot. Around 100 people stormed Guangzhou's central police station while the international media, sure that the men were dead, complained of China's continual violation of human rights.

'The raids started again,' Kabba said. 'My wife opened the door to the police, who wanted to see our visas, but I had their papers with me. The policemen started shouting at my children, who were in tears, telling them they'd go to prison – even though my family is registered with the immigration authorities. They knew our papers were in order.'

In October 2009 Mo Lian, deputy director of border control operations for Guangdong province's public security department, told Xinhua news agency that 70 per cent of foreign nationals detained in 2008 for illegal immigration and overstaying their visas were from Africa. In the first half of 2009 the figure rose to 77 per cent. After what Africans call 'harassment' and 'a conspiracy', a black market began. According to Ladji, you can buy a 'genuine' visa: 'Some Africans are paying as much as $2,600. They simply use private agents to bribe the authorities.'

'By trying to contain immigration, the Chinese government is pushing people into the arms of the African networks, which are just growing stronger,' said Ojukwu Emma, president of a Nigerian community association in China. 'Newly arrived immigrants sell their passports for cash. When they are deported, they just go home, change their identity and come back. Others end up in drug trafficking or prostitution. This kind of thing gives Africa a very bad name.'

So Emma tries to keep Guangzhou's African community in line with strong-arm tactics. 'Our community is fighting lawlessness. We've created the "peace-keepers", a band of 50 young men with machetes who catch African criminals and hand them over to the police, to protect our image.'

CHILDREN RUN AWAY

Thanks to this initiative, Emma was able to sign, in November 2009, an 'amnesty agreement' with the local government, applicable to every African who gives himself up to the immigration authorities. 'On 8 March 2010, 400 Nigerians whose visas had expired left China. I also negotiated the fine down to $300, half what it had been. Which means I'm down at the immigration office every day, along with many other African community leaders...As soon as they have the money, those who leave in this way will be able to return legally.' He did not mention the plight of those who are unable to pay the fine or the cost of their plane ticket home (the Chinese system doesn't provide repatriation for free). They go straight to prison and, according to some reports, are put to work in state factories. The government will not say how many Africans are in this predicament.

The resulting tensions stigmatise the African community by presenting it to the local population as having no respect for the law. 'Chinese people have always feared Africans. To preserve society's wellbeing the authorities believe that they must protect their people from too big an invasion,' said a professor at Guangdong University, speaking on condition of anonymity.

In her family history, *Wild Swans: Three Daughters of China*,[7] the Chinese writer Jung Chang describes how Chinese schoolchildren in the 1970s were taught that Africans were less developed and were unable to control their instincts. As in the West, most Chinese people see Africa as it is depicted in the media, overwhelmed by AIDS, famine, wars and drought – a world with no future.

The Chinese may be no more racist than any other nation, but they are less reluctant to show it. Vincent, a Nigerian who has lived in China for five years, said, 'Even if it's worse in Indonesia or Malaysia, you get insults like "black devil". On public transport, people hold their noses, and some children run away when they see me in the street. You just have to live with it.' Jean-Bedel, a

Congolese student, said: 'When you go to hospital, even if you only have a little fever, they always take an unusually large number of vials of blood from you, and automatically test you for HIV. They don't do it with their own people. They also put on gloves with a great show of taking precautions before examining you. It's only for blacks.'

Taxi drivers often ignore Africans. 'Those black devils are into drugs and prostitution,' said one. 'They even try to haggle over the fare. I never stop for them. Anyway, I can never understand where they want to go.'

TRYING TO INTEGRATE

Most African migrant workers make no attempt to integrate. Research by Brigitte Bertoncello, a professor at the University of Aix-Marseille, and Sylvie Bredeloup, research director at the Institut de Recherche pour le Développement in Paris, found that they live on the margins of Chinese society, preferring to create an enclave where they can behave as they choose. The Africans blame the Chinese: 'It's difficult to get closer because most Chinese denigrate us and don't believe we are their equals,' said Barry.

Mao Zedong advocated a different definition of otherness, as the historian Frank Dikötter recalled: 'In an often-quoted speech delivered in 1963, Mao claimed that "in Africa, in Asia, in every part of the world there is racism; in reality, racial problems are class problems". Official propaganda fostered the idea that only westerners could indulge in racism, the Chinese having become the leaders of victimised "coloured" people in the historical struggle against "white imperialism".'[8]

Replace the concept of class with that of economic success, and you describe today's China. 'If western racism is about genetic dispositions, Chinese prejudices and racism are more about achievements and standing in the world as applied to individuals or groups,' said Yan Sun, professor of political science at the City University of New York.[9] As in politics and the law, racism often stops where business begins. In the business centres and freight zones of Africa Town, the Chinese have realised that the Africans can contribute to their country's prosperity. In the rest of China, Africans are always exposed to hostile reactions. In the words of Deng Xiaoping, it is 'One country, two systems'.

Undeterred by the way Guangdong authorities have tightened the immigration laws or by Chinese chauvinism, Africans living in

China are building bridges between their host country and home countries. Perhaps they have found a way through the four walls of the pictogram that represents the word 'country' in Chinese. Popular uprisings against Africans, as at Nanjing University, Beijing, in 1988, no longer happen. Then, Chinese demonstrators attacked African students and poured into the streets chanting 'Death to the black devils!' Their excuse was that a Chinese student had been beaten to death, but they were also angry at Africans' interest in Chinese girls.

Since then, mixed marriages have become more visible around Xiaobei Lu, as have mixed-race children. 'Thanks to China opening up to the world there is now some hope for coloured foreigners here,' said Yane Soufian. 'We are learning their customs and we obey their laws.' Soufian, from Niger, arrived eight years ago 'almost broke and knowing only black tea, not green'. He has been married for five years to Hanna, a Chinese woman, and they have a ten-month-old son, Arafat. 'My in-laws never opposed our marriage. Their only fear is that, some day, we'll go back to Niger. My wife trusts me because she understands that Africans who stay in China have shown they can adapt. They fight for themselves and have joined the modern world. We have a lot of respect for our wives and help them with the daily chores.'

Standing in the square of the Sacred Heart Cathedral of Shizhi in Guangzhou, Ojokwu Emma estimated that there are between 300 and 400 mixed marriages. 'I'm hoping to create an organisation to help prevent divorces,' he said. Some Africans only marry to obtain a residence permit. Ladji confirmed this: 'To be able to start a business you have to marry a Chinese woman. That's what my brother did and it's what we all dream about.'

Africans are learning Chinese, in China, at university or in one of the many Confucius Institutes opening up across Africa and are taking on the role of mentors, even of educators. Barry recalls how ill equipped the host nation was: 'The arrival of the Africans taught the Chinese how to look for business opportunities. The secretaries we had here didn't speak a word of English. Our presence started a craze for learning languages – English and French. The Chinese didn't know the basic rules of international trade. They knew nothing about documentary credit. They paid for everything cash in hand. That's no way to do business.'

Spontaneous, non-institutionalised exchange makes for bonding between communities. When encouraging South-South development, China should not forget that when a less developed country takes off, there is usually increased human exchange with the industrialised country to which it is linked. China will need to find a way to encourage such development without harming its image, especially as criticism of Chinese immigration to Africa does not permit any hardening of its own policy on immigration.[10]

We could be seeing the emergence of a new transnational African business class that might flood sub-Saharan Africa with low-cost products from China. This model has its limitations. In a café at a Chinese shopping centre, a Burundian observed, 'China is flooding Africa with goods that are four or five times cheaper than those imported from Europe. Of course, that helps to boost purchasing power, but it means we are not making anything ourselves.' African economies suffer from unfair competition (non-payment of customs duties, dumping). It is this practice, rather than cooperation agreements based on an exchange of infrastructure for resources, that feeds the fears of Chinese neo-colonialism. China may be pursuing its own interests under the pretext of non-interference in the internal affairs of its economic partners.

'China is trying to keep things at government level,' said Barry, 'but the Chinese people will soon realise that it's better for business to deal directly with ordinary Africans.' China would prefer Africans to do business with China without living here, yet 90 per cent of Guangzhou's Africans act as intermediaries between the African continent and Chinese factories. Without them, there would be no business.

The Chinese economist Yan Xuetong said: 'At the moment all of China's attractiveness comes from its economic power. But that cannot last. Money worship is not attractive enough. You need moral power.'[11] Beijing has everything to gain from looking after its African population. 'The door to the Chinese market has only opened a crack, mostly because visa requirements are so tough,' said Zango, a trader from Mali. 'The future is elsewhere – India, perhaps.'

Translated by Robert Waterhouse

Tristan Coloma is a journalist.

1. Adams Bodomo, 'The African trading community in Guangzhou: an emerging bridge for Africa-China relations', to be published in *The China Quarterly*, School of Oriental and African Studies, University of London.
2. Mark Leonard, *What Does China Think?*, HarperCollins, London, 2008.
3. Hubert Escaith (dir.), *International Trade Statistics 2009*, WTO, Geneva, 2009. Chinese exports to Africa were worth $50.84 billion (up 36.3 per cent on 2008); imports from Africa $56 billion (up 54 per cent). Hydrocarbon fuels accounted for 71.7 per cent of imports, metals for 14.1 per cent.

4. Around 33 per cent of Africans in Guangzhou are from Nigeria, 10 per cent from Mali, 8 per cent from Ghana, 6 per cent from Guinea; the remainder are mainly from the Democratic Republic of the Congo, Senegal, Ivory Coast, Niger, Tanzania, the Gambia and Cameroon (Adams Bodomo, op. cit.).
5. Zhigang Li, Desheng Xue, Michael Lyons and Alison Brown, 'Ethnic enclave of transnational migrants in Guangzhou: a case study of Xiaobei', *Acta Geographica Sinica*, China, 2008.
6. Jiang Zhuqing, 'China issues "green card" to foreigners', *China Daily*, 21 August 2004.
7. Jung Chang, *Wild Swans: Three Daughters of China*, Harper Perennial, London, 2004.
8. Frank Dikötter, *The Discourse of Race in Modern China*, C. Hurst & Co., London, 1992.
9. Yan Sun, 'Millennia of Multiethnic Contradictions' in the forum 'China's Changing Views on Race' of the New York Times' Room for Debate, 13 December 2009.
10. According to Jean-Raphaël Chaponnière, a researcher at the Agence Française de Développement, there are between 480,000 and 750,000 Chinese nationals in Africa.
11. Quoted by Mark Leonard, op. cit.

❖ ❖

OCTOBER 2011

'ALWAYS BE PUNCTUAL AND DON'T COUNT THE WORK YOU ARE DOING'

Filipino maids for export

In the Philippines 12 per cent of GDP comes as remittances from nationals abroad. Many of those are maids, sent all over the world into domestic service to support their children back at home. The Philippines government is even sponsoring their training.

Julien Brygo

Béatrice, a Franco-Belgian expatriate, lives in the gated community of Stanley Knoll, named after the explorer Henry Morton Stanley, in a house that overlooks Hong Kong Bay. She, her French husband Paul, a senior executive with a French bank, and their four children have lived here, half an hour from the heart of 'the most free economy in the world',[1] since 2005. She does not have a job, but does humanitarian work for a French NGO, swims in Stanley Bay and plays tennis. They need a maid to help with their house and children. 'Lennie is so devoted,' says Béatrice. Leonora Santos Torres looks after the children, cooks and cleans. She is one of the 290,600 foreign maids currently working in Hong Kong. Like most of them, she lives in a room less than 5 square metres, on call day and night. Béatrice has not set foot in a supermarket for four years, and says she feels 'liberated' by not having to do domestic tasks. She is still surprised when the maid dries her swimsuit as soon as she returns from the beach. Béatrice and Paul pay Leonora $650 a month to be available 24 hours a day, six days a week, a quarter of the cost of such help in France. 'It's $144 more than the minimum wage for maids in Hong Kong, based on at least 10 hours' work a day,' said Béatrice. They add $80 a month for food, because Paul does not want Leonora helping herself from the fridge. 'That's the law in Hong Kong,' said Béatrice.[2] '$650 is a good salary. Some expat families pay $860–$1,000 a month. They're destroying the market for the rest of us.'

Leonora, 47, is from the northern Philippines tourist province of Luzon, and has a diploma in telegram transcription. She left three of her five children in the village of Calatagan in 1999 to work in Hong Kong to support her family. 'Every month I send four-fifths of my salary, minus the Western Union transfer costs [$3.5 per transaction], to pay my three children's university fees. Education in the Philippines is so expensive we have to make sacrifices.' 'Sacrifice' is a word you hear again and again when talking to Filipino maids. 'We are usually not free to come and go in our employers' homes, the food is rarely enough and we are completely dedicated to the family. Many of my compatriots live in terrible conditions,' said Leonora. They may be verbally or physically abused, subjected to their employers' whims, underpaid and exploited. According to the Hong Kong Labour Department, 10 per cent of domestic workers lodge complaints against their employers every year for non-payment of wages, infringement of contract, ill treatment or sexual harassment (25,000 complaints a year). Leonora was badly treated by a Hong Kong family ('They wanted me to give up my day off') before she walked out after six months, then by a Chinese family she was with for six years, where the grandmother used to beat and insult her. Her current employers are good to her, she said. Many domestic workers don't dare complain because they only get 14 days to find a new placement, or leave Hong Kong, once a contract has terminated.

'GIVE THANKS TO THE LORD'

'It's in their genes,' said Béatrice, explaining her employee's devotion. 'Filipino women are very good with people. It's in their culture to be devoted. And they love children. That's what they enjoy doing, because their lives are not much fun. What keeps Lennie going is her involvement in the parish.' Like many Filipinos, Leonora is a devoted Christian who 'draws strength from her relationship with the Lord'. Her moral code fits in well with her employers' rules: 'I listen to the Lord, who does not distinguish between rich and poor.' In her little room she has a computer connected to Skype, Facebook and Yahoo!, a baby monitor, and photographs of her own children. A large picture has pride of place above the computer, with the words: 'Give thanks to the Lord for His love endures forever.'

Every year more than 100,000 Filipinos go abroad to work in the service industry. President Ferdinand Marcos (1965–1986) started exporting manpower in 1974, when the economy was derelict, and he saw an opportunity in the rapid development of the Gulf states after the 1973 oil crisis. In 1974, 35,000 Filipinos found jobs abroad. It was meant to be temporary, but 35 years later this trickle has turned into a flood, involving more than 8.5 million Filipinos, mostly women – just under 10 per cent of the population and 22 per cent of the working age population. According to the World Bank, foreign workers contributed 12 per cent of the Philippines' GDP in 2010 with $21.3 billion in remittances.[3] This is the fourth highest number of foreign remittances after China, India and Mexico.

Most of the permanent and temporary diaspora (of whom a quarter are illegal) are in the US, Canada and the Middle East. A million are in Saudi Arabia, even though it announced a ban on Filipino and Indonesian maids last July. Gloria Arroyo, the former Philippines president (2001–2010), described them as 'modern heroes'. In 2006 (after Israel's bombing of Lebanon, where 30,000 Filipino workers lived), she launched the 'supermaid' programme.[4] She wanted to train domestic servants 'in the language of their employers', and educate them, through a national diploma, in the use of household appliances and first aid. The aim was to do away with agency fees, ensure that every maid earned at least $400, and reduce the institutional violence (economic as well as physical) affecting women. Five years later there are training colleges all over the country, but the promise of basic rights for Filipino overseas workers has proven empty.

WELCOME TO LITTLE HONG KONG

'Welcome to Little Hong Kong,' said Michelle Ventenilla, one of four teachers at Abest, one of the Philippines' 364 registered private training centres for domestic servants, in Manila. The small brick villa resembles a typical upper middle class home in Hong Kong, with a saloon car, an aquarium with rare fish, western-style bathrooms and bedrooms with pink curtains and bright green walls. Since 2007 Abest has 'exported' 1,500 domestic workers to Hong Kong, which is only two hours away by plane. The school's fees are $212, and it is linked to a recruitment agency.

It was the day of the final exam, and candidate number five, a frail-looking woman, sweated as she carried a porcelain tureen in both hands to the table, and then mimed serving a bowl of soup. Lea Talabis, 41, was one of around 100,000 candidates per year to sit National Certificate II, after 216 hours of training. The inspector from the Technical Education and Skills Development Authority (TESDA), Rommel Ventenilla,[5] watched the candidate as she performed the table service test. Talabis, a former primary school teacher who became a maid to support her family, approached her fictitious boss and asked: 'Would you like some soup, sir?' Ventenilla nodded his head and grunted. Talabis hesitated – after serving him from the left, should she take the tureen back to the kitchen, or leave it for him to help himself? Confused, she lowered her eyes and put the tureen down on the sideboard.

The examiner gave her a second chance with the question and answer part of the test. Indicating the table, laid out for a typical middle-class Hong Kong family with three placemats, fish and meat knives, and glasses, he asked: 'How much water do you pour into the glass?' Talabis moved to his right-hand side carrying a carafe, and filled his glass three-quarters full. Ventenilla validated the test and Talabis went back to the kitchen. The final part of the exam could include making the bed, washing the floor, cleaning the aquarium, ironing clothes or washing the car.

'The final mark is made up of 20 per cent skill, 20 per cent theory and 60 per cent behaviour,' said Michelle Ventenilla, indicating that future maids are tested less on their medical, housekeeping or cooking abilities than on their capacity to obey the rules. 'We don't use the term maid any more,' said Susan de la Rama, head of the programme. 'We now say "domestic helper". We don't want the Philippines to be labelled a country that exports maids, as it was a few years ago.' The second definition of a Filipino woman in the 2005 Merriam-Webster dictionary is 'maid'. This angered the Filipino government, prompting it to professionalise the industry.

'Many employers are looking for domestic workers who are polite, respectful, patient and quiet. Here we try to get them used to the excitable temperament of Hong Kong employers. You have to be patient, and work from the heart,' said Ventenilla, delivering a key point of the super maid programme. Above the aquarium (symbol of social success within Asian families) is written the college slogan: 'Cleanliness is next to godliness'. On the classroom wall, a poster distinguishes winners (those who 'look for solutions' and say to their bosses 'let me do it for you') from losers (those who 'look for someone to blame' and 'always have an excuse' for not doing what they are asked). The Code of Discipline stipulates: 'DO NOT ARGUE with your employer'; 'Do not talk to other maids'; 'Do not show a temper or long face when scolded by your employer'; 'Contact your agency whenever you have problems and don't rely on your friends'.

A FACTORY FOR WORKERS

There is no chance of socialism here: no union, no strikes, no political meetings, no questioning the basis of servitude. 'Always be punctual,' says chapter six of the manual, while the 'Things Not to Do' section lists 'Don't count the work you are doing'.

'These schools are a disgrace to our country,' said Garry Martinez, chair of the NGO Migrante International in Manila. 'Every day the bodies of six to ten Filipinos who have died working overseas are repatriated. The Philippines has become a factory producing workers.'

Ten years ago Talabis worked as a maid with a middle-class family in Hong Kong, but she came back 'to bring [her] skills up to standard', and to get National Certificate 2, which allows her to work overseas legally. She had resolved to go abroad again, leaving her fisherman husband and two children. 'I'm doing it for them. In Hong Kong I would earn twice what I earn here as a teacher.' She acknowledged that the college taught her to obey and submit to the boss's rules, but it didn't surprise her: 'It's to make sure we complete our contracts, because we get into debt to become maids.'

She had to use her savings to pay the agency fee of $1,839, the equivalent of six months of her teacher's salary. 'I paid cash and got no receipt. The agency is approved by the department for Filipinos working abroad, but they were clear – take it or leave it. I had to pay the fee if I wanted to work in Hong Kong.' She hoped her husband and children would join her later. Her eventual aim was to go to Europe, like 10 per cent of her fellow expatriates.[6] 'I don't want to be a maid all my life,' she said. Three weeks later, after she had arrived in Hong Kong, she said she was delighted because her employers told her to think of them as her second family. But the best thing was that the house had Wi-Fi: 'Every evening I can use the web cam to talk to my children and husband. For the moment I'm very happy.'

Joseph Law, 65, opened the door to his 13th floor apartment on Elegant Terrace, a building with caretakers and a swimming pool in Mid-Levels, a fashionable part of Hong Kong. 'Elena!' he shouted to the maid. 'Julien is a French journalist. He's writing an article about the daily life of Filipino maids in Hong Kong. Go and make us some tea with milk.' Joseph showed me his shirt: 'I like them well ironed, with a crease down the middle.' He flopped on to his leather sofa: 'Do I like being waited on? That's a good question. I admit I have always preferred being waited on than doing things myself. I've been hiring foreign maids for the last 35 years, and my favourite by far are the Filipinos. They speak better English, are less risky than the others and are generally much more devoted to their job.' His apartment and his appearance are impeccable, thanks to Elena's hard graft. 'I pay her the legal minimum: $3,580 HK [US$459],'[7] said Law, former assistant manager of the Hong Kong fire brigade, now chairman of the official Employers of Overseas Domestic Helpers Association, the enemy of the six maids' unions in Hong Kong.

Elena Meredores is 51, has an 18-year-old daughter in the Philippines, and has been a maid for more than 16 years. She entered the room wearing cropped trousers and a T-shirt wet from doing the washing up, and put a tray with two cups and a teapot on the table in front of her boss. After acknowledging a complaint from Law ('Next time I have guests, bring a bigger tray'), she perched on the edge of the sofa. 'Why are salaries so low?' Law continued. 'It's because Filipinos like Elena have no qualifications and low skills. Isn't that right Elena? No qualifications.' She lowered her eyes and agreed: 'That's right, sir.'

DOCTORS, TEACHER, GRADUATES

Sensing that she felt obliged to agree with him, Law told Meredores to speak 'freely'. She laughed, then said: 'No, sir, you can't explain our low salaries by saying we are under-qualified or have few skills. Many of my fellow maids are doctors, teachers, university graduates, but they are obliged to become maids to support their families. And the government has created training centres to train them.' Law dismissed these schools ('They are the biggest joke, and the biggest source of dispute between employers and employees') and asked: 'Elena, I think 50 per cent of foreign maids in Hong Kong enjoy a peaceful and harmonious relationship with their employers, like you and myself do. Don't you agree?' 'I would say 15 per cent, sir,' she replied. 'No, come on, 15 per cent?' said Law, irritated; 'be fair, Elena.' 'Many employers claim to have a good relationship, but it's a lie. They say that just to show off. Not like you, Mr Law.' He interrupted her: 'Hong Kong is paradise for foreign maids. Paradise!'

When I drew a comparison between his monthly income of more than $14,000 and his maid's salary, he got angry. 'Hong Kong is their dream location. They get an employment contract, a minimum wage, and on top of that they get room and board, plane tickets, health insurance and long-service payment after five years. The whole package costs employers an average $5,500 HK [$705] a month. That's a lot of money.' He conceded that most employers were upper class, but he said giving small gifts helped to even things out: 'Every year I give her presents. At New Year, Chinese New Year, isn't that right, Elena?' Meredores recalled getting a brown envelope at New Year, containing almost $60.

At the end of 2010, the Philippines' government announced that Overseas Filipino Workers (OFW) would have to pay $200 HK ($25) insurance, and it intends to introduce a minimum wage of $400 for its ten million overseas workers. It's a proposal that angers Law: 'I warn the Philippines and Indonesia: if they carry on adopting such stupid policies, and demanding higher salaries, I will call for the embargo on Chinese maids to be lifted.'[8] He has cause to be nervous: both the Philippines and Indonesia – who are the most aggressive defenders of overseas domestic workers – announced in June 2011 that they intended to ratify the International Labour Organisation's convention on decent working conditions for maids. 'We employers are strongly opposed to this convention, because it is impossible to count hours in this kind of work,' said Law.

Early next Sunday morning, Meredores went to the Catholic church. 'I'm going to pray for my family, and also for Law's family. You mustn't be selfish in your faith.' Afterwards she went to the big weekly gathering of Filipino maids in the financial district, where Hong Kong and Shanghai Banking Corporation (HSBC) has its headquarters, between the Bank of China and Van Cleef and Arpels jewellery. Tens of thousands of maids like Meredores meet at the foot of this steel and glass skyscraper every Sunday. 'We meet here because we have nowhere else to go on our day off. All week we are alone, cleaning their apartments, then once a week, we can free ourselves of our employers. That gives us our dignity,' she said.

That week a fashion parade had been organised by the federation of Filipinos from Benguet province in the northern Philippines to celebrate Mother's Day. The theme was 'women as daughters, wives and mothers'. This promotion of women in stereotyped gender roles has led millions to become domestic servants. Filipino women in their 40s and 50s – nurses, housemaids – paraded across the podium, opposite Bank of America, hoping to win titles such as 'most beautiful secretary'. Fifty metres away, thousands of maids waved their Western Union flags: the company that handled most of the $21 billion sent in remittances in 2010 had organised a concert of Filipino singing stars for the Fiesta at Saya festival.

Two bronze lions flank the HSBC tower, representing the bank's founders A.G. Stephen and G.H. Stitt. The lion on the right, Stitt, has a serious expression, while the other one, Stephen, seems to be roaring with pleasure. Over the years it has become a favourite meeting place for expatriate Filipinos. 'I like having my photo taken in front of the laughing lion, because it represents our hard work,' said Gorgogna, who is a maid on a low salary, after 22 years in the country. The lion, symbol of employers and their wealth, has eaten well, and looks up towards the top of the HSBC tower, while at the bottom, thousands of domestic servants savour their day off. 'To the Chinese, the lion symbolises money,' said Gorgogna. 'If it weren't for us, it wouldn't be so well fed.'

Translated by Stephanie Irvine

Julien Brygo is a journalist.

1. The Index of Economic Freedom measures ten criteria (business, trade and fiscal freedom, government spending, monetary, investment and financial freedom, property rights, corruption, labour freedom) in 183 countries. In 2011 Hong Kong was rated number one.
2. Employers who do not feed their maids should pay a food allowance of $96.
3. 'Remittances to PH ranked 4th biggest in world', http://www.ofwguide.com/, Manila, 11 November 2010.
4. 'Housemaids to supermaids soon!', http://www.ofwguide.com/, Manila, 24 August 2006.
5. No relation to Michelle Ventenilla.
6. In 2009, 41.7 per cent of the 8,579,378 Filipinos abroad worked in America (33.5 per cent in the US, 7.4 per cent in Canada), 28.2 per cent in the Middle East (13.5 per cent in Saudi Arabia, 7.1 per cent in United Arab Emirates), 12.5 per cent in Asia and 8.4 per cent in Europe. Source: Commission on Filipinos Overseas.

7. The minimum wage was frozen at $3,580 HK ($459) between 2009 and 2011, but was re-evaluated in June 2011 at $3,740 HK ($480); that is below the pre-financial crash 1999 figure of $3,860 HK ($495).
8. The British authorities in Hong Kong declared an embargo on Chinese domestic workers in the 1970s.

❖❖❖❖❖❖❖❖❖❖❖❖❖❖❖❖❖❖❖❖❖❖❖❖❖❖❖❖❖❖❖❖❖❖❖❖

APRIL 2010

EXPLODING CITIES, NEW SUBURBS

Greater Hanoi swallows the countryside

Hanoi is now ranked ahead of Shanghai, Beijing, Tokyo and Seoul as the place to shop in Asia. It has annexed vast areas of farmland on which to build suburbs served by motorways. But the lives and homes of ordinary Vietnamese, rural or urban, aren't improving that fast.

Xavier Monthéard

The Vietnamese architect Hoang Huu Phe made a passionate case for a policy of all-out urban development in Hanoi: 'Some people in government still see a city only as an administrative entity. Luckily this backward-looking attitude is on the decline. We need to build an attractive, hi-tech capital with an international outlook. After all, the Americans built Las Vegas in the middle of a desert.'

His opinions carry weight: he is the director of the research and development division of Vinaconex, Vietnam's biggest state-owned construction firm, typical of the flourishing enterprises of the post-communist era. His sky-blue office is hung with futuristic blueprints alongside photographs of completed buildings and a hi-tech video screen. Phe claimed to have no concerns about property bubbles: 'We must use property speculation as a driving force. Our determination will protect this city from the laissez-faire approach that has led to cosmopolitanism in Bangkok or Manila, which you could call westernisation. I am trying to use market mechanisms to make my dream come true.'

Last year, the online magazine *Smart Travel Asia* ranked Hanoi the continent's sixth-best city for shopping, after Hong Kong and Singapore but ahead of Bali, Shanghai, Tokyo, Beijing and Seoul. Vietnam is in. In 2008 property projects there attracted more than $28 billion, or almost half of all direct foreign investment in Vietnam.[1] Property prices in its larger cities have shot up. Can this really be the battered post-communist Vietnam that Noam Chomsky believed would need a century to recover, if it ever did?[2]

In August 2008 Prime Minister Nguyen Tan Dung announced that, with immediate effect, Hanoi would absorb Ha Tay province and a number of adjoining towns. Overnight it tripled in size to more than 3,300 km². According to Laurent Pandolfi of the Hanoi Cooperation Centre for Urban Development, 'Even though the decision was made very quickly and has strong political motives, it is not short on logic. It is consistent with a policy of urbanisation, and one hopes that it will supported by large infrastructure projects, such as the future subway.' The government also commissioned a US-Korean organisation to draw up a new urban plan within a short (some would say impossible) time frame.

DECOLLECTIVISED LAND

Why the fuss over 'Greater Hanoi'? To understand, go back some 20 years. Since 1986 Vietnam has had a policy of economic opening up, similar to China's *doi moi* (renewal). In 1990 the political bureau of the Communist Party acknowledged the family as an autonomous economic entity of production and enterprise and proposed the allocation of land to family units. This was the beginning of decollectivisation. A new law in 1993 allowed private individuals to hold land-use rights on renewable long-term leases (initially of 15 years). These rights can be sub-leased, sold and inherited, although the Vietnamese state reserves pre-emption rights to prevent the theoretical possibility of land grabbing by the urban bourgeoisie. Important property reserves remain in the hands of the Communist Party, the army and communist mass organisations such as the Fatherland Front and the trade unions.

In 1993 the market value of land was low but exports have quadrupled in 15 years and some 10,000 foreign companies are now operating in Vietnam. As a result, the old rice paddies have become goldmines. Commercial ambitions are beginning to conflict with historical legacies, such as the allocation of colonial villas to families that distinguished themselves in the war against the US, or the reservation of vast estates for the military. The property developers want land that the city can no longer supply.

According to its advocates, the development of Greater Hanoi will require the construction of satellite towns. This will open up the mountainous areas to the west while reducing population density in the capital, and will connect Hanoi to the flow of international commerce while providing it with modern housing. One name sums up this: Splendora. This complex is under construction in North An Khanh, in the former province of Ha Tay. A motorway will pass close by, leading to the Hoa Lac High-Tech Park, where Vietnam's Silicon Valley is to be built. Vietnam National University, Hanoi, will be transferred to Hoa Lac and provided with a campus. The park is expected to attract a range of high value-added green technological industries.

At harvest time last year, farmers were using sickles to cut rice around where the motorway was still under construction. Children led buffalo and horses and goats roamed among the concrete blocks. Signboards advertised residential complexes in varying stages of completion, including Splendora and the Singapore-designed Tricon Towers, three 44-storey buildings offering 732 condominiums with swimming pools, a medical centre and a kindergarten.[3] So far nobody had dared touch the village cemeteries that lay scattered among the paddies, mournful reminders of the old Vietnam.

The promotional videos I saw showed big developments with green spaces and lakes, all in 3D. Fast roads would allow traffic to flow through a mix of skyscrapers, smaller buildings and detached houses. The videos depicted a serene shopping experience in superstores, far from the tumult of the city centre or the boorishness of the suburbs. 'But do you see any nurseries or schools or sanitation equipment in these videos?' asked Pham Van Cu, a geographer at Vietnam National University, Hanoi. 'Where are the ordinary people, where is the economic activity? Such projects put the investors' interests first. The state will lose resources, services will be privatised and people of modest means will become dependent on the service companies... rich people pay other rich people: they're the only winners.'

These medium- to high-end developments do target the well-off, the 10 per cent who earn 30 per cent of the national income and like to stroll around Hanoi's West Lake on Sundays. Developers hope they will leave the city centre for more spacious accommodation and the calm of the suburbs, in the US sense of the word. There is one problem: the farmland between the residential developments, motorways and industrial zones will be cut off from its irrigation systems. The new developments are built on mounds, which heighten the risk of floods in the lower-lying villages of this densely populated alluvial plain. And as Vietnam is in a monsoon zone, it rains a lot. Regulations governing construction of such mounds in built-up areas require developers to install drainage systems. But when the state withdraws to the point of transferring control of urban and rural planning to investors, who is to keep watch? In return for building road infrastructure, the government rewards the developers with parcels of adjacent land. It even delegates the compulsory land purchases to them.

This was the case in Hoa Muc, a village closer to the centre of Hanoi affected by an earlier redrawing of administrative boundaries. When it was reclassified as an urban district in 1997, land prices rose. Three years later the authorities – that is, Vinaconex – began construction on the Nuong Chin-Trung Hoa residential development. 'Hoa Muc was one of the many villages in Vietnam whose inhabitants pursued both agriculture and crafts. Here it was brick-making,' said the Canadian sociologist Danièle Labbé. 'When the state decided to build Nuong Chin-Trung Hoa, it issued compulsory purchase orders for the villagers' agricultural land, leaving them just their houses and a small patch of ground to cultivate. The state negotiated the level of compensation via the People's Committee (the municipal authorities) and the mass organisations. The inhabitants knew that villagers in other newly urbanised districts who had resisted had been treated badly, so they gave in. Since 2003 the state has directly entrusted the developers with the task of making these compulsory purchases. There have been promises of new jobs and vocational training, which have not generally been kept. At Hoa Muc the financial compensation, though far below market rates, was decent. But in other places the conflicts have reached deadlock.'

SOCIAL TRANSITION

The Hanoi People's Committee, whose members are urban, is trying to deal with problems of which it has little understanding – those of rural districts. The social risks are considerable. 'It's not easy to make the transition from country to town without preparation, especially when it happens quickly,' stressed Labbé. 'It's very hard to find a new job. And we're talking about a village that's only four kilometres from the city centre and has been linked to it for centuries. What will it be like for those living further out?'

The destabilisation of peri-urban areas also threatens the commercial city centre, whose development has relied, since at least the 17th century, on continual exchange with a peripheral belt rich in agriculture, crafts and industries. At the end of the 1980s, this traditional arrangement, which had been shattered by the communist period and the war, was revived, and the city with it. The '36 streets and corporations' quarter is typical. Famous for its commercial vitality, it draws vital components from the countryside into the city. Ornate and brightly coloured residential buildings, surrounded by a maze of structures with many internal courtyards and hidden floors, overflow with merchandise. Each street has its speciality and often its own smell: coffee roasting, the odours of traditional pharmacopoeia (with spices such as cinnamon, aniseed and ginger beside medicinal ingredients). There are streets for office equipment, second-hand clothes and cut steel. Restaurants alternate with businesses, many of them the 'dust restaurants' that offer a typically Southeast Asian sociability: Hanoi people like to eat outdoors, in spite of the noise and crowded conditions. They sit on low stools to be as close as possible to the ground. The traffic roars and the division between the pavement and the roadway is notional. Cars (still few in number) jostle for space with thousands of motorcycles.

NUMBER ONE EMPLOYER

The emergence of family micro-units working in services and retail has just about made up for the loss of jobs in the public sector and farming. A poll of several thousand households found that the informal sector is now the number one employer in Hanoi (30 per cent) and operates as an enclave economy, relatively cut off from formal business channels.[4] I saw some of this informal sector. It included an old itinerant saleswoman trotting along so as not to bend under the weight of her wares; two stately women on bicycles, carrying star fruit and custard apples; and Man, a young moto-taxi (motorcycle taxi) driver, providing a vital service in a city where public transport is in its infancy. He spends ten hours a day in heavy pollution – and danger, given Hanoi drivers' idiosyncratic interpretation of traffic rules. During a break, he treated himself to a lungful of smoke from a beautifully decorated pipe. A pouch of low-quality tobacco only costs a few US cents. But, like everything else, it has become more expensive. 'I can still manage two meals a day. But I have to be careful. My partner does manicures; she's not rich either. I don't have enough money to get married, so I smoke and drink less. But it'll take years to scrape enough together.'

His worst problem, besides the inflation that keeps raising the cost of basic essentials, was accommodation. He was renting a cubbyhole of 10 m² for $52 a month, water and electricity included.

Coming from the provinces, Man had little hope of finding anything better: everything had been taken by native Hanoians. A young woman about to complete a doctorate in sociology was in a similar predicament. She bowed her head in embarrassment, so acutely did her social circumstances contrast with her professional aspirations. She was still living in shared accommodation with a communal toilet and shower. 'I've studied for ten years, I do research for a prestigious institute, but nothing is coming onto the market. In fact it's the opposite. For the past two years, it's been impossible to find accommodation. The university's halls of residence are jam-packed. It's not right that the government should give students so little support.'

According to Nguyen Thi Thieng, of the population department at the National Economic University in Hanoi, 'Studies show clearly that migrants now settle in the outlying districts whereas, until 2007, they gathered in the central districts of Ba Dinh and Hoan Kiem. They can no longer find housing in the areas where they work.' Dispossessed farmers sometimes turn makeshift landlords. As Danièle Labbé explained: 'On the little patches of land they have been left with, the inhabitants of Hoa Muc have erected simple buildings to rent to students and workers who don't have the means to live in the centre. It's very big business.'

This is because demand is rising while developers' projects make it ever harder to get access to property by causing prices to rise. According to the April 2009 census, the city now has 6.5 million inhabitants – as many as the whole of neighbouring Laos. Even though the basic family unit has stabilised at four people,[5] demographers expect a national population increase of about one million a year over the next few years, most of the growth in cities.

EVERYONE FOR HIMSELF

At a conference in Hanoi in September 2009, Martin Rama, the World Bank's chief economist for Vietnam, was enthusiastic about Vietnam's progress in poverty reduction, which he pronounced to be even faster than China's, claiming that the ratio of the population under the poverty threshold had fallen from 58 per cent in 1993 to only 16 per cent in 2006 and even lower since. Nguyen Nga, who was involved in humanitarian and economic development projects for 20 years, was less sanguine: 'To understand Hanoi, you have to remember the misery of the 1980s. When I looked at children then, I used to tell myself they were learning to cope with inequality along with hunger and that they were making it part of themselves. And that's what happened. Those children are 20 now, and know no other culture than "everyone for himself". They want their share of material wealth, but their sensitivity is atrophied; their dreams are impoverished.'

When autumn comes to Hanoi, it's wedding season, because the moon, a symbol of fertility, is at its purest and most brilliant. It's customary at this time of year to give presents of little round biscuits representing the celestial body. The origins of the custom are lost in antiquity, but last year, the 4,646th of the traditional calendar, the most highly prized biscuits were those bearing the logo of the Sheraton Hotel. Have the Americans finally conquered Vietnamese hearts and minds, 35 years after the war? The time of ideological divisions is long past. Nationalism, abandoning its communist past, is going back to its roots. According to the historian Nguyen The Anh, 'the country is returning to a time before French colonisation. Especially where the structure of government is concerned. The ruling caste, whatever you want to call it, can be compared to a self-proclaimed mandarinate, minus the Confucian virtues. As for the people, they are reviving the old cults.'

I noticed a group of workers from the provinces who had been restoring a 17th-century temple. Surrounded by the mud and the incessant noise of the capital, their makeshift camp was built around a statue of the local guardian spirit, a deified popular hero, which generations of squatters had left intact. Flowers, fruit, cooked food and joss sticks were heaped up at its feet.

Translated by Tom Genrich

Xavier Monthéard is a journalist.

1. See Hanoi Statistical Office, *Hanoi Statistical Yearbook*, Hanoi, 2009.
2. See Noam Chomsky, *Understanding Power: The Indispensable Chomsky*, edited by Peter R. Mitchell and John Schoeffel, New Press, New York, 2002.
3. See Minh Ky, 'Tricon Towers: a new face for Hanoi', *Vietnam Economic News*, 11 September 2009.
4. See Jean-Pierre Cling, Le Van Dy, Nguyen Thi, Thu Huyen, Phan T. Ngoc Tram, Mireille Razafindrakoto and François Roubaud, 'Shedding light on a huge black hole: the informal sector in Hanoi' (PDF), GSO-ISS/IRD-DIAL Project, Hanoi, April 2009.
5. With 2.08 children per woman nationwide and 1.83 in urban environments; see United Nations Population Fund, *Viet Nam Population 2008*, Hanoi, April 2009.

❖ ❖

March 2011

Why the battle for Algiers is being lost

Death of the Casbah

The new protests in Algeria recall a history of resistance, of which the Casbah was the proud symbol. But this heart of Algiers, famous in the fight for independence from the French, is being neglected by Algeria's rulers who don't want anyone to remember what it stood for.

Allan Popelard and Paul Vannier

Algiers shuts down for the evening after about 8pm. The waiters clear away the tables and chairs from the pavements outside the cafés; shopkeepers roll down the shutters. The centre is deserted, except for the police checking drivers at roadblocks. Memories of the 'black years' of the civil war remain vivid – booby-trapped cars, bombs outside cinemas.[1] The state of emergency is still in place and prohibits public gatherings. The state's desire to contain the Islamists has perversely driven it to meet some of their demands: the authorities closed 1,200 bars in Algeria between 2006 and 2008.[2] Every year the number of public spaces decreases, and people spend more of their leisure time at home; every balcony now has a satellite dish.

Cheap restaurants bring some life to popular central districts such as Bab El Oued and Belcourt, but as night falls the only places open are big hotels and exclusive nightclubs in the smart neighbourhoods; only the middle classes can get together in the recreational venues they have built for themselves. In Sidi Yahia, below the wealthy district of Hydra, the street is dotted with boutiques and trendy cafés where boys and girls can meet – cafés in the city centre and in working class areas are almost exclusively for men. Private initiative has transformed this pocket of the city, which until recently had few houses, and Sidi Yahia is now a favourite meeting place for the fashionable young.

Working-class areas have been abandoned, and nowhere can this be seen more clearly than in the Casbah. It has been a UNESCO world heritage site since 1992, yet this historic heart of Algiers is falling apart. Buildings are being replaced with piles of rubble. Scaffolding and metal and wooden posts prop up cracked walls. In some houses, walls that were meant to screen families from the gaze of neighbours and passers-by have collapsed, making public the intimate details of their daily lives. Broken patios, smashed china and ripped panelling show something of the scale of the disaster. Few venture into this labyrinth of steep alleys and narrow steps. For many who live in Algiers, the Casbah is unknown territory. Most of its residents left after independence, preferring the more modern and comfortable apartments vacated by the Europeans. Others replaced them, exiles from the countryside, who broke down the doors of the empty homes and squatted. The Casbah became a place to be lived in only until somewhere better was found. But it started to deteriorate after the old families left. Some new inhabitants deliberately wrecked their homes so they would be rehoused; and causing water damage is still common practice. Lahsen, a member of the Casbah Foundation, a preservation group, says 350 houses have been destroyed in this way. The authorities have done nothing, apart from restoring a few buildings, like Mustapha Pasha's palace.

Yet for locals and visitors alike, the Casbah is Algiers. This city was built by the colonial French, and at twilight when the white buildings turn grey, it looks so much like Paris; the Casbah is all that remains of its Arab and Ottoman heritage. So why do the authorities not value it?

A PLACE OF MILITARY DEFEAT

Perhaps because the Casbah has a name for depravation: a place of smugglers and prostitutes, immune to the moralising of the authorities and also of the Islamists, who are quick to praise the uncorrupted values of the peasants compared with the dissolute morals of city dwellers. Yet it really has more to do with the way in which the leaders of the ruling FLN (National Liberation Front) defined and constructed their political legitimacy after the war of independence. They did not do this on the basis of democratic, multi-party elections, but connected their legitimacy to history, rooted in the war against the French. The resistance fighters in the Casbah were integral to that war, although during the Battle of Algiers in 1957, they were almost destroyed by General Massu's French paratroopers, and it took them two years to reorganise. The Casbah is a place of military defeat.

The Algerians won the war politically, but not militarily. After Colonel Houari Boumedienne seized power in 1965, the army obscured this. There is no official celebration of the Battle of Algiers, while the protests against President Charles de Gaulle's visit to Algiers in December 1960 are commemorated. The Casbah is struggling to find its place in national history, fighting against politically induced forgetfulness, even amnesia.

'If you took Algiers, you took Algeria. Every competing group fought to control the capital,' says the French historian Benjamin Stora. When the residents of Algiers saw Boumedienne's tanks rolling into the city in 1965, they thought director Gillo Pontecorvo was filming another scene for his film *The Battle of Algiers*. Only later did they realise the tanks were Algerian, not French, and manned by real soldiers. Another battle for Algiers was beginning – less violent but just as decisive for the country's future. In the months after independence, people from the outside put down those on the inside. After removing them from power, they erased them from history.

'Why are they letting the Casbah fall to bits?' The former resistance fighter (who did not wish to give his name) answered his own question: 'Since independence, most of those in power have not pursued revolution. So what interest do they have in honouring those in the Casbah who really fought for it?' The Casbah is 'a symbol, an affront that recalls the 1965 coup and the illegitimate origins of the Algerian state'.

Ruined and marginalised, the Casbah represents the great gulf between the Algiers of the 1950s and 1960s, when it was the focal point for the emancipation of the colonised, and what it has become today – a city hostage to the ruling oligarchy.

TOWER BLOCKS AND SLUMS

The city's shape and layout spatially express bureaucratic ambition. The city is spreading. Huge dormitory towns have sprung up on the outskirts, eating away the fertile land of the Mitidja plains. The city has opened up, disgorging people into the suburbs. The wealthiest have left the centre for the chic districts higher up; the working classes live in slums and tower blocks on the outskirts.

The state tries to gain legitimacy through the redistribution of urban income, as it did with oil revenues. Madani Safar Zitoun, a sociologist at Algiers University, said that in 1962, apartments left empty by the departure of the French pieds noirs were regarded as spoils of the colonial war, to be redistributed by the state to the people, creating a tacit pact between them. 'Yes, we live in an authoritarian state,' said Zitoun, 'but it works differently from Tunisia or Morocco. Here, everything is based on clientelism. The state ensures social harmony by giving away some of its wealth in housing grants, which can amount to 50 per cent of the value of an apartment. It doesn't even demand rent from the 70 per cent of social housing tenants who don't pay. The secret of the government's longevity is the way it manages social housing. It suits everyone.' Mohamed, who is in his 50s, welcomed us to his two rooms with kitchen where he lives with his wife and five children. He was proud that he had built his house with his own hands – cement floor, sheet metal roof, brick walls, electricity and air-conditioning: 'all mod cons'. Nothing he said belied his contentment, even if all round his house, a maze of alleys, it was one big slum.

This area was built in the 1990s in the eastern suburb of Bab Ezzouar, and is home to 350 people. Rubbish is piled near the outlet of a makeshift sewer. Rickety huts have gradually been transformed into more solid structures. Some have two storeys and look like small houses. Large families fill the tiny rooms. Most are peasants fleeing the poverty of the countryside, but there are also businessmen, teachers and policemen, like Mohamed. 'You don't only come here because you are poor,' he said. 'Look at the car parks, they're full.'

A few years ago he was still living with his parents. So were his seven brothers, their wives and children, and it became impossible for them all to stay. Without enough money to buy or rent (rent for a two room flat in a working class suburb is equal to the minimum wage) many people, particularly young couples, live in illegal slums. It takes 20 years to get a council house, but only five if you live in the slums. Everybody in Algiers knows that, and it has consolidated the power of these areas, although they are a relatively small proportion of the city.

HOUSING GREW WORSE

Algeria has not been able to deal with the housing crisis left by the French. On the eve of the war of independence, 125,000 native Algerians already lived in slums.[3] Since then the situation has worsened. In 40 years, the population of Algiers has tripled – through natural growth, urbanisation and the 1991–2001 civil war which drove many to seek refuge there.

The civil war helped spread clientelism through land use. Both the FIS (Islamic Salvation Front) and the FLN fought brutally for control of the city and its inhabitants, and tried to make political capital from the sudden rise in demand for housing. When FIS representatives triumphed in the municipal elections in June 1990, they allowed people to construct their own homes without title deeds or building permits. The Bab Ezzouar slum looks like a Wild West town, with sandstorms blowing down empty streets, nothing there but a bakery and a half built mosque, and a few small postmodern-type buildings, ochre in colour with Greek columns.

Even after the electoral process was halted in 1992,[4] local politicians continued with the same system. Throughout the civil war they continued to allocate land for housing to ensure public support and their political survival. Or just survival.

Once the war ended, people were no longer the principal beneficiaries of urban revenue. President Abdelaziz Bouteflika repeated the refrain of his predecessors and promised to build a million new homes in five years, and made eradicating illegal housing a priority of his 2009 election campaign. This July, the Bab Ezzouar slum was knocked down and its inhabitants re-housed in new apartments on the outskirts of town. But west of the city, on the Bologhine Heights, a favela-like slum on the side of the hill is now home to thousands. There is no planning, and new arrivals keep coming.

The frequent protests in poor districts suggest that the national pact between the politicians and the people is falling apart. Nordine Grim, a journalist at *El Watan* newspaper, said the housing crisis was not due to an imbalance between supply and demand, but to the stupidity of the authorities. 'In Algeria, there are 7.2 million homes for 34 million inhabitants. The average household has five people, so we should be able to house everyone at an acceptable level. The crisis is not only about availability but distribution. The real issue here is clientelism and corruption.'

EVERYONE WANTS A SLICE OF THE CAKE

Within the governing administration, powerful groups vie for control of urban revenue. Mohamed Larbi Merhoum, former winner of the Algerian national prize for architecture, is familiar with this. In 2007 he entered a competition to build a university centre in Algiers. His submission was ranked first for technical aspects, but was rejected when cost was taken into account, even though it was three times cheaper than the winning entry from a Tunisian firm.

'The difference between us was that they demanded 90 per cent of the fee be paid abroad in foreign currency, while I wanted to be paid in Algeria in dinars.' Once money leaves the country it is difficult to track, so part of the payment to the Tunisian firm could have been diverted and transformed into commission. Merhoum took the decision to the national contract commission. The competition was relaunched, but Merhoum was effectively excluded. The project was awarded in 2009 to a South Korean firm, for twice Merhoum's fee. Everyone wants a slice, giving rise to convoluted internal politics, as opaque as the planning system. 'There are three layers of supervision,' said Merhoum. 'The ministry of town and country planning, the ministry of town planning, and the prefecture. The fortunes of each, the personal ambitions of their officials and their leverage have a huge influence on how projects are run in Algiers.' Rivalry for control of areas that can bring power and profit is so intense that it leads to paralysis on some work sites. Local politicians, he said, are 'excluded or compromised by hidden processes, so they never become an opposition force'.

The unfinished Algiers Museum of Modern Art (MAMA) on Larbi Ben M'hidi Street shows the degree to which the ruling classes use urban policies for their private interests. In 2006 the government decided to open a museum of modern art – the first in Algeria, the second in Africa – in the former Galeries de France, an early 20th-century neo-Moorish building.

The architect was chosen in a national competition: Halim Faidi, of Algiers, who had been awarded a medal by the French academy of architecture. But when Algiers became Arab Cultural Capital in 2007, the ministry of culture ordered Faidi to build a provisional structure urgently. The complete museum would come later, they promised. So he put aside his original plans. But after the provisional museum's inauguration, the works never began again. 'At the moment there is not even an office on site for the director, or a storeroom for the works of art. Safety standards have not been respected – what would happen if there was a fire? How can we hope to get collections from foreign museums in these conditions? The ministry tells the public this is a museum, but at best it's only a gallery. It's all window dressing.'

Algiers' white façades are just a screen on which is projected a shadow theatre. The ruling oligarchy has pulled the threads of the city's fabric to shreds.

Translated by Stephanie Irvine

Allan Popelard and Paul Vannier are geographers.

1. On 11 December 2007 two car bombs were used against the headquarters of the UNHCR and the Supreme Court in Ben Aknoun, a suburb of Algiers, killing dozens.
2. *El Watan*, Algiers, 1 December 2008.
3. Estimate by Jacques Chevalier, former mayor of Algiers. Cited by Benjamin Stora, *Le nationalisme algérien avant 1954*, CNRS Editions, Paris, 2010, p. 192.
4. In the first round of general elections in 1991, the FIS took 188 seats and were poised to win an absolute majority in the second round. The elections were cancelled, triggering the country's long, violent civil war.

❖ ❖

JANUARY 2010

DESCENT OF DETROIT

America's slow ground zero

Detroit is a city in decline, shrinking, segregated, and now one of the poorest in the US, with a third of its people below the poverty line and health indicators equal to those of a developing country.

Allan Popelard and Paul Vannier

'Can you smell it?' asks Dave, as five piles of cinders smoulder across the road from his house. Dave, 30, lives on 7 Miles Road in one of Detroit's poor districts, part of a 10 km-wide belt running between the skyscrapers of the city centre and the wealthy suburbs. The cinder piles are all that remain of five houses that were lived in only two months ago. 'Another one burnt down last night. Every week one gets torched. They do it to get the insurance, so they can move to the suburbs. No one wants to live around here anymore.'

Detroit's urban ghettos are being eroded bit by bit, leaving only fragments behind. In some blocks only two or three houses remain inhabited. The area has become a wasteland of burnt-out cars, empty parking lots and disused factories. Derelict homes are consumed by shrubs and trees. A once dense urban landscape is decomposing, turning into a rural wilderness where the crowing of cockerels and the buzz of crickets reverberate.

Detroit is shrinking: 35 per cent of its municipal area is uninhabited[1] and it is the only city in the world to have lost more than half its population – almost a million people – in half a century.[2] It is only around the university that you see a few pedestrians, or at the end of the school day, on the main avenues of Woodward, Michigan or Gratiot. The sub-prime crisis has increased the problem.

Michigan's largest city was one of the worst affected by the sale of sub-prime mortgages – variable rate loans offered by neoliberals keen to give the poorest in society access to the property ladder, so they could join the consumer society. The failure of thousands of borrowers to keep up the rising monthly payments led to repossessions – 67,000 between 2005 and 2008, according to the city council.

Capitalism's latest crisis affected the people of Detroit particularly badly, as they were hit both by the financial meltdown and the fall in production that followed. The collapse of the banking system reduced access to credit, so consumption decreased, causing a dramatic fall in car sales in the US. The Big Three – General Motors, Ford and Chrysler – which are all based in Detroit, were hit badly. Over-indebted, under-capitalised and out-competed by Japanese manufacturers, GM, Chrysler and Ford owe their survival to the government's federal rescue plan. But the plan didn't prevent job losses.

Unemployment almost doubled in Detroit between January 2008 and July 2009, rising from 14.8 per cent to 28.9 per cent. The real rate may be over 40 per cent, according to Kurt Metzger, director of the Detroit area Community Information System.[3] 'It's worse than it used to be,' says Dave. 'I manage by doing odd jobs here and there. My wife can't find work though. GM and Chrysler are about to go under, Ford is just holding on. There are no more factories here.' The abandoned skyscrapers downtown are like empty flagpoles, symbols of decline.

ARSENAL OF DEMOCRACY

Detroit's specialisation in car manufacturing made it particularly vulnerable to fluctuations in the economic cycle and changes within the capitalist system. Fordism made this city the centre of industrial capitalism. Mass production, introduced during the first half of the 20th century, was hungry for labour, so relatively high wages were offered attracting workers to the car industry: blacks fleeing the racism of the south, and immigrants from abroad, notably Greece and Poland. Detroit was in its heyday during the Second World War, 'the arsenal of democracy' as Roosevelt put it, at the heart of the US war effort.

But things changed after 1945 when Detroit started losing contracts and jobs. US capitalism entered the post-Fordist era, and industry relocated from the Northeast and Midwest to the south, where the unions were weaker and manpower was cheaper. The mass ownership of cars and changes in the methods of production meant less activity took place in urban areas. A polycentric urban model began to emerge, with employment and services based in the outskirts. Attracted by new job opportunities and the American dream of owning your own home, the white middle and upper classes moved to the suburbs.

But fear and racism also played a part in this migration. Although whites had started leaving the inner city with the de-industrialisation of the 1950s, the majority left after the black riots of 1967, when 43 people were killed and the army sent in the tanks. Detroit's apocalyptic image and new nicknames of Murder City and Devil City became self-fulfilling prophecies.

Fear and racism also played a role in the economic segregation of the city. The power of the city's negative image – just think of the film *Robocop* which is set in Detroit – explains why it is the only large city in the US whose city centre did not go through a process of gentrification, or become multicultural. It is one of the poorest cities in the US – a third of people live below the poverty line – and one of the most segregated with almost nine out of ten of its inhabitants black. This US-style apartheid is not evident between one district and another, as in other US cities, but between the inner city and the suburbs.

On 8 Miles Road, the wide avenue at the northern limit of municipal Detroit, the central reservation marks the boundary between two worlds. On one side lie the wealthy homes and manicured lawns of the suburbs; on the other, rows of slums housing the unemployed and people excluded from the private health care system.

In the city centre the disabled and homeless wander the streets, like Beckett's Molloy, who kept plodding on with his crutches and his bicycle. The city of the car is also the city of the electric wheelchair. The health indicators for the local population are equal to those of a developing country: infant mortality is 18 per 1,000, three times higher than in the rest of the US, and the same as Sri Lanka.

'When you lose your job, you lose your health insurance,' explains Dave. 'So once you're unemployed you stop going to the doctor. At the corner of the street you can get medical care for $20, but someone in your family has to be working and act as your guarantor.

But don't expect anything more than a routine visit, and you'll be the last person in the waiting room to be seen.' With the new rise in unemployment, public health is expected to get even worse.

AN URBAN GHETTO

But how do you reverse this trend when the physical arrangement of the city in the form of a ring is part of the problem? It perpetuates social inequality by hemming the proletariat into an urban ghetto. Eighty-six per cent of jobs are in the outskirts, but a quarter of the city's inhabitants don't have a car (the official figure is 33 per cent, but Metzger points out that many people drive without insurance and so are excluded from the statistics). It is not easy getting around without a car in this city built by, and for, the automobile, dominated by motorways and wide avenues. Mobility is a social issue. Those who cannot join car-pools resort to the transport of the poor: buses with bike racks. But with the city on the edge of bankruptcy,[4] Detroit's mayor, Dave Bing, has made drastic cuts to the transport budget: 113 bus drivers laid off, some routes cut, lower frequency on others.[5]

The structure of the city also explains why Detroit's poor are excluded from health care. Many GPs have moved to the suburbs where they can earn more. And while the city is at the forefront of medical research, with some of the best hospitals in the US, it is only the suburban rich who can afford them.

So for many here the health care reform promised by President Obama is a question of life or death. Louise used to work for the city council. She lives in East Side, a run-down African-American district. 'I am 74 years old, so the health insurance debate really concerns me,' she said. 'I voted for Obama because I thought he could make a change. You know, I really need it. My doctor said I needed a scanner. Medicare [the government programme that insures people over 65] covers me for 80 per cent. But what about the other 20 per cent? I can barely afford to pay for my medicine. Do I need to choose between my medicine and the scanner? Is that it? I worked for 29 years. I paid tax. It's not fair.'

In this Democratic heartland, 97 per cent of the electorate voted for Obama. One year on, Luther Keith, president of Arise, an organisation offering free health care and schooling to the poor, remembers that day with emotion: 'There were parties everywhere. It was extraordinary. It felt as though something wonderful had happened to a member of the family. It was like Joe Louis beating

Max Schmeling in 1938!' he says, referring to the black boxer who became a hero when he defeated the German, and is honoured with a statue in the city.

But even in such a centre of African-American culture and civil rights struggle as Detroit, it is the Democratic candidate's economic and social programme that counts, not his ethnic origin. 'We didn't vote for Obama because he was black, we voted for him because of his policies, in particular his promise to reform the health care system,' everyone tells us. Electoral support for the Democrats in Macomb County is a textbook case in American political science, and reveals the economic and social determining factors in the Detroit metropolitan area.

'LIKE THE AIR WE BREATHE'

Detroit's citizens remain sympathetic towards the new president, for the moment, but they are concerned by the obstacles being put in his way: 'Things take time. If you look at what Obama has done in the last few months, it's more than any president did before him,' says Keith. 'But, obviously, there's a lot of work to be done. And it's not easy for people who have lost their jobs to say everything will be okay.' People see Obama having to compromise with the lobby groups, the Republicans and even the opposition within his own party. Hope among his supporters has turned into patience. If he fails, Keith warns, 'disappointment will be huge'.

People are turning to the federal government as a last resort, because the municipality has no more room to manoeuvre. Its tax base collapsed when the middle classes and capital fled, and now it is almost bankrupt. The Democratic city council seems powerless to prevent the cycle of poverty. The question of whether to integrate the metropolitan area has still not been resolved: the residents of the suburbs refuse to share their wealth, while the black inhabitants of the inner city don't want to see their hard-won political power diluted in a metropolitan authority that would care little about them.

Despite the disaster, there are no strikes in the factories or protests in the street. Instead the poor, broken by the 'casino economy', cram into the games halls built by construction companies offered tax breaks by the council – its main development policy at the end of the 1990s. The city seems to have left behind its radical past: the strikes of 1937 and 1945 that led to the election of the first black mayor, Coleman Young in 1973,[6] the abolitionist networks, the civil rights struggle, the emergence of Black Power and the African-American revolts of 1833, 1918, 1943 and 1967.

Even United Auto Workers, the all-powerful automobile trade union, has given up the fight, going as far as to agree with the bosses at GM and Chrysler not to strike in times of crisis. No one seems to be rebelling against a system that has created Detroit as its most advanced end product. 'Capitalism is America,' says Keith. 'It built this town: the Motown record label, the cars we drive...Capitalism is everything – everything you have, and in a way, everything you don't have. It's like the air we breathe – we can't change it.'

Businessmen at the Tech Town enterprise zone and politicians are banking on the green economy. The elite has always believed in a bright future, in innovation and the perpetual cycle of 'creative destruction'. This 'Renaissance city' is built on liberal optimism: every time it is down it finds renewed vigour in the political theories of Schumpeter. The Renaissance Centre, conceived by Henry Ford II and built only four years after the riots of 1967, is the most glaring symbol of this. It has been the headquarters of General Motors since 1995. Businessmen enjoy lunch in the comfortable restaurant on the 73rd floor. Before them lies a panorama of devastation and a landscape of relics ingrained with the marks of violence.

'For many Americans, Detroit is Ground Zero,' says Keith. Not the ground zero created in a moment of searing intensity, but a zero reached gradually, in an account that never stops being debited. Detroit is the product of a system that makes you wonder how it stubbornly keeps on going – through the blindness of the oppressed, or the cynicism of the oppressor? 'Optimism is our only solution,' Keith concludes, smiling.

Translated by Stephanie Irvine

Allan Popelard and Paul Vannier are geographers at the Institut français de géopolitique, University of Paris-VIII.

1. *Detroit Free Press*, 7 September 2009.
2. In 1950 its population was 1.8 million, but now it is between 912,062 and 777,493 depending on the census. The discrepancy between the two figures is the source of vigorous debate: the political influence of the city and the amount of subsidy it receives depend on its population.
3. Only people registered with the employment agency are counted in the unemployed figures.
4. The city's debt reached $300 million in 2009, with a deficit of $80 million; *Detroit Free Press*, 11 September 2009.

5. *Detroit Free Press*, 11 September 2009.
6. The first black mayor of Detroit (1973–93) and a member of the Democratic Party, he asserted the city's black identity by renaming streets and erecting monuments to prominent members of the civil rights movement, such as Harriet Tubman.

❖ ❖

May 2010

Urbanisation and the need for sustainable development

The world has become a city

The 2010 UN World Urban Campaign wanted to tackle the problems of overcrowding and slums. But as more and more people move to ever-larger cities, how are we to create liveable urban spaces?

Philip S. Golub

More than half the world's people live in towns and cities for the first time in history. Over 3.3 billion people live in cities – 500 million of them in cities of more than five million or in mega-cities of more than 10 million. According to United Nations Population Division estimates, the rate of global urbanisation will increase considerably in coming decades, reaching 59.7 per cent in 2030 and 69.6 per cent in 2050. Old and new urban centres will absorb most of the anticipated demographic growth.

This large-scale transformation will primarily impact on the most populous poor and emerging world regions. The rate of urbanisation in the most developed countries, already intensely urbanised, will only increase slightly, from 74 per cent today to around 85 per cent by mid-century, pushing the possibility of further urban expansion to the limits.

Latin America – an exception among emerging regions because of its widespread urbanisation in the early 20th century – is already mostly urban. But Africa and Asia are facing a veritable upheaval. Africa's urban population, which multiplied tenfold between 1950 and today (from 33 million to 373 million), is expected to reach 1.2 billion in 2050, 63 per cent of the total continental population. Meanwhile, Asia's urban population, which jumped from 237 million in the mid-20th century to 1.645 billion today, should more than double, reaching 3.5 billion. More than half of the population of India, three-quarters of that of China, and four-fifths of that of Indonesia will be living in cities.

As Lewis Mumford presciently argued 50 years ago, the world has 'become a city' – or a constellation of expansive urban spaces that constitute the nodal points of globalised economic and social interactions.[1] The extensive urbanisation of the poor and emerging world regions is revolutionising longstanding ways of being and doing; and it will intensify over this century. Large-scale urbanisation – the cause and consequence of the migrations that it stimulates – is restructuring social relations and producing sharp new stratifications. At the ecological level, it is accentuating the transformation of local and planetary ecosystems.

To grasp the scope of the phenomenon, it needs to be seen in historical perspective. Mass urbanisation is coextensive with the Anthropocene, a concept that designates the new geophysical era introduced by the 19th-century industrial revolution and the intensive use of fossil fuel resources that has led to a fundamental modification of the habitat.

URBAN SURGE

Prior to this rupture, economic and social life had, for millennia, been dominated by the slow rhythms of traditional economies based on agriculture. In Mumford's words, the villages and early cities of the pre-industrial era had 'a symbiotic relationship with the natural environment'. Society impacted nature at local level without modifying eco-systemic equilibriums. From the Neolithic agricultural revolution, which opened the way for sedentary population concentrations, to the industrial revolution in the 19th century, the urban share of the world population remained fairly constant at around 10–12 per cent.

According to Paul Bairoch, who revised previous estimates upwards, the rate of urbanisation varied between 9 per cent and 14 per cent depending on regions and epochs.[2]

Over the course of this long pre-industrial period some very large cities came into being: Babylon, Rome, Constantinople, Baghdad, Xi'an, Beijing, Hangzhou, Nankin. Some of these great cities were the hearts of empires and contained tens of thousands or even hundreds of thousands of people. (In 1300 AD Beijing contained 5–600,000 inhabitants.)

Medieval Europe witnessed what Bairoch called an 'urban surge' with the formation of a network of merchant cities and city-states of 20,000 inhabitants or more. But this development did not fundamentally modify the equilibrium between city and countryside or revolutionise social relations. In 1780 there were fewer than a hundred cities with more than 100,000 inhabitants; neither in Europe nor elsewhere was the urban phenomenon dominant. Social reproduction was everywhere founded on agriculture.

The industrial revolution, requiring a concentration of work and capital, called for a new division of labour and led to unprecedented urbanisation. Britain's urban population rose from 20 per cent in 1750 (high compared with the rest of Europe) to 80 per cent in 1900.

Britain, though well in advance, was not an isolated case. The urbanisation rate of the newly industrialised countries (Japan not included) multiplied tenfold between 1800 and 1914 – three times greater than the rate of demographic growth. Overall, according to Bairoch, the rate of urbanisation in Europe increased from 10 per cent in 1800 to 35 per cent in 1914. Industry accounted for nearly half of urban employment.

The evolution reflected urban migration from the countryside induced by redundancies and rises in agricultural productivity. The transformation was violent – think of the deplorable work and living conditions of children and adults inserted in the industrial machine in the second half of the 19th century. Even so, urbanisation was part of a slow evolution leading to a general increase in living standards that became apparent in the 20th century.

AWAY FROM EUROPE

The urban experience in colonial or peripheral regions was different. Coupled with the territorial expansion of the West, the industrial revolution instituted a new international division of labour; long-distance trade played a growing role. Describing this first wave of globalisation Marx and Engels wrote in *The Communist Manifesto* in 1848: 'Old established national industries...are dislodged by new industries...that no longer work up indigenous raw material but raw material drawn from the remotest zones; industries whose products are consumed, not only at home, but in every quarter of the globe. In place of the old wants, satisfied by the production of the country, we find new ones requiring for their satisfactions the products of distant lands and climes. In place of the old national seclusion and self-sufficiency, we have intercourse in every direction, universal interdependence of nations.'

Interdependence, which was asymmetric, and structured around uneven centre-periphery relations, reconfigured the economies and spaces of dependent or colonised world regions. Their integration in the new world market disrupted traditional linkages between city and countryside, weakening or tearing apart traditional domestic economic circuits. It encouraged export-oriented production of primary products – cotton, sugar, opium, cereals, minerals. Over time, as a result of the restrictions imposed by the mercantile colonial pacts, this led to stagnation or regression in living standards. (India, the world's leading producer of textile products before 1750, underwent thoroughgoing de-industrialisation.)

Urbanisation mostly remained weak. But the new structure of international trade and uneven 'development' generated demographic inflation in coastal cities, which became warehouses for the primary products destined for the world market. The result was economic de-continentalisation in favour of coastal urbanisation: the populations of Mumbai, Kolkata or Chennai grew in the middle of the 19th century, just as the cities of inner India got smaller. This also happened in sub-Saharan Africa and northern Africa, where coastal colonial cities came to dominate the urban landscape.

The rapid urbanisation of these world regions in the 20th century, particularly after 1950, occurred in the absence of economic 'development'. There are exceptions, notably the large urban ensembles of the newly industrialised countries of East Asia (Seoul, Taipei, Singapore, Hong Kong, Shanghai), whose expansion marks a successful exit from the third world. But in most other cases the disorderly, uneven urbanisation of the post-colonial periphery resulted from the interaction between internal economic and social disequilibrium, often inherited from the social structures of the colonial era, and world market forces.

Large scale population flows from rural to urban areas, stimulated by rural poverty, have led to the creation of immense and increasingly unmanageable urban areas in sub-Saharan Africa, Latin America and South Asia. Their continuous demographic and spatial expansion is coterminous with mass unemployment, massive slums, inadequate or failing infrastructure and formidable ecological problems (Lagos, Dakar, Mexico City, Caracas, Kolkata, Jakarta, Manila). In these extraordinarily stratified spaces, there is extreme polarisation between pockets of extraordinary wealth and great mass poverty, a phenomenon that has produced what Mike Davis calls 'a planet of slums'.[3]

MEANING AND PURPOSE

The great urban centres of even the richest countries are also 'dual cities' incorporating the South in the North.[4] Sharply segmented at social level, they concentrate an important mass of ancillary workers and excluded peoples, who (not accidentally) often came from the former colonial periphery. But the social inequality of the so-called global cities of the North, which concentrate wealth, culture and knowledge (New York, Los Angeles, London, Tokyo), cannot be compared with that of the urban centres of the South.

Urbanisation concentrates and expresses the tensions and contradictions of industrialisation and globalisation. In the words of Henri Lefèbvre: 'Urban society, which is the meaning and the purpose of industrialisation, forms itself while seeking itself.'[5] The complete urbanisation of the world, an irreversible phenomenon, raises inescapable questions about the future of our societies. Will we be able to produce public goods – education, culture, health and a healthy environment for all? Or implement sustainable development strategies that ensure collective wellbeing and allow for the expansion of individual freedoms?

The appropriation of the urban areas by citizens has been an issue for well over a century: it is by definition a polarised and politically dominated space. The creation of the great urban centres in the industrialised countries at the end of the 19th century and beginning of the 20th, juxtaposing wealth and misery, gave rise to much creative thinking. Attempting to resolve the problem of Victorian slums, reformers proposed urban decentralisation by building smaller, more liveable constellations, which would have allowed for smoother population management. China and India are moving in this direction today.

Later on, Mumford and others imagined a programme of urban decongestion through regional and sub-regional planning founded on the use of local resources and short supply chains. The aim was to arrive at ecological equilibriums in local and regional settings (what we call sustainable urban development today). These intellectual efforts remained stillborn. Still later, in the 1970s and 1980s, the concept of community development and 'community design' briefly flourished; this would have allowed for people's appropriation of their community spaces. The question of urban citizenship and of the creation of liveable urban spaces is now one of the major challenges of the coming century.

Translated by the author

Philip S. Golub is a lecturer at the University of Paris VIII and author of *Power, Profit and Prestige: A History of American Imperial Expansion*, Pluto Press, London, 2010.

1. Lewis Mumford, *The City in History: Its Origins, Its Transformations, and Its Prospects*, Harcourt Brace International, New York, 1961.
2. Paul Bairoch, *De Jéricho à Mexico: villes et économie dans l'histoire*, Gallimard, Paris, 1985.
3. Mike Davis, *Planet of Slums*, Verso, London, 2006.
4. Manuel Castells, *The Informational City: Information, Technology, Economic Restructuring and the Urban-Regional Process*, Cambridge University Press, 1989; *Dual City: Restructuring New York*, Russell Sage Foundation, New York, 1991.
5. Henri Lefèbvre, *La Production de l'espace*, Anthropos, Paris, 1974.

Index